Praise for *Finding Mañana*

"It's impossible not to admire the boldness, the candor, the moral toughness of Ms. Ojito's writing. In this wonderful memoir, she ransoms herself from the seductions of nostalgia, and reclaims instead the beleaguered Cuba of her childhood—a Cuba that is all the more interesting for not being looked at through the prism of longing and desire." —*The New York Times*

"In *Finding Mañana*, Mirta Ojito goes a long way in righting the Mariel story and bestowing some belated dignity on this ragged stepchild of exile history." —*Los Angeles Times*

"Ms. Ojito's book is filled with the anguish of separation and the tragedy of living under a merciless regime. But it also celebrates familial bonds and undying love—not to mention freedom itself, a gift too often taken for granted by those of us who have never had to live without it." —*The Wall Street Journal*

"The insight Ojito brings to bear, coupled with the crispness if her prose . . . make this memoir required reading for anyone interested in the history of post–Batista Cuba or Cuban–American relations." —*The Washington Post*

"*New York Times* reporter Mirta Ojito melds the personal with the political in a moving account of her family's departure from Cuba. She also provides a solid historical context for those five months in 1980 when 125,000 Cubans arrived in Florida, a mass exodus that came to be known as the Mariel boatlift." —*People*

"Ojito's historical reconstruction is fascinating. . . . (She) has created a poignant and poetic memoir of an important moment in Cuban and U.S. history." —*The Washington Times*

"This is much more than one Cuban exile's bittersweet tale; it's the memoir of an entire era." —*The Times-Picayune* (New Orleans)

"Ojito's book . . . is unlike most entries in the genre of the modern memoir. More than a novelistic exercise in creative recollection, it's a skillful blend of reportage and family history about a pivotal international event." —*Sun-Sentinel* (Fort Lauderdale)

"Like many Cuban exiles, Ojito says she left part of her soul in Cuba. The good news is the rest of it came over with her intact. Plenty of it went into this book." —*St. Petersburg Times*

PENGUIN BOOKS

FINDING MAÑANA

Mirta Ojito was born in Cuba and came to the United States in 1980 in the Mariel boatlift. In 2001, she shared the Pulitzer Prize for national reporting for a *New York Times* series on race. She has also received the American Society of Newspaper Editors' writing award for best foreign reporting. Ojito now teaches journalism at Columbia University in New York City. She can be reached at www.mirtaojito.com

FINDING MAÑANA

A MEMOIR OF A CUBAN EXODUS

✦

Mirta Ojito

PENGUIN BOOKS

PENGUIN BOOKS
Published by the Penguin Group
Penguin Group (USA) Inc., 375 Hudson Street,
New York, New York 10014, U.S.A.
Penguin Group (Canada), 90 Eglinton Avenue East, Suite 700, Toronto,
Ontario, Canada M4P 2Y3 (a division of Pearson Penguin Canada Inc.)
Penguin Books Ltd., 80 Strand, London WC2R 0RL, England
Penguin Ireland, 25 St Stephen's Green, Dublin 2, Ireland (a division of Penguin Books Ltd)
Penguin Group (Australia), 250 Camberwell Road, Camberwell,
Victoria 3124, Australia (a division of Pearson Australia Group Pty Ltd)
Penguin Books India Pvt Ltd, 11 Community Centre, Panchsheel Park, New Delhi – 110 017, India
Penguin Group (NZ), cnr Airborne and Rosedale Roads, Albany,
Auckland 1310, New Zealand (a division of Pearson New Zealand Ltd)
Penguin Books (South Africa) (Pty) Ltd, 24 Sturdee Avenue, Rosebank, Johannesburg 2196, South Africa

Penguin Books Ltd, Registered Offices:
80 Strand, London WC2R 0RL, England

First published in the United States of America by The Penguin Press,
a member of Penguin Group (USA) Inc. 2005
Published in Penguin Books 2006

3 5 7 9 10 8 6 4

Portions of this work first appeared in By Heart/De Memoria: Cuban Women's Journeys In and Out of Exile edited by
Maria de los Angeles Torres (Temple University Press, 2003); The New York Times; and The New York Times Magazine.

Photograph credits: Chapter 2: Bob Mark; 4: AP Photo/Charles Tasnadi; 5: AP Photo; 7: Napoleón Vilaboa; 8: © Murry
Sill/The Miami Herald; 9: Sam Howell; 10: Historian's Office of the United States Coast Guard; 11: © The Miami Herald.

THE LIBRARY OF CONGRESS HAS CATALOGED THE HARDCOVER EDITION AS FOLLOWS:
Ojito, Mirta A.
Finding mañana: a memoir of a Cuban exodus / Mirta Ojito.
p. cm.
Includes bibliographical references and index.
ISBN 1-59420-041-6 (hc.)
ISBN 0 14 30.3660 2 (pbk.)
1. Ojito, Mirta A.   2. Ojito, Mirta A.—Childhood and youth.   3. Cuban American women—Biography.
4. Cuban Americans—Biography.   5. Immigrants—United States—Biography.   6. Mariel Boatlift, 1980.
7. Girls—Cuba—Biography.   8. Cuba—Biography.
I. Title.
E184.C97O45 2005
973'.04687291'0092—dc22
[B]
2004057322

Printed in the United States of America
Designed by Michelle McMillian

To Arturo,
and to
our children:
Juan Arturo,
Lucas,
and Marcelo,
my true home

Contents

Author's Note

Throughout the reporting of this book I've asked my "characters" to remember in great detail events that transpired twenty-five years ago—in some cases even longer than that. I'm fortunate that many of them have very vivid memories. Some even kept written records and photographs of their participation in what turned out to be historic events. All depictions of the events that I didn't witness, including dialogue, have been double-checked with more than one source whenever possible. There are a few instances in which I've had to rely on only one source, either because the second party in a private meeting is dead or because the Cuban officials involved were unwilling to cooperate despite my repeated requests to interview them. Because quotation marks in journalism indicate that the words were spoken exactly as cited, I've opted not to use them unless I'm quoting from a published source, or I witnessed the exchange and took notes.

Those who don't have revolutionary genes, revolutionary blood,
a mind or heart which can adapt to the effort and heroism
of a revolution aren't wanted here, they aren't needed.

—FIDEL CASTRO, DURING A MAY 1 SPEECH
IN HAVANA, 1980

We will continue to provide an open heart and open arms to refugees
seeking freedom from Communist domination and from economic deprivation,
brought about primarily by Fidel Castro and his government.

—PRESIDENT JIMMY CARTER,
MAY 5, 1980, WASHINGTON, D.C.

Prologue

HAVANA, 1980

THE POLICE CAME on May 7 when I was about to have lunch: a plain yogurt, sweetened with several spoonfuls of sugar, fried yellow plantains, and an egg-and-ketchup sandwich on half a loaf of Cuban bread. I was wearing a *bata de casa*, a housecoat, over my painstakingly ironed school uniform: a blue skirt with two white stripes around the bottom hem, signaling I was in eleventh grade, and a starched white poplin blouse, which I didn't want to stain with grease.

I was just smoothing the pleats of my skirt over the back of my thighs when I heard the steps on the stairs that led to our second-floor apartment. I could tell that at least three people were coming up. By the way one of them paused after every other step, I knew that she was our downstairs neighbor and the president of the neighborhood watchdog committee. Two other people, agile and strong, led the way and knocked on the door before I could alert my mother, who had been sewing a dress and now stood, perfectly still, next to the sewing machine. Her maroon skirt was littered with pieces of yellow thread.

On the red plastic clock above the television set, it was fifteen minutes past eleven in the morning. I waited for a signal from my mother, but she didn't move. Then our neighbor spoke.

Mirta, she called out, a little out of breath. Open up. It's the police. You are leaving.

My mother swallowed and opened the door. A burly government officer, unshaven and dressed in olive green pants and a white T-shirt with large sweat rings under his arms, walked in. Without introducing himself, he read our full names out loud: Orestes Maximino Ojito Denis, Mirta Hilaria Muñoz Quintana, Mirta Arely Ojito Muñoz, and Mabel Ojito Muñoz.

Are these the names of the people who live here? he asked. My mother, who had started to tremble, nodded.

There is a boat waiting for you at the port of Mariel, he said, pausing a bit to gauge our reactions. He went on, Are you ready and willing to abandon the country at this time?

Yes, my mother said, her voice merely a whisper.

"Abandon" the country, he had said. I knew why the officer had chosen that word, and I refused to let it taint my family. I was sixteen: angry, opinionated, and politically aware. "Abandonment" was not a word I associated with us.

I GREW UP KNOWING that one day I would leave Cuba with my family. My parents had met in the late 1950s, just as revolution was brewing in the mountains of eastern Cuba and in the hallways of the universities that dotted the island. Unlike many other Cubans, who supported Fidel Castro's ascent to power in 1959 and then changed their minds, they had never really believed that a thirty-three-year-old in dirty fatigues and a scraggly beard could make their world better. They were indifferent to his promises, just as they had been somewhat blind to the injustices of the dictator whom Castro had deposed, Fulgencio Batista. My parents, who were poor and simple folk from the countryside, had never been fans of Batista, but they believed a good government was one that stayed out of the way and allowed individuals to work hard to provide for their families. Batista did that. Fidel did not. Fidel demanded loyalty.

When Castro came to power, my father worked at a store selling cloth by the yard to women who made their own dresses at home, as was fashionable then. He had aspired to be a traveling salesman, zigzagging the island in a company car, selling cloth to merchants in small towns. But shortly after the new government confiscated the store as part of its grand plan to build what it called "an egalitarian workers' society," my father was assigned to a truck-driving job. No one had asked him for his opinion, his plans, or his illusions. It was assumed that he would want to aid the revolution because, he was told, in doing so he would help his country.

Fiercely independent and completely apolitical, my father decided that he couldn't live in a place where government edicts, not his wishes or abilities, determined the kind of job he would perform for the rest of his life. In April 1961, around the time Castro announced in a televised speech the socialist nature of his regime, my father began making plans to join his older sister in the United States. In October 1962, he and my mother rushed their wedding date so that they could apply for a U.S. visa together. But then the Missile Crisis set the world on the brink of nuclear war, shadowing the first week of my parents' honeymoon and putting an end to their emigration plans. From the window of their ocean-front hotel room in Havana, they saw tanks rolling by and thousands of soldiers marching behind. The country was prepared for an American invasion that, to my father's chagrin, never came.

When the crisis ended a few days after it began, the United States government tightened an economic embargo declared against Cuba in 1960—which meant, among other things, that I was reared on Russian baby food and that Russian cartoons, not Walt Disney's animated movies, informed the better part of my childhood. The United States all but stopped issuing visas to Cubans, and life in Cuba became even more difficult than it already was. Food was scarce, and the country was politically and economically isolated, except for the help of the Soviet bloc.

Then, in a speech in September 1965, Castro suddenly announced that he would not stop anyone from leaving the island if Americans traveled south to the port of Camarioca, on Cuba's northern coast, to pick them up. Scores of Cuban-Americans in Miami mobilized to charter boats, taking about 2,800 relatives in 160 vessels before the boatlift was stopped. President Johnson took Castro at his word and immediately set up an airlift program, baptized as the "Freedom Flights." More than 270,000 Cubans left the island in the seven and a half years that the Freedom Flights cruised the skies over the Florida Straits.

We were not among them. The government would not authorize the exit of any male under the age of twenty-seven who had not completed his military duties. In 1965, when I was not yet two, my father was twenty-six. He was told he had to wait a year before he could apply for an exit visa. As his May birthday approached in 1966, my mother made me a sky blue corduroy jacket, appropriate for the winter land she imagined would greet us. It was double breasted, with large covered buttons and a round neck that hung in the back, cape style.

The day after my father turned twenty-seven, he mailed a certified letter to the government's emigration office, formally requesting permission to leave the country. He kept the receipt in the drawer of his night table, under the packs of Populares cigarettes he smoked. Every day my mother would quickly scan the mail looking for the only two envelopes that would bring joy to our lives: a letter from one of my father's sisters—by then two were living in the United States— or a fat, official-looking envelope that would mean we were a step closer to resume living the lives my parents were certain had been robbed from them. Letters from my aunts were common sights in the mailbox, some of them carrying tiny white socks for me or shiny Gillette blades for my father. But the government's envelope never arrived.

The following year my mother took the sky blue coat out of the plastic bag she had wrapped it in and allowed me to wear it for a Sunday trip to her sister's house. It was a chilly morning in January, and we'd had hot chocolate for breakfast. On the crowded bus to my aunt's house, I became sick and threw up, ruining the coat that I should have worn for my trip north.

FROM 1966 UNTIL we left in May 1980, the main topic of conversation at home and with friends who shared my parents' obsession was if and when and how we would leave Cuba. With the United States closed off to immigrants from Cuba after the Freedom Flights stopped in 1973, our chances were slim. We knew that some desperate people took to the treacherous waters of the Gulf of Mexico, braving dangerous currents and sharks to make it to Miami. Once in a while, we would hear stories of those who made it, but we never heard of the ones who did not. The ocean was not an option for my family. By nature, my mother was pessimistic; my father, cautious. Neither knew how to swim. Nor could we go the other route and request a visa through Spain, because we had no relatives in that country and no one in the family had even bothered to trace our roots to a Spanish ancestor.

At last something extraordinary happened. A deeply religious man with a commitment to upholding human rights assumed the presidency of the United States in 1977 and announced that he wanted to revamp his country's foreign policy. There was no need to have enemies; antagonism had no place in the world he envisioned. Almost immediately Castro saw in Jimmy Carter an ally, the U.S. president who would finally acknowledge that Castro was the rightful president of Cuba, an *americano* who would give him the recognition he craved. Members of Congress started traveling to Cuba; officials from both countries began discussing issues of maritime boundaries and fishing rights; an American journalist questioned Castro on Cuban television about the prisoners he kept throughout the island; and young Cuban-Americans returned to their homeland to pledge their support and youthful enthusiasm to the revolution their parents had refused them. In late 1978, with the blessing of the Carter administration, Cuban-Americans began a dialogue with the Cuban government that led to the release of hundreds of political prisoners and the visits of thousands of exiles, who in 1979 returned to the island, loaded with gifts.

The visits were a jolt to the country and its people. For almost a decade, Cuba had lived in complete isolation from the Western world. No one could get in; no one could get out. God and the Beatles were forbidden, men with long hair were arrested, homosexuals and artists were sent to labor camps. Anyone who expressed a desire to emigrate was immediately ostracized, harassed, and denied jobs and higher education. Those who openly and defiantly disagreed with the government were jailed or executed. Neighbors spied on neighbors, and everyone was expected to give up all allegiances for the good of the revolution, including obligations to the family and loyalty to friends.

In that milieu of angst and distrust, the government had surprised us all by welcoming back exiles. People were stunned and confused and began to look for a way to escape. Embassy break-ins became everyday occurrences. By Christmas of 1979, there were more than a hundred Cubans sheltered in Latin American embassies in Havana.

Despondent that so many people seemed eager to abandon his socialist paradise, Castro retaliated by using the only weapon he had: In a repeat of the 1965 Camarioca boatlift, he threatened to flood South Florida with refugees. In April 1980 he invited Cuban exiles to return to the island to pick up their relatives at the port of Mariel, west of Havana. President Carter, preoccupied with myriad domestic and international crises and a faltering reelection campaign, initially ignored the threat. But Miami Cubans, desperate to be reunited with their relatives, once again raced to Havana's shore.

My father's older brother, Uncle Oswaldo, was one of them. On May 7, 1980, the day the police knocked on our door, our names must have finally made it to the top of the emigration list. That day, within a matter of minutes, we left our home, our neighborhood, our lives. We left the way one leaves a cherished but impossible love: our hearts heavy with regret but beating with great hope.

I RETURNED TO that apartment in January 1998—seventeen years, eight months, and ten days after we had last walked away from it. When the short, slim woman who lived there opened the door, I mumbled a teary introduction and looked over her head, straight into my past: the old refrigerator was huffing in the kitchen, its door now kept shut by an ingeniously placed wire hanger; the ironing board, the one I used so many times to keep my school uniforms crisp, was hidden behind the kitchen door, just where we used to keep it; and my mother's colorful water glasses, the ones we could never touch because they were reserved for special occasions, were still gathering dust on the shelves in the living room. Their new owner, just like my mother, didn't use them for fear they would break.

Memories assaulted me in a way I had not anticipated.

I had gone back to Cuba as a reporter to cover Pope John Paul II's historic visit to the island, not to dissolve into tears at the sight of a chipped floor tile or a faded burgundy couch. Wearing my press badge, I'd felt powerful and even somewhat detached. But no plastic piece of identification hanging from my neck could protect me from my past. That old apartment, that block, that leafy neighborhood—Santos Suárez, with its graceful houses and tiny gardens—was still home.

◆ ◆ ◆

BACK IN NEW YORK, I began to dissect the forces that had made me and thousands of Cubans like me become enamored of the revolution. From a very early age, I had been well versed in the rhetoric of sacrifice and martyrdom favored by our leaders, mainly Fidel Castro. To be revolutionary was to be Cuban. To be Cuban was to be revolutionary. Castro's revolution was our all-compassing national project, his ideas our gyroscope. In his relentless march toward communism, everyone had a task, a duty, as he often told us. The adults contributed with their sweat and loyalty, while we, the children, were expected to turn over our souls.

Yet I hadn't even seen Castro until 1991, when, as a reporter for the *Miami Herald*, I managed to interview him once outside his hotel room in Guadalajara, Mexico. Though I had grown up obeying Castro's dictates and knew, firsthand, the spirit-crushing pain of living under a leader intent on controlling the will and the mind of his people, I felt nothing but elation for having scored a scoop as I shook his large but limp hand.

In interviews with former Cuban officials who had defected to Miami, I always made it a point to ask about the moment in which they knew they could no longer be faithful to Castro, but I had never pondered that question for myself. When had it all become unbearable? Was it in fifth grade, when I was forced to renounce God? Or when the government acknowledged that it had kept thousands of men and women jailed simply because they opposed the revolution? Or perhaps it was much later, during my last weeks in Cuba, when the violence against those who wanted to escape had left me with no choice but to face a country, a people, I no longer recognized.

In my memorized version of events, Mariel had simply happened to me, to all of us—in Cuba, in Miami, and in Washington. After fifteen years as a reporter in Miami and New York, mainly covering issues of immigration, I was familiar with the consequences and the broad outlines of the boatlift: the dates, the statistics, the impact—the good and the ugly—and the television images of desperation and hope, but my own story was a blank.

Why, I began to ask myself, had the boatlift really taken place? More than 125,000 Cubans arrived in South Florida during the span of five months in 1980, an election year, making it the biggest mass exodus in this hemisphere in recent history. Why had Castro encouraged it? Why had President Carter allowed it?

ONE MORNING, aboard the Grand Central shuttle that took me to work in Times Square, I began to read a story in the *New Yorker* about a woman who had a prosthetic arm, with perfectly shaped nails. An image of perfect square nails on the fingertips of a fake arm assaulted my brain. Whom did I know who had a fake arm? The captain of the *Mañana*! I remembered, the Good Samaritan who had brought my family to Key West when the fishing boat that my uncle had chartered had broken down at Mariel. I should find the captain, I thought, if only to thank him. What had brought him to Cuba anyway? And who was he?

That quest became the impetus that led to these pages, the story of my journey—from red-beret-wearing communist pioneer to a soaking-wet, filthy refugee stepping onto the docks of Key West, too young and bewildered to fully comprehend the events that had swept me ashore and given me new life. This book is also the story of what I have learned since then: that a handful of men and women, acting alone and often selfishly, altered the history of two countries and changed the course of thousands of lives.

In Mariel, I've discovered, we were all protagonists—from Bernardo Benes, a deeply religious Cuban Jew, who changed the nature of Cuban-American relations, to Héctor Sanyustiz, the unemployed bus driver who in the spring of 1980 rammed a bus through the gates of the Peruvian embassy in Havana. More than 10,000 people followed Sanyustiz's lead and flocked to the embassy to seek asylum. Ernesto Pinto-Bazurco Rittler, a German-born Peruvian diplomat with a distaste for conflict, set out to save their lives. So did Napoleón Vilaboa, a down-on-his-luck used-car salesman in Miami who left for Cuba on the first vessel of the Mariel boatlift and inspired thousands to follow him. Mike Howell, the captain of the *Mañana*, was one of them, though he had never heard of Vilaboa when he sailed to Cuba to pay his debt with God.

They are the people who inspire this book, the characters that allow me to take the tale of the boatlift beyond the realm of politics and into the intimate spaces of private lives. As I got to know them, as I teased out the details of their personal histories, I saw how each frame of my own life bears the ghostly imprint of my characters' actions. By alternating between my recollections and theirs, between my roles as protagonist and reporter, I've set out to bring those images into focus.

These are their stories, and, therefore, mine.

ONE

Worms Like Us

My elementary-school graduation in 1975, with my
sixth-grade teacher, Rita, and the school principal, Iraida.

*W*HAT IS IT? I yelled, reluctantly dragging myself up the steps that led to our apartment. What do you want? I demanded as I yanked the door open. I had been playing at my best friend's house across the street when my mother's voice, calling from our balcony, had shot through the windows, forcing me to abandon our game and race home.

My little sister looked at me expectantly but didn't say a word. A feeling of dread overcame me, and I began to search my mother's face for clues.

Years of studying her face had made me an expert at deciphering her moods. With a quick glance at her mouth or her brow, I could tell what kind of day awaited us. A frown by itself was a sign of boredom or tiredness; a frown accompanied by squinting eyes spelled anger and warned of consequences for misbehaving. An unlined brow, and sometimes even sparkling eyes, meant a respite from her relentless pessimism or her sadness. On the days of the sparkling eyes, I could expect any surprise from my mother: a dead mouse floating in a pail of water, a warm rice pudding, a new blouse stitched together from the remnants she had saved from her work as a seamstress, or the promise that, come 7:00 P.M., I would be allowed to watch my favorite television show at a neighbor's house.

Today was different, though. Today, she seemed happy. Her round face, framed by shiny black hair, was open and warm, soft and glowing with the luminosity of an antique white satin wedding gown. Her slightly slanted dark brown eyes sparkled. She didn't even seem to have registered my alarmed tone. Oh, no! I thought, we got our exit papers. And my heart sank, because in the summer of

1974, when I was ten, nothing would have lifted my parents' heart—and broken mine—more than receiving authorization to emigrate to the United States.

I don't remember a time when I didn't know that my family's most cherished aspiration was to someday, somehow leave Cuba, as most of the people we knew had already done. My earliest memories are not of making friends but of losing them to the United States. All my parents' friends and many of our relatives had left by the time I was six. We would take a walk in the neighborhood, and suddenly my mother would notice the telltale official yellow piece of paper sealing shut someone's main door, and just like that she would know she'd lost another friend—and, by extension, so had I. Marcelo and Mery and their two girls, the family downstairs, left first. Mery used to cut my mother's hair; Marcelo, my father's. Then it was Gladys and Ñico from around the corner. Gladys was my mother's second cousin; her oldest daughter was my friend and classmate. Later it was Alicia and Miguel's turn. They lived just a block away and were my parents' best friends. Their sprawling, book-filled house was a magnet of interesting, fun people who on many evenings had made my mother laugh and my father forget his life for a while.

Eventually my parents, my sister, and I would sit to plan our weekend and realize that we had no one to visit anymore. My mother started listening to radio soap operas to fill the silence of her days. My father preferred to stay home, spending an entire Sunday afternoon shining our shoes. I began to befriend the elderly people in the neighborhood, the ones I thought were too old ever to leave. I spent hours at the dark Colonial-style home of five sisters, old maids, who were fond of saying they wanted to be buried in Cuba. I figured that unless they got sick and suddenly died, their burial plans granted a certain longevity to our relationship.

After a while wanting to leave became a way of life. It meant that my father scanned the paper for news of conflicts with other countries, calculating which enemy nation would be most likely to welcome fleeing Cuban refugees. My sister and I rarely got to wear our nicest outfits, because my mother saved them, pressed and covered in plastic, so we could look elegant upon landing in Madrid, which was the plan for a while, or New York, which was always the dream. As we got older, she stopped doing that and instead saved the thickest fabrics she could find, calculating that any place north of Havana was bound to be frigid. Both my parents avoided any kind of political affiliation because, as they would explain to different recruiters who came to our home to encourage them to join in the spirit of the revolution, why get involved? We are waiting for our exit papers, you see, they'd say. And the men and women who dutifully tried to make communists out of my parents would open their eyes wide and exclaim, Ooh! surprised at their honesty and somewhat envious of a family with an actual plan.

But as I stood in front of my mother that day, silently praying that the urgency in her voice was not linked to our emigration plans, I detected only joy, no nervous edge to her gestures. It wasn't the papers, then, I realized. That's when I saw my father's back. He was kneeling on the floor, his large brown hands toying with what looked like a black box. I leaned forward, but all I could see at first was the top of his head, covered by curly black hair, which he carefully combed back every morning with brilliantine. Then his long nose, which cleaved his narrow face in half like the arm of a sundial and hung in a perfect right angle over his thin mustache. I stood on my toes and finally saw what he was hiding from me: a television!

Oh, my God! I yelped and jumped on my father's wide back, hugging him tightly from behind.

I had wanted a television set for so long that I'd begun to think I was never going to have one. All my friends had one, old black-and-white relics from the time American products could be purchased in Cuba. And here was ours. Finally. Black-and-white as well, but shiny and new, with an incomprehensible Russian word on the top right side.

I jumped up and down. My sister joined me. My mother, too. My father explained that for two hundred pesos, or about one and a half times his monthly salary, he had bought a coupon from a friend stating that he had donated an old American TV to the government. Armed with the fake coupon, my father spent another seven hundred pesos, a fortune for us, to buy the Russian box; without the coupon he couldn't have done it. It was all sort of illegal, but my father was confident he wouldn't get caught, he said, sounding more hopeful than certain, more embarrassed by the deal than triumphal. Still, with the help of my mother, he had accomplished a major feat. For years my mother had tucked away every peso she earned at the sewing machine so that our family could afford small luxuries such as fried chicken every Sunday for lunch, occasional dinners out, and now, finally, a television.

I was reminded daily of the life my parents used to have before the revolution, of the life they claimed I should have had. My parents often talked of bathing with fragrant soaps, of using shampoos that actually cleaned long hair like mine, of American-made appliances that lasted for years, and of a sticky magical concoction, called Vicks VapoRub, that cured all coughs and unclogged stuffy noses. The cobalt blue glass bottle of one, the last one my parents bought before American products disappeared from pharmacies, still sat in the middle of our medicine cabinet. All the possibilities of capitalism, of life in pre-Castro Cuba, were encapsulated for me in that squat little container of a salve so old that it had lost its scent.

Life in the late 1950s had been joyous, my parents told me. On weekends they rode around the city on clean, practically empty buses, just to kill time. In the evenings, television shows were entertaining, not educational like the ones I was forced to watch because nothing else was on. Their favorite shows gave prizes away. Imagine that! my father used to tell me. You would climb up a waxed pole, and if you made it to the top, you'd win a mattress or a couch. If you found a plastic rooster in the laundry soap, you could win a house. A whole house! Imagine that! But I couldn't imagine, and so my father took me to the one house in the neighborhood that still bore the sign of the soap, Jabón Candado.

When I walked about my neighborhood, I used to go out of my way to find that house, to marvel at its construction, to scrutinize all the details of its ornate façade—crevices and niches and Doric columns, a relic of times past. A disabled girl in a wheelchair lived in that house, and every day her parents placed her on the front porch to let her catch the afternoon breeze. She sat there alone in her pink, ruffled dress and watched me while I looked at her house. Her mother would come out sometimes and, assuming I was curious about the girl, invite me in. She'd ask me, Do you want to be her friend? But I didn't. I wanted only to live in her house or, at the very least, to visit it. I yearned to touch the symbol of Jabón Candado, an open lock attached to the façade to remind people that someone in that house once had the good fortune of finding a plastic rooster nestled inside a bar of soap.

+   +   +

IN MY WORLD there was no such thing as good luck. My family lived in a one-bedroom apartment for which my parents paid twenty-five pesos a month, or a little less than 20 percent of my father's salary. Because the government had confiscated all private property, we never knew who the original owner of the apartment had been. As far as we knew, it was ours. No one could kick us out, as my teachers often told me capitalists used to do to the poor who couldn't pay the rent. But we also had no chance to win a house or even a bigger apartment by testing our luck. In my world people earned the right to have things through hard work and the right political attitude, not because they were lucky.

The people I knew earned coupons to buy plastic blenders or Russian-made washing machines by working long hours in their jobs six days a week and then volunteering to work on Sunday for the good of the country. They cut sugarcane in fields far from their homes, helped build homes for those who didn't have any, or labored overtime in factories to meet production quotas and maybe even earn the right to buy a refrigerator. My father worked hard, harder than many others, I knew. And yet until the day my father brought that black Russian box home, I had never switched on a television set.

Go ahead, turn it on, my father said, as if reading my mind. Gently.

A simple switch of a button to the right, and a light appeared on the center of the screen, where it flickered for a while, and then, as if by magic, the screen opened.

There was nothing on; programming didn't start until later in the day. We sat on the couch smiling, watching vertical stripes on top of a large horizontal stripe until we got bored. At 5:45 P.M. an old Argentine film came on, and we all watched attentively, eating bread with oil and salt, our favorite snack.

An hour later, just as the movie was nearing its end, the power went out. A nightly blackout, a few hours without electricity, was a common occurrence in Cuba, and especially in my neighborhood, Santos Suárez. There were no diplomats where we lived, no foreign students, no Eastern European comrades—the only outsiders who visited Cuba then—so my neighborhood was a convenient one to keep in the dark. No one complained. To whom? For what? Most people did what we did that night: went out to their terraces or balconies, sat in their rocking chairs, and rocked the boredom and frustration away.

I was so grateful for that precious black box that when the lights went off, I ran to my parents' bedroom, threw myself on the pink bedspread, facedown, eyes squeezed shut, and promised myself that once I started sixth grade in September, I would watch TV only after I had completed my homework and memorized my lessons of the day.

When I told my mother later about my promise, she shook her head silently. If she thought I was exaggerating, she didn't say. She knew that the previous school year had been a torment for both of us. I needed to prove, if only to myself, that—at least academically—I was beyond reproach.

I HAD HAD TWO teachers in fifth grade, one for science and math, the other for literature and history. The arrangement was a novelty, because up to then I'd had only one teacher for each grade and revered all of them. So it was perhaps out of habit and goodwill that I felt an instant connection to my two new teachers the moment they walked into class the first day. They were young and pretty. Tania had long black hair, down to her waist, and she always wore very short dresses. Eradia was thin and dark, with the delicate features of a bird. She had short, curly black hair and a wide smile that revealed shiny white teeth.

Sometime during the first week of classes, Tania posed a question I had never been asked before.

Who here believes in God? she asked, looking over the entire class.

Without thinking I raised my hand. So did Ivón, the chubby girl who sat next to me and was in my Saturday catechism class. We were the only ones with our hands up. Ivón blushed deeply. Under the weight of so many eyes looking in our direction, she slowly lowered her hand, letting it rest delicately on top of her desk.

And who goes to church? Tania pressed on.

I left my arm up, mainly because I knew that my teacher already knew. The fact that I went to church, I was sure, was in my student record, the one kept by school officials for each child from kindergarten on. Also, because denying God was not allowed in my family. There were categories of lies at home. We were never to flaunt the fact that we had relatives in the United States, but we were not to deny them either. We didn't have to announce to the world that we believed in God, but, if asked directly, we would affirm it. And to anyone who asked we would always say that we were waiting for our exit papers to leave the country because we wanted to join my father's siblings abroad, which was only half the truth. We weren't to reveal that my father had issues with a revolution that he felt robbed people of their souls.

The lies were necessary because any perceived ideological flaw could potentially mark a family as counterrevolutionary, an enemy of the revolution. Having a relative in jail for opposing the revolution; communicating with relatives in a Western country, especially the United States; having had a great deal of money or influence under the previous regime; believing in God and openly going to church; and wanting to leave the country could earn one the label of counterrevolutionary. Once so branded, life in Cuba became even more difficult. A mistake that would cause anyone else to receive a reprimand could land a counterrevolutionary in jail.

Three years earlier, when Uncle Oswaldo had sent us a package from Madrid, my mother had instructed me to lie about it. It's a family issue, she'd said. I understood her comment as permission to lie. A package wasn't worth the aggravation of being honest. If anyone asked where I got the canary yellow dress I wore on special occasions, I was to say that my neighbor, who often traveled to the Soviet Union, had brought it back for me. Admitting to having received a package from *el exterior*—the official shorthand used to describe anything not produced, sold, or controlled by the revolution—offered the government ammunition to cast aside a family as counterrevolutionary.

And so my parents went about their lives carefully, trudging on the ever-narrowing space where their personal convictions didn't interfere too much with their obligations as conscientious parents who had to teach their children to obey rules they abhorred. With tact and good nature, they managed to remain undetected, or ignored, by those who thought apathy was almost as subversive as an attack against the revolution.

They never went to La Plaza de la Revolución, the square where Castro delivered his endless speeches, but they were helpful to neighbors and often worked without pay on Sundays, pouring cement to repair cracked sidewalks or planting trees in community gardens. Despite their obvious political shortcomings, they were respected and even admired by some of the most militant members of the neighborhood. Our downstairs neighbor, a woman who moved in after Marcelo and Mery left for the United States, had fought in the mountains with Castro, and her husband periodically received military training in the Soviet Union, yet she talked to my mother every day as the two washed clothes on their patios, their voices muffled by the floor that separated them and the sound of the water splashing in the sink.

Perhaps I should have lied then when asked about faith, but thus far my teachers had been kind to me, and in their kindness I had found a refuge from the dichotomy of my life. I could believe in God and Fidel. I could read Karl Marx and Mark Twain. I could play Angela Davis, the 1960s black radical, in a school play and sing in the church choir Saturday afternoons. Every day I tested my balance on an ideological tightrope, torn between school, where I was constantly told that the revolution had been built so that children like me could have a better future, and home, where the very mention of the word "revolution" caused my parents, particularly my father, to grimace. I had no reason to believe that my fifth-grade teachers would upset that balance.

To them, though, I was damaged goods, a smart kid who would never amount to anything because the counterrevolutionary attitude of my parents held me back. Teachers, especially ambitious young ones who aspired to join the Communist Party, aimed to shape the "New Man" that Che Guevara had dreamed about out of the pliable clay of a child's character. But I, the daughter of professed *gusanos*—"worms," the term applied to those who had not integrated into the revolutionary process and wanted to leave the country—was not moldable material.

My teachers knew that my father had been opposed to my becoming a Pioneer when I was five, the age at which Cuban children swear before the flag, in an elaborate ceremony, to grow up to be like Che Guevara: *"Pioneros por el comunismo. Seremos como el Che"*—Pioneers for Communism. We will be like Che. It had taken my mother two years to convince my father to let me wear the then white-and-blue Pioneer neckerchief to school; she sensed I wasn't going to thrive in school unless I became a Pioneer. When I finally did, at the beginning of third grade, my mother attended the ceremony; my father did not. I bet my teachers noted that, too.

How can such an intelligent girl believe in God? Tania asked me in a mocking tone. Does God put food on your table? Noooo, Fidel does. Does God give you your books and pencils so you can come to school? Nooooo, the revolution does.

I lowered my head in silence. I had been marked.

In the Cuba of the 1970s, even children knew that no loyalty was more important than that owed to Fidel Castro and the revolution. Before I learned my multiplication tables, I had memorized Che's final letter to Castro, the one in which he tells him he has to leave Cuba because he was made for the struggle, not for the spoils of victory. I was told that Nixon was an evil man before I learned who Hitler had been or what he had done. I could recite Castro's speech at his 1953 trial for leading an attack against a Batista military barracks before I ever laid my eyes on a poem by Lord Byron or Pablo Neruda. In school we were often reminded of how many children went to bed hungry or died of treatable diseases in places like Nicaragua, Ethiopia, and even Alabama, and we were made to memorize slogans such as "*Fidel es mi papá y Cuba es mi mamá.*" I mouthed the words but never uttered them aloud.

FROM THE DAY TANIA discovered I went to church, she began to make fun of my mother.

She waltzes in and she says, Miss, how is my daughter doing? How are her grades? Is she behaving in class? My teacher would say, walking from the center of the room to the door, holding her hand in midair, the way my mother did, straining in vain, with her short, thick neck, to look like my mother. My mother was so tall and elegant that this woman couldn't possibly ever look like her.

So there I sat, first to the teacher's right, surrounded by my giggling classmates, not knowing if I should laugh at her for looking so ridiculous or cry at the caricature of my mother she had created.

Why doesn't she ask about *all* the kids in the class? Tania asked, emphasizing the word "all," stretching the vowel to make it match the sweeping arch of her arms over the entire class of thirty. Why is she so individualistic, so bourgeois? And why does she insist in calling me *señorita*?

To be polite was to be bourgeois, a sin in Castro's Cuba. My teacher wanted to be called *compañera*. She wanted my mother to become a "combatant mother," a much-politicized version of the hard-driving PTA leader. I had begged my mother to join the mothers' group and to start using the words that the government had popularized. But she eschewed any kind of organized effort, and her thin lips seemed to be built for softer words, like "Miss" and "please" and "kindly." "Comrade" was harsh. "Combatant" was a military word.

Oxen have partners, my mother used to tell me. We are people. I don't have a *compañera*, and I don't wage war.

The weeks of school went by. My mother never knew that *la señorita* Tania— so young and innocent-looking—was mocking her in front of the class. I dared not tell her, for I feared her reaction. If she talked to the teacher, I was certain, the mockery would never end.

ONE SATURDAY, as my parents were dressing for their weekly outing to the movies, my mother asked me why I hadn't yet selected my clothes for church. Every Saturday my parents walked my sister and me to our weekly catechism class, and then they would quickly leave for the movies. By the time the movie ended, my sister and I were taking communion. My parents waited for us in the back pews, hoping no one noticed they had missed mass. Neither one of them had been brought up in a particularly religious home. Yet they insisted that my sister and I go to church because, they said, nothing bad could ever happen to us there.

But I wasn't so sure anymore that church was good for me, and I told my mother just that as she was slipping on her black high-heeled sandals. She got up from the bed, looked me in the eye, and asked why.

I just don't like it, I said. It's boring, and I have to confess, and I don't have any sins, so I make them up, and I'm tired of that. My eyes welled with tears.

My parents were stunned at my words.

And I think my sister shouldn't go either, I went on through sobs. It's not good for her.

My sister Mabel, four years younger than I was, would do as I said, I was sure of that. From the time she was born, my mother had made me feel that I was as responsible for her safety and well-being as my parents were. In return I had her loyalty. Mine was the hand she held on to as we crossed the street during family outings, and mine was the shoulder she sought when she was sad or conflicted. I wanted to spare her the humiliation and pain my admitted faith was putting me through. My parents looked at each other but didn't say anything. My father finished combing his hair and, finally, spoke.

Okay, then, he said. Get dressed anyway. You are going to the movies with us.

We went to see *Los Incapturables*, a Russian film with Spanish subtitles about a band of four youths who roam Russia in search of adventure. We laughed until we cried. And we never again talked about God, the church, or religion in our home.

In class I began to sit in the back and rarely raised my hand anymore. My grades started to slip, not dramatically, but enough for my mother to notice, which made her visit the classroom even more and question the teacher in greater detail, which made Tania intensify her mocking. Eventually I feigned headaches to avoid going to school. Soon enough the headaches became real.

For every day that I missed school, Tania had a special punishment for me. I was to complete, at lunchtime, five hundred lines of whatever humiliating sentence she could come up with: I will not talk in class. I will not miss class. I will not be late. My mother learned to imitate my handwriting so she could help me finish the assignments on time. I began to skip lunch to complete my lines, or if I did manage to eat, I would throw up on the way back to school for the afternoon session.

One day the teacher asked me to stay after class and accompany her to the principal's office. I wondered what I had done this time to deserve such humiliation. The principal, a stocky and stern woman named Iraida, was waiting behind her desk when we arrived. In front of her, she had a file with my name on it. She said something about being concerned for my future, worried that my behavior

would derail my plans, thinking that my family was jeopardizing my opportunities for advancement. My future, she told me, was in peril.

But I tell you what, she said. There just may be something we can do about it.
Compañera Tania here has something for you.

Tania handed me a yellow envelope and asked me to take it home and make
sure that my parents answered each and all questions in the pages it contained
and to return it to her the next morning. I thanked her and the principal, because
I felt that I had been given the responsibility to save my future. It was, quite literally, in my hands.

I went home thinking I would lock myself in the bathroom to read the papers
before handing them to my mother. But the moment my mother saw my face, she
asked me what had happened. I took the envelope from my book bag and handed
it to her, not telling her what the principal had said about my uncertain future.
She glanced at the papers before laying them on the dining table; for once her
face betrayed nothing. Accustomed to leaving important decisions to my father,
she said he would take a look at them when he came home from work, which he
usually did after eight, exhausted from driving a delivery truck.

When he arrived that night, he, too, ignored the papers at first. I was aching
to read them but didn't dare to touch them. I reminded my father to answer all
the questions, just as the teacher had instructed. We'll see, he said.

I went to bed but didn't sleep. Because my sister and I shared the couch in the
living room, I could see my father hunched over the papers by the light on the
dining table. He stayed up half the night, sometimes reading, sometimes thinking, holding his brow with the first three fingers of his left hand, as was his custom when events overwhelmed him. I peered at him from under the sheets,
pretending to sleep. Sometime before dawn he pushed the papers away and went
to bed.

In the morning he simply told me he couldn't answer the questions, and he
showed me why. The questionnaire asked every detail of our lives. Did we have
relatives in the United States? What were their names and addresses? Did we
communicate with them? How often? Did we go to church? Every week? Every
day? Did we know any counterrevolutionaries? Did we go to La Plaza to hear Fidel speak? Did we volunteer when the revolution needed us? One hundred and

fifty-four questions that were impossible to answer but perhaps dangerous to ig-nore. To discard the questions could send the signal that I was desperately trying to avoid: that as the daughter of avowed *gusanos*, I was beyond redemption. There was nothing I could do for the revolution, and therefore there was nothing the revolution could do for me.

No one has the right to invade our privacy like this, my father said. I knew not to go further.

He rolled up the papers and put them inside one of the glasses from an orange-and-green set my mother kept in the cupboard. I skipped school that day, complaining of stomach pains. The next day my teachers asked me if we had filled out the questionnaire. I said my father was working on it. They asked again the next day, and the next. Until one day they stopped asking. The papers remained inside the cupboard for as long as we lived in Cuba.

THE SCHOOL YEAR ENDED, as did all my years in grade school, with a student show. Teachers would pick their favorite students and coach them to display their talents on graduation day, when awards were issued along with the diplomas. I'd had such a chaotic year that I knew I wouldn't receive any special awards or be picked to perform in any of the shows. My class had organized a fashion show representing the countries of the world. There were girls dressed in flowing white Panamanian dresses, elaborate Spanish dancers' costumes, and even Japanese kimonos. Others wore short, skin-colored smocks and feathers in their hair; they were American Indians. A black girl wrapped her lithe body with a colorful curtain from her living room to represent Africa. Another wore baggy pants and a veil around her face; she was the Cuban version of an Arabic country.

I stood on the sidelines pretending to enjoy the preparations for the show as much as if I were participating in it. But I couldn't, because for the first time I had not been chosen. I was no longer good enough to play a Vietnamese farmer, harvesting rice with a stick while pretending to dodge American bombs, or even Angela Davis, a role I had played before, clad in a black plastic miniskirt, my hands bound by paper chains while the people of the world swirled around me and clamored for my freedom. I had danced and sung and recited revolutionary poems from the time I could read. I had played the role of Cuba, the motherland, wrapped in a flag, my head topped by a tiny red hat.

And yet there I stood that day in July 1974, watching my classmates giggle as they put on their costumes and the girls brushed each other's hair while the boys fiddled with the sound system. The salty taste of my tears surprised me, and I ran to the bathroom to hide. On my way back to the show, I ran into Eradia, the teacher who had stood by while Tania made my life miserable that year. She grabbed me by the waist and said, There you are!

Here I am, I replied, bracing for the worst.

I've been looking for you, she said. I have no one to play the role of Cuba, and you are perfect for it.

But I don't have a costume, I said, my mind racing, my heart beating fast. Could I run home and fashion a dress with my mother's magical sewing machine before the show started in ten minutes? Probably not.

You don't need one. You'll play revolutionary Cuba, she said, gesturing toward my outfit.

I was wearing black cotton pants and a long red polyester blouse with ruffles in the front. Red and black were the colors of the 26 of July Movement, the group that Castro had led in his quest for power.

Yes, I said, yes! And I ran to the stage, jumping on instead of climbing the stairs. I took my place in line just as the music began. When Eradia read my name and said, And now, *compañeros* and *compañeras*, here's the Cuba of today, the Cuba of all of us, revolutionary Cuba! I took a gracious bow and looked over to my mother, who suppressed her surprise and politely smiled back from the audience.

My graduation gift from my teachers that day was a large book titled *Moncada*, the name of the military barracks that a group of young men, led by Castro, had attacked in their first attempt to overthrow the government of Batista in July 1953, twenty-one years before I graduated from fifth grade. The shiny cover had what I thought were splashes of black and white paint until a boy pointed out that the black was really blood, the blood of the martyrs who had died so that I could enjoy the freedoms I was told I had. Inside the book were pictures of the dead revolutionaries who had accompanied Castro in that failed mission. Some had been tortured beyond recognition, eyes gouged out, fingernails pulled off, faces smashed by fierce blows. I closed the book quickly but thanked my teachers anyway. When I got home, I hid the book on the tallest shelf I could find, so that I would never again have to see what happens to revolutionary young men and women with convictions.

THE VERY FIRST DAY of sixth grade, I met Marta, a short, toothy girl with bright eyes and freckles, who quickly became my friend. Like me, she took school seriously and always carried a book with her. Marta lived with her grandmother, Carmelina, a kind old woman who taught piano and French to a select group of children. To study with Marta's grandmother was a privilege, a sign that you were ambitious and smart enough to garner the attention of the most educated woman in the neighborhood. Before the revolution she had gone to school abroad, in France and the United States, where she had majored in philosophy. She knew history and geography and geometry as intimately as she knew the contours of her house.

I already knew of Carmelina's reputation, and I liked Marta a great deal, so I immediately told her that I wanted to do my homework with her. Kathy, who was my oldest friend, also came along. A partnership was forged. Every day after school, we would go home and shower quickly and then rush to Marta's dining room, where, at the head of a long wooden table with thick, carved legs, her grandmother awaited. First we would do our homework with her guidance, then review the day's lessons. She would push us to think critically, to go beyond the chapter at hand. We would stay at that table until Carmelina was certain that, for that day at least, we understood the world as she saw it. She would often finish the evening by playing the piano as we sat on the posh but faded couches of her living room and looked at paintings of English hunting parties on the walls.

My grades improved so dramatically that I could entertain thoughts of going to the country's top university preparatory school, the Vocational School Vladimir Ilich Lenin. There were three girls who had a good chance that year. I was one of them; the other two were Kathy, whose sister already attended the school, and Marta, whose parents everyone said were members of the militia, the group of men and women who wore the olive green fatigues favored by Fidel and who performed important but drudging work for the country. I had the best grade-point average in sixth grade but no brilliant older sister or family connections, as my mother would often remind me. In the days leading up to the announcement, the three of us were nervous but tried not to show it. We knew that only one of us would be chosen, and yet we continued to study together. Now that we were certain to graduate with top honors, Carmelina had relaxed her rules and allowed us to play on her vast terrace, from which we could see the rooftops of the entire neighborhood. She even made us cookies and allowed us to bang on the old piano ourselves.

But my mother remained wary. They'll never pick you. Remember that, she would say, and then add for good measure, If you expect the worst, you won't be disappointed when it comes; you'll be prepared. And if it doesn't, you'll be thrilled.

At the end of the school year, when the principal called out the name of the sixth-grader selected to go to the Lenin school, I was prepared for the worst, as my mother had taught me, but also hoping for the best. It was not to be. Marta's name was called. Everybody rushed to congratulate her, including me.

WHEN THE TIME CAME to register for middle school, my student record had been sent to the wrong school. I had to retrieve it personally and carry it to the school I had been assigned. I was told not to open the package or dare peek at the pages of my record.

The first thing I did when I got home, of course, was to figure out a way to read my records. It was easier than I'd thought. The white notebook with my name printed in bold black letters was inside a plastic envelope sealed only with a simple staple. I carefully removed the staple by separating the two legs with a kitchen knife and pulled the notebook out, trying not to smudge the immaculate covers with my fingers.

I had been told many times by my teachers that from kindergarten on, a detailed year-by-year record was kept of our grades, our strengths and weaknesses, our disposition. What I had never been told was that my record as a student would also include a fair amount of information about my family. Page by page, in handwriting that I recognized as that of my grammar-school teachers, my record revealed every detail of my life.

Father won't let her become a Pioneer, my first-grade teacher had written.

Mother takes an extreme interest in the child, even sitting in class to learn modern mathematical concepts. She has a sixth-grade education from the years before the revolution, the teacher went on.

Child likes to read, wrote my second-grade teacher, a man who used to give me books about the Vietnam War as rewards for my good grades.

She is precocious. She shows potential but won't participate much in political activities, wrote my third-grade teacher. She has relatives in the United States, and the family regularly communicates with them.

This student still goes to church, wrote Tania.

Excellent grades but needs to become more involved in revolutionary activities, wrote my sixth-grade teacher.

By the end of the report, I was holding the notebook away from my face so my tears wouldn't stain the pages. Now I knew why I had not been picked for the school of my choice. I'd never really had a chance. Mercifully, I was alone in the house. I didn't want my parents to conclude that their ideology was hindering my education. I slipped the notebook back into the plastic envelope, slowly pushed the staple through the holes, and, with the back of the knife, pressed it closed.

SOMETIME LATER THAT YEAR, the president of the block committee approached my father one day at dusk, just as he was coming home with a bagful of potatoes he had purchased from a farmer, a forbidden transaction then. When are you going to join us? she asked him, eyeing the illegal potatoes. My father froze in place. He knew that she could call the police right there, but he hoped she wouldn't. After all, he had been buying food on the black market for years, and so far no one had said anything. This time was different, though. He could sense it. The president of the block committee was upset because ours was the only one in the neighborhood that did not have 100 percent participation. And

all because of the Ojito family, she said. My family's reluctance to join was upsetting her record. If she wasn't able to make revolutionaries out of all her neighbors, she would be perceived as a weak, untrustworthy leader.

How much longer do you think I can protect you? she said.

My father understood the implicit threat. Soon after, my parents became
members of the Committee for the Defense of the Revolution, and I became a
junior member of sorts, volunteering to distribute vaccines for children, helping
to weed community gardens, and knocking on doors reminding people to attend
the next block meeting.

On October 6, 1976, after years of relative peace between Cuba and the
United States, terrorists planted a bomb in a Cubana de Aviación plane on its
way from Venezuela to Cuba. The plane blew up in midair, killing all seventy-
three people on board—including most of the members of Cuba's youth fencing
team. The pilot of the plane was the father of one of my eighth-grade classmates.
Our school, and the nation, was in mourning; it was Fidel's finest hour. This was
exactly the kind of disaster he needed to stoke the flames of nationalistic ardor.
We had gotten too lax, he told us. Too sure of our revolution, our accomplish-
ments, our resolve. But we must never forget that our enemies lay in wait.

The country was thrown into a revolutionary frenzy from which it was impossible to escape. Though I had never felt especially drawn to Fidel and had
managed to avoid listening to most of his speeches, I felt a duty to go with the
rest of my classmates to La Plaza de la Revolución to hear him give a eulogy for
the victims. When the buses came to school to pick us up, instead of hiding in a
closet or a bathroom as I used to do, I boarded, sat by a window, and sang my
heart out, defying the enemies of the revolution to try our might.

I didn't get to see Fidel. Hundreds of thousands of people thronged the
square and the streets of the neighborhood that surrounded it. As I made my
way through the crowds trying not to lose sight of my friends, I could hear
snatches of Fidel's speech, booming overhead. Blood. Principles. Death. Yankees.
Once again he was blaming the United States.

Fidel's fury frightened me. My chest tightened, and I began to feel an urge to
get away. I forged ahead but couldn't move. Too many people. I couldn't even
think of going back. A mob was pressing at my back. Making a sudden turn to

the right, I became separated from my friends and ended up seeking shelter in a funeral home. There a family was in mourning for a young man who had killed himself with his father's gun. From the foyer of the funeral home, I could see his swollen head protruding over one end of the casket. It was the first dead body I had ever seen, and I felt a surge of bile rising up my throat.

I ran away and didn't stop running until somehow I boarded a city bus that was practically empty because everyone or nearly everyone was at La Plaza, from which I'd just escaped. I rode the bus until it reached its final destination. I was so confused I had no idea where I was. When the speech ended and the buses resumed their normal routes, I found one that eventually took me home.

BEFORE THE YEAR was over, the newspapers began writing a great deal about the man who had won the race to the White House, Jimmy Carter. Cuban newspapers always paid exaggerated attention to the comings and goings of the *americanos*, but this Jimmy Carter was getting more attention than most. He was a man, it seemed, with whom Fidel could communicate. He would control the crazy Miami Cubans or the CIA assassins or whoever it was that had murdered the fencing team, the government assured us.

Despite the news that held the nation transfixed, our lives went on as usual, preoccupied by the lack of food and other inexplicable consequences of defying the United States. We lived in a country of mysteries, of mirrors, of magicians. Large quantities of eggs could appear in the market one morning, as if all the hens of Cuba had gone into a production overdrive, and then suddenly eggs would disappear for weeks. The Americans must have poisoned the chickens, people would say. A store in Old Havana would receive a large shipment of hand soap, and lines that snaked around the shaded porticoes of the city would form for days; then there would be no soap for months. A crucial ingredient for soap must have been held up by the embargo, we would hear. Butter would come and go. Vanilla ice cream was plentiful, but strawberry was rare; the tropics were not kind to berry plants, we were told. There always seemed to be plain yogurt in the stores, but not enough milk. We had bread, but, though the ocean surrounded us, never fish.

Cuba's leading cookbook author taught us to make meatballs without meat. She suggested using *gofio*, a sort of parched cornmeal. We had the best health care of the Americas, we were repeatedly told, but for a while cavities went unfilled because amalgam was nowhere to be found; dentists were using it as plaster to even the cracking walls of their homes as there was no plaster—or cement or tiles or paint—in the stores. Fidel would talk for hours about how the farmers were meeting production quotas despite the *americanos*, but the next day no one could find plantains anywhere in Havana.

We lived in fear of the enemy. We lived defying the enemy. The enemy was always the United States. My father would caution me that though the American government might have made mistakes, the people were good. They were people who, like us, worked hard and went to school and obeyed the rules but who, unlike us, were rewarded for their efforts. Over there, my father would say, always pointing with his index finger to an imaginary land just north of our terrace, it is possible to buy a ham-and-cheese sandwich every day on a man's salary and possible, too, to treat yourself to something lacy and ruffled, like the dresses I favored, without having to sacrifice a month's meat ration to acquire it.

And you know what's even more important? he'd ask, then answer the question before I could reply. What's more important is that no one will ask you what you bought and why. No one will care what you do or what you think.

In the sixties and seventies, the Cuban government called this implicit promise of a better life under capitalism *diversionismo ideológico*, an ideological betrayal punishable by expulsion from schools and jobs as well as, in some instances, detention and even imprisonment. Out of respect and curiosity, I let my father explain his theories about the United States without interruption. But at the time I was still enthralled by the possibilities of socialism, and I knew, as much as a fourteen-year-old can profess to know, that revolutionaries like me should not allow the trappings of capitalism to cloud their judgment.

Then, in May 1977, an extraordinary event took place in Cuba. A U.S. journalist, a woman named Barbara Walters—a name I could hardly pronounce—had come to Cuba to get to know us, we were told, and to interview our leader. Back then, ordinary Cubans like us had not been in contact with Americans for almost two decades. Once again I was grateful that we had a television set. The sight of that woman hurling questions in English at Fidel for almost five hours, questions that no one had asked him before, left me speechless. What about political prisoners? she wanted to know.

When I was little, I had heard a story about a young man in the neighborhood who was sent to jail and later executed by a firing squad for conspiring against the revolution. His bride had gone crazy, the story went; she spent her days in a catatonic state, looking out the window of her imposing but crumbling house across from our apartment. I thought of my mother's cousin, whom I remembered vaguely. He had been in prison on an island south of Havana, and my father had flown in a small plane to see him several times. The man fled Cuba in a boat as soon as he was released. The son of my father's closest friend at work had also been in prison, sentenced to thirty years for trying to leave the country illegally in a raft. I had always thought that those were isolated incidents, aberrations of a regime that felt threatened by its enemies to the north. Yet here was Fidel on television admitting that he held maybe two or three thousand political prisoners in Cuba's jails. Not only that, he said that, at one point, more than fifteen thousand Cubans had been jailed for political reasons. Finally Ms. Walters asked Fidel to say a few words in English for the American people. His words were instantly translated to Spanish. He said that the *americanos* were hardworking people, honest people, even idealistic. Fidel added that he hoped the people of Cuba and the people of the United States could be friends. That, he said, was his sincere hope.

When we turned off the television, my father remained pensive in the darkened living room. The message was clear, he said. Changes were coming. If Fidel were willing to talk to his enemies, who knew? Maybe we could dare to dream again. Not about the kind of radical changes that would make us want to stay in Cuba, my father said, but dream about obtaining the one thing he wanted more than anything else in life: a visa to the United States. All he needed now—all Fidel was after, really—was a little push, a hint from Washington or from Miami that the Americans were willing to listen. But who, my father wondered, citing an old proverb, who would be the one to place the bell around the cat's neck?

TWO

Bernardo Benes:
Our Man in Miami

Bernardo Benes during a meeting with Cuban political prisoners
in Havana. He's holding up a sign that says "agent of Fidel" to show
the prisoners that his efforts to liberate them were
not well received in Miami.

*F*ROM HIS WINDOW in the small plane, Bernardo Benes could see the outlines of the distant palm trees against the darkness. The plane was about to land at a small military airport in Havana. His mind was racing, his emotions were riding a pendulum, and he was overcome by anxiety. What would his beloved Havana look like? What would happen to him, to his mission? This was not how he had imagined his return to Cuba. Benes had left Cuba in 1960 as a twenty-five-year-old lawyer convinced that Castro had to be ousted from power by force. He was returning in 1978, as a forty-three-year-old prominent Miami banker on a peaceful mission.

The Russian airplane that was taking him back touched the runway. The palm trees now seemed huge and perfectly clear. Benes went down the stairs first, followed by some of Castro's closest associates, and was immediately overwhelmed by the smell, that sticky, suffocating mix of sea salt and diesel fumes so particular to Havana.

It was 9:00 P.M., and a persistent drizzle clouded his vision. Ten black Mercedes-Benzes awaited them. Too many cars, Benes thought. Uniformed men stood next to one of the cars. A breeze swayed the palm trees, and the rustling sound of their leaves under the raindrops reminded him that yes, he was finally home.

He held his breath to avoid crying. Benes had no time for sentimentality. In his office at the Palace of the Revolution, Fidel Castro awaited.

THE IMPROBABLE ROAD that took Benes back to Cuba had begun to unfurl six months earlier during a family vacation in Panama. He was eating breakfast with his wife and children at the Panama Hilton Hotel in August 1977 when a waiter approached the table with a message. Someone wanted to speak to him. Urgently.

On the line was Alberto Pons, a friend in the retail business whom Benes had met during his frequent travels to Panama. The two had radically different views on Cuba. Pons, who had emigrated from Cuba in 1953 and held a variety of positions in the Panamanian government of Omar Torrijos, had befriended some of the officials who worked in the Cuban embassy in Panama. Benes had settled in Miami, with the thousands of emigrants who had started to flee Castro's regime in 1959. The only officials he was friendly with were elected and tended to live in Washington, D.C.

Pons was well aware of their differences, but he also knew that the two shared a passion for Cuba. And that's the reason he was calling: Two of his Cuban acquaintances had traveled to Panama and told him they wanted to meet Benes. Pons figured that whatever mission they had in mind would require generosity of spirit and plenty of courage. Benes, he knew, had both.

Bernardo, there are some Cubans here who want to see you. Can you have lunch with us today at one?

Sure, Benes replied, thinking that his friend had organized a get-together with fellow emigrants.

As if he could read his mind, Pons corrected him. These are Cubans from Cuba, not from Panama.

Benes paused. Why would Communist Cubans want to talk to him?

He was, he knew, what most people would consider a prosperous, well-connected man. He was the vice chairman of the board of Continental National Bank of Miami and a rising star in the Democratic Party, with friends in high places; Congressmen Dante Fascell and Claude Pepper had been to his Miami Beach house for cocktails. The year before, he had been director for Hispanic affairs for the Carter campaign in Florida and he had been invited to President-elect Carter's intimate victory party in Atlanta and to the inauguration in Washington.

His carrot-colored hair, freckles, and Jewish faith helped Benes move easily among the members of Miami's establishment. His Cuban accent and easy, folksy manner made him feel comfortable among his compatriots, arguing louder than they did when necessary, hugging longer and tighter than most, blowing cigar smoke in the air as he talked of returning to a free Cuba one day. On his daily calendar, in any given week, his secretary could schedule an appointment with the publisher of the *Miami Herald* as well as a meeting with a factory worker who wanted financial help to send his daughter to college. If one had to pick a Cuban with access to both the White House and the exile community in the Miami of the 1970s, Bernando Benes was that man.

Yet Benes was also an avowed *gusano*. Over the years he had helped finance covert operations by exiles intent on infiltrating the island to initiate revolt from within. He had raised money to build a monument to the Cuban exiles killed during the Bay of Pigs invasion, and he had testified before Congress against Castro. He had no doubt the Cuban government knew that as well.

Intrigued, Benes agreed to meet at Panamar, his favorite restaurant. Fifteen minutes after the appointed hour, Pons arrived, accompanied by the men from Cuba. One was of a slight, compact build with a certain air of aristocracy about him; the others were short and stocky. All wore regular street clothing. They were amiable, and Benes felt relaxed, as if he were among friends, which surprised him. After all, these were exactly the kind of men that Cubans in Miami feared and despised; these were Castro's men. The type of men who had helped him remain in power for eighteen years by lining his enemies against walls to face firing squads. Castro and his men, these men in front of Benes now, had desolated a nation that had once been grand and prosperous, a place where the Cuban peso had been as valuable as the American dollar.

Still, for three hours Benes drank beer and ate lobsters and fresh sea bass with the Cubans, talking about the old times, common acquaintances, and their university years. Pons paid the check. At the end of the meal, Benes, still uncertain as to what they wanted, agreed to meet them at Pons's house that evening.

The next day's sunrise found all five men deep in conversation and drinking scotch in Pons's sunken living room. In ten hours they had discussed everything from the embargo the United States kept against Cuba to the successes of Miami's Cuban-exile community. As the evening and then the night progressed, Benes had the sense the Cubans were sizing him up, judging his char-

acter, scrutinizing his personality. It was clear they wanted to reach out, and
they wanted Benes to be their emissary to Miami's exile community. Benes, on
the other hand, wanted to know when Castro would be willing to forgive his
former enemies and empty his jails of political prisoners. And, equally important, when would Cubans be allowed back to their beloved land? But he didn't
ask. He saved the questions for the next meeting the men told him they were
sure to have.

FAMILY AND COUNTRY were more important to Benes than anything else.
His father, Boruch Benes, had never lost his sense of nostalgia for the land and
family he abandoned when, at seventeen, he left Russia and boarded a freighter
for Cuba to escape the misery of his life. In Russia he'd had to scavenge in the for-
est for edible roots. He arrived in Havana in 1923, with $20 in his pocket. With
that money he bought cloth to make handkerchiefs, because, though unskilled,
he could sew and he could sell. To young Boruch, Cuba—still giddy from its
hard-won independence from Spain only two decades earlier—was a place
where everything seemed possible for anyone, even a Jewish immigrant who
spoke no Spanish.

With the profits from the sale of the handkerchiefs, the senior Benes bought
more cloth to make cheap undershirts. Those, too, sold briskly. After a few
months, he had a profitable underwear business that eventually made him a
wealthy man. He learned Spanish, changed his name from Boruch to Boris, married Dora Baikowitz, a Lithuanian-Jewish immigrant, and had three children
with her; Bernardo was the youngest.

Despite their prosperity, being Jewish in the Cuba of the 1940s was not easy
for the Benes family. Bernardo's mother hired a professor of Yiddish and Hebrew
history who traveled every Wednesday from Havana to their home in Matanzas—about a two-hour drive—to keep the children connected to their heritage.
Because there was no synagogue in Matanzas, the Benes home became the meeting place of the few Jews who lived in the city and those who passed through it
on their way to other provinces. Bernardo and his siblings, whose milky white
skin and red hair made them stand out among their peers, sometimes were

brought to tears when their friends told them that Cuba was for Cubans, not for foreigners like them. Their father comforted them by reminding them they had nothing to complain about. Compared to other countries, such as the Soviet Union, where families were torn apart by war and hunger and, worse, communism, Cuba was a beautiful, wonderful country of opportunities and prosperity. It was a message Bernardo kept close to his heart.

Bernardo became interested in politics when, at around age thirteen, he read a magazine article about how a minister in the democratically elected government of Ramón Grau San Martín had stolen money from the taxpayers to support his lavish lifestyle. Young Bernardo was outraged and began to take note of other instances of corruption the press reported.

Then, in March 1952, Fulgencio Batista, a former army sergeant who had been president of Cuba in the 1940s, deposed the government of Carlos Prío Socarrás through a coup d'état. The coup was seen as a major setback for the democratic momentum the country had maintained for almost twelve years. The opposition to Batista grew slowly among both the middle class and university students. It did not reach its peak until July of 1953, when Fidel Castro, then a twenty-seven-year-old lawyer, and a gaggle of young men attacked a military barracks in Oriente, the easternmost province of the island. Castro and his men were defeated, and he was sent to jail. But in 1955 Batista declared an amnesty and released all political prisoners, including Castro, who promptly left for Mexico to regroup and returned with a guerrilla army to overthrow the government.

For the next three years, the island was in upheaval. There were rallies and protests against Batista everywhere. The opposition set off bombs in bars and theaters, and shots were often heard in the middle of the night. Benes did not participate in any of the violent protests. Raising money was his specialty, so he became a treasurer of the Directorio Estudiantil Revolucionario, one of the groups fighting to depose Batista.

ON NEW YEAR'S EVE 1958, Batista fled Havana. Soon after, Castro declared his triumph. Benes rejoiced, thinking that democracy would resume as soon as the last flames of war and its rhetoric were extinguished. He also thought that he would be able to continue working as a corporate lawyer—by then he was twenty-four, married, and making more than $20,000 a year, a considerable sum at the time—going to baseball games in the evenings and playing poker with his friends on Saturdays.

Benes was so enthusiastic about the new regime that he began to work as a legal adviser in Castro's treasury department. His father cautioned him that Castro was a communist. Forget about it, Dad, he would say.

Then came the summary trials and, to Benes's horror, the televised executions of counterrevolutionaries and the arrest and imprisonment of Húber Matos, a much-admired *comandante* of the revolution who dared to challenge Castro's communist leanings. As early as March 1959, the government began confiscating private businesses. A year later Benes's father was ordered to abandon the office from which he ran his textile business. He was not even allowed to take the framed pictures of his children from his desk.

A month after the confiscation of his father's business, on a Friday in November 1960, Benes left his law firm carrying his briefcase, which contained only a ticket to Miami, his government identification, and an American visa he had applied for and received long before. He walked through the airport as if he were a government official engaged in an investigation. No one stopped him as he boarded a plane to Miami. Like his father before him, Benes had fled his country of birth alone and with little money, $215 sewn into the shoulder of his jacket. And, like his father, he left his home with a broken heart.

Because he left on a Friday, Benes's absence went unnoticed by the authorities. The next day, his wife and son, who also had U.S. visas, joined him in Miami, but Benes never forgot how much he had missed them in the few hours he was separated from them and how much he had feared he might lose them. He resolved, during his time alone in a Miami Beach hotel, never to let politics or war keep him apart from the ones he loved.

In the years that followed, Benes concentrated on making a living. The young bourgeois, who just a few years before had dropped out of the University of Maryland because the beds were too hard, started working in Miami as a punch-card operator at Washington Federal Savings and Loan, making $65 a week.

Benes turned that job into a stepping-stone for his ambition. Within six months he had risen to the vice presidency of the bank.

IN MIAMI, Benes became a walking billboard for the success of the Cuban-exile community. He was the director of a housing-loan program for South and Central America and the Caribbean that turned thousands of poor people into homeowners, and he helped start the Hispanic branch of Big Brothers and Big Sisters of America, specializing in training mentors for newly arrived refugees. His picture and name appeared in the local newspapers almost weekly, with stories that ranged from what he liked to do on lazy summer Sundays to what he thought about the county's health-care system.

Cuba, however, was never far from his thoughts, and through the years those thoughts evolved. He stopped believing that war was a viable solution. Faced with the inertia of successive U.S. administrations toward the government of Fidel Castro, Benes had come to the conclusion that the best tactic for Cuban exiles was to rely only on themselves. After all, Cubans had elevated Castro to power. Maybe it was Cubans who had to bring him down. And perhaps the best way to right the wrongs that Castro had committed was by getting close to his side, by talking to those who surrounded him, not by antagonizing them.

But Benes needed a platform. He couldn't just arrange to meet a Cuban official to instigate the overthrow of Castro. What he craved was an issue, a not-too-controversial topic that could get him close to Castro's inner circle.

Benes found his cause the day a friend called to ask him for help in buying a full-page advertisement in the *Miami Herald* to inform people about the plight of political prisoners in Cuba. Benes had good contacts at the paper who could perhaps sell him the ad at a discounted rate. At the time members of the exile community were disappointed with the paper's near-total lack of coverage of Cuban events. A few exiles had even chained themselves to the marble columns at the entrance to the newspaper's building in downtown Miami to demand news coverage of the prisoners.

Benes accompanied his friend, and as he heard him state his case to the newspaper's executives, he was transfixed to see the man argue so passionately for the freedom of people he didn't even know. Benes had heard the stories of Cuban prisoners before—about men who were isolated for months in cells so small they had to crouch and the almost daily beatings of those who had once fought along-side Castro—but somehow he had not yet embraced their cause.

It wasn't that he was indifferent to pain. Benes was familiar with the dilemma of scores of exiles who longed to travel to Cuba to visit a sick mother for the last time or to bury a grandmother. Through his contacts in Washington he had occasionally intervened, but the answer had always been the same. There was nothing Benes or anybody could do for the families. Cubans who had chosen to leave the island were not welcomed back.

That bothered Benes, who was surrounded by family and couldn't imagine how he would feel if his father had died in Cuba, far from him. As he tossed and turned some nights, thinking about the prisoners and the suffering of their rela-tives in Miami, an idea began to form in his mind. He couldn't change Castro's regimen; he couldn't alleviate the tension between the two countries. But, he thought, perhaps he could find a way to free political prisoners while facilitating travel to and from the island to reunite families.

And so, when he saw Jimmy Carter for the first time during a campaign meet-ing in Florida in 1976, and Carter told him he was worried about Cuban politi-cal prisoners and thought that the travel ban to the island ought to be lifted, Benes knew instantly he had to help this kind peanut farmer from Georgia make it to the White House.

WHEN BENES RETURNED from Panama in 1977, after his encounter with the Cubans, he was excited but scared. Talking to Cuban officials in foreign countries somehow felt un-American, even un-Cuban. He knew that many of his fellow exiles wouldn't approve. War was still the prevailing thought in the minds of most exile leaders, Castro still the enemy. Yet the prospect of meeting with Cuban agents thrilled Benes. He felt important, chosen in a biblical sense. A deeply religious man and a history buff, he had a finely tuned sense of the un-expected ways in which personal lives and history sometimes intersect. It must be fate, he thought, that Castro has decided to extend an olive branch precisely now, when Benes was, as the *Miami Herald* had anointed him, one of South Florida's most influential citizens. Perhaps he could play a role. In his mind, if he played his cards right, this approach by the Cubans could lead to fundamental changes in Castro's government. Benes was sure he had nothing to lose and perhaps much to gain. He resolved to share the details of his encounter in Panama with his partner in the bank, Carlos "Charles" Dascal, another Cuban Jew who had fled Cuba in the sixties.

Benes wanted someone else to know about his meeting in Panama, someone who could serve as a sounding board and, if necessary, as a witness to his intentions from the outset. He called a friend who worked for the CIA and gave him the names of his lunch companions—José Luis Padrón, Amado Padrón, and Antonio "Tony" de la Guardia—and full physical descriptions. Less than eight hours later, the CIA man was at Benes's desk in the bank with surprising news. The men were not consular officials, he told Benes. Two of them were part of Castro's inner circle, the ones he often turned to for sensitive, secret, highly important missions abroad.

Benes was shocked. These were precisely the men he'd been yearning to get close to. The agent urged him to continue the talks and to keep notes. His case was transferred to the Federal Bureau of Investigation, where Benes was told to report to a Mexican-American agent whose nom de guerre was "Taco." To keep Benes's identity secret, the Cubans gave *him* a nickname as well: Benito. Cuba's consul in Kingston, Jamaica, Ramón de la Cruz, was to be their contact. Through him meetings were arranged in Nassau, Mexico City, Kingston, and Panama City. Through his friend Congressman Fascell, Benes also went to the White House and passed on the message that Castro wanted to talk. His message was referred to members of the National Security Council. With little enthusiasm and no hope for any agreement of substance, they gave Benes their tacit blessing, making sure he understood he was not representing the U.S. government but acting as a Cuban-American, alone.

Yet every time Benes returned from a meeting, he shared his notes with his FBI handlers in Miami and Washington and reported to his primary State Department contact, Peter Tarnoff, the right-hand man of secretary of state Cyrus Vance.

IN THE SUMMER OF 1977, just as Benes and Pons were meeting secretly with
the Cubans, the U.S. and Cuban governments were putting the final touches on
an agreement to open what they called "interests sections" in each other's countries. The interests sections were quasi embassies, designed for countries to
maintain relations when formally they had none. All American diplomats had
left Cuba in a rush in January 1961 after Castro, in a speech, called the U.S. embassy in Havana a "nest of spies," and demanded that the United States reduce its
embassy staff. As the diplomats were packing to go, a crowd began to form
around the building: desperate visa seekers pleading for stamps on their passports before the last Americans left Cuba for good.

   Much had happened since. Years of antagonism, isolation, and an economic
embargo had not yielded the desired results: a softening of Castro, a democratic
government on the island that sits just ninety miles from the southernmost point
of the United States—too close for an unfriendly nation. Instead Castro had become a sort of godfather of the left, sending highly trained troops to Angola and
Ethiopia, as well as financing covert operations in Latin America to fight imperi-
alism, much to the dismay of the United States.

   A month into his administration, President Carter gave his team at the National Security Council a list of countries he wanted to resume full relations
with; Cuba was at the top of the list. Around that time the Cuban government
proposed, and Washington eagerly accepted, a series of meetings about fishing
rights and maritime borders. Limited in scope as they were, the secret meetings
held in New York and Havana broke ground. Though other treaties had been
signed through the years between the two governments, these talks marked the
first time since 1961 that representatives from the United States and Cuba sat
across from each other in a climate that seemed conducive to their beginning to
talk about the real issues that bitterly divided the two countries.

   During the first encounter, on March 24, 1977, in a mezzanine-level room of
the Hotel Roosevelt in New York City, U.S. officials began by laying out the administration's hopes: the release of Cuban and American prisoners from Cuba's
prisons and the withdrawal of Cuban troops from Africa. The Cubans retorted

by saying they had agreed to meet only about maritime concerns, and the demands were dropped, but not for long. The second round of talks took place in April, in Havana.

Carter's agenda was straightforward. He deeply cared about human rights, and he wanted them to be the centerpiece of U.S. relations with the world, including Cuba. In the early days of his administration, Carter emphasized that the release of political prisoners was the key element in his Cuba policy. Carter lifted restrictions on travel to the island and allowed exiles to take money to their relatives there—part of the administration's broader strategy to make it clear that a Cold War mentality would no longer dictate every White House foreign-policy decision.

Cuba's motives were less clear. Castro himself had said he wanted better relations with the United States and a lifting of the embargo that for almost two decades had hurt the country's economy. But he had never made the kind of political concessions that would allow the United States to implement a gentler policy toward Cuba. What's more, to stoke the ideological flames of his revolution, he needed the United States to continue its antagonism toward Cuba. Nothing brought a people together more than resistance against a powerful and unrelenting enemy. After years of battling unfriendly administrations, however, Castro must have felt he was ready to extend an olive branch, and Carter must have seemed to him the right American president with whom to negotiate. Negotiations were important because the Cuban government wanted to depend less heavily on the Soviet Union, which supplemented Cuba's economy at a cost of $8 million a day. Courting the exiles was crucial because Castro knew that the White House would not move forward on any initiative that would alienate Miami's Cubans. Ultimately Castro wanted recognition, a much-delayed but still crucial nod of approval from his neighbors to the north.

The political gamble made sense at the time. After eighteen years in power, Castro deemed his revolution and reputation solid. He was a leader of the Non-Aligned Movement and, by extension, of much of the Third World. He no longer faced a visible internal opposition, since most of his early opponents had been killed, jailed, or exiled. His intelligence experts told him that exiles were not monolithic in their political opinions; many were eager to back any initiative that would bring them closer to their families and to the country they'd left behind. In the end Castro must have thought he had nothing to fear from an aging, busy community intent on turning their exile nightmare into the American dream. He could negotiate with the United States and the exile community from a position of power and magnanimity. He just needed an intermediary, a person to understand his message and deliver it intact.

EARLY IN 1978 the men who had first contacted Benes in Panama said it was time for him to meet with Castro. Though the possibility of a reunion with Castro had not been raised before, Benes was not surprised at the offer. No matter how many times he talked with Padrón and de la Guardia and how much they agreed on the need to improve relations between Cubans on both sides of the straits, Benes knew that nothing would be accomplished without Castro's personal intervention. His trip was arranged for February 12. On the appointed day, Benes and Dascal first traveled to Kingston, Jamaica, where a black Mercedes picked them up and took them to the home of the Cuban consul, who had been their contact for months. There a Cuban agent handed Benes a black wig and a black mustache and took his picture without the thick prescription eyeglasses he always wore. In thirty minutes Benes and Dascal had new passports. At dusk, accompanied by Padrón and de la Guardia, they boarded a sixteen-seat Russian plane. Two hours later the plane landed in Cuba.

The ride to the Palace of the Revolution, where Castro awaited them, took less than fifteen minutes on the nearly deserted roads of Havana. Before he realized where he was, Benes heard a loud noise, and a garage door concealed at the end of a small incline suddenly opened. He and Dascal were rushed out of the car and swiftly placed in an elevator, flanked by Padrón and de la Guardia.

They rode up to the third floor in silence and disembarked in a hallway. A door to Benes's left was opened from the inside. Framed against the backlight of the room stood the uniform-clad figure of Fidel Castro.

How are you, Benes? Castro asked, already extending his hand.

How are you, Fidel? Benes answered.

Castro offered him a cigar.

Benes made a flat attempt at a joke: I'm here to collect the million dollars you took from us when you confiscated my father's underwear business, he said.

Nobody laughed.

It's a joke, Benes said, looking from one face to the other. Castro smiled faintly.

The two sat across from each other on fat leather chairs and, without making any more small talk, immediately began to discuss the need to improve relations between Cuba and the United States and the hopes Castro had placed on Carter, whom he praised for his religious beliefs and his interest in human rights. Though Castro had long declared organized religion a threat to the revolution, he'd been educated by Jesuit priests and still professed to respect, even admire, leaders, such as President Carter, who were guided by faith-based principles.

Castro's office was devoid of personal touches, Benes noticed. The furniture was simple, wood and leather. Everything seemed to be some shade of brown, and several bookshelves were crammed with hundreds of books. The meeting ended late. Castro made his points. It was agreed that Benes would come back.

For the next year, Benes would secretly travel to Cuba fourteen times. The Cuban consul in Jamaica arranged the meetings. Each time, Benes met with Castro for eight to ten hours of friendly and relaxed chats. Once, when Benes noticed that Castro wore Florsheim boots, he told him that such a public man ought to wear a better shoe. He asked Castro for his shoe size and, at their next reunion, gave him a pair of Johnston & Murphy boots worth $650. After admiring them for more than ten minutes, noting the strong stitching and the flawless black leather, Castro seemed to accept the gift with pleasure.

During one of his trips to Cuba, Benes took a solitary trip to the Jewish cemetery in Guanabacoa, a neighborhood of Havana. It was a hot summer afternoon, a Sunday, and he was the only visitor at the dilapidated and dusty cemetery. Walking through the aisles of graves, Benes stopped before each one that bore a name he recognized from his extended family or from his parents' circle of friends and placed a stone on the headstone, an ancient Jewish ritual. Then he sat down on a granite and marble tomb and looked up at the trees; their shade offered no respite from the heat, their leaves barely moved. Suddenly he started to cry. Softly first, then sobbing loudly. His chest heaved, and tears drenched his already sweaty shirt. He wondered why he was crying. Because he was happy, he thought, that's why. He realized that what he was doing was good and noble, that his secret conversations with Castro were the natural outcome of everything he'd worked for in his life, everything he'd believed in.

On another trip Benes went prepared with proof that Cuban exiles were turning Miami into a vibrant community. He had hired a television cameraman and asked him to film a one-hour special about the successes of Miami Cubans. When Castro saw the tape, he slumped back in his chair and didn't say a word. To Benes he seemed thoughtful, somewhat depressed.

In the Cuba of the late 1970s, little was known about the United States. Castro's security apparatus had infiltrated some Miami organizations, but the information gathered was mostly political and ideological, not sociological. Benes was showing Castro, for the first time, how Cubans in Miami really lived. It was vastly different from the way Cubans lived on the island, enduring food and housing shortages, frequent blackouts, and the constant repetition of the false promise that in a few years their lives would improve.

By contrast, Cubans in Miami were intent on re-creating the "paradise" they'd lost in 1959. They opened bakeries, restaurants, and shops that bore their old Havana names. Professionals—from engineers to musicians—reinvented themselves in a city that was quickly becoming the displaced capital of Latin America, due in no small part to the hard work of the newly arrived Cuban immigrants. In 1978, when Benes began to meet with Castro, there were more businesses in Miami owned by Cubans than the total number of businesses that had existed in the city in 1959. Spanish-language bookshops, theaters, and newspapers seemed to sprout overnight. Former top Havana physicians reclaimed their patients on this side of the Florida Straits, Cuban teachers taught Spanish to English-speaking children in Miami Beach, and famous actors hawked cars and cleaning products on Spanish-language radio and television stations. A stretch of Tamiami Trail was baptized as "Little Havana," and the local baseball stadium was named after Bobby Maduro, a famous Cuban baseball club owner.

Benes intuited that with his visits to Cuba he was opening doors between

Cuba and Miami. Castro seemed to be understanding exiles better. He was clearly impressed with the wealth accumulated in Miami and must have wanted some of it to be spent on his island. As a gesture of goodwill, he was prepared to release thousands of prisoners and to allow exiles to visit their relatives in Cuba. But both Castro and Benes needed the approval of Washington and the support of Cuban-Americans. After all, Benes was just one man.

Castro proposed a dialogue, a meeting of Cuban-Americans with Cubans on the island. Benes was asked to help with the logistics and to handpick a few of the guests to what soon came to be known as *el diálogo*. Other exiles, who had developed their own ties to the regime over the years, were also asked to provide names for the list, but ultimately the Cuban government had the final say regarding who would go to Havana and who would not. The only Cubans who wouldn't be accepted back were the hard-core counterrevolutionaries, Castro announced, though he said he believed that the counterrevolution had "become so weak that nobody knows if it really exists anymore."

In a press conference on September 6, 1978, to announce the dialogue among Cubans, journalists repeatedly asked Castro what had prompted his change of heart toward exiles. "The revolution will be twenty years old soon," he said. "From our point of view, it is absolutely consolidated and irreversible. We know it, the government of the United States knows it, and I think that the Cuban community abroad knows it, too. This is an important factor." Then Castro went on to explain that the 1977 return visit of fifty-five young Cuban-Americans, many of whom had left the island as toddlers in their parents' arms, had helped soften his view of the Cuban community abroad. The young Cubans, members of a group called Antonio Maceo Brigade, were obviously sympathetic to the revolution and had made him rethink the term he had long used against those who emigrated. From then on, Castro announced, they would no longer be called worms. "We don't stand to gain anything out of it; that is, we aren't looking for any advantage or anything like that; we are acting on principle," Castro concluded. "We are following a policy, and it seems to us that this is the policy that has to be applied at this moment."

The way Benes saw it, though, Castro was taking a risk.

* * *

WHILE BENES WAS CONDUCTING his amateur diplomacy in Havana, the White House had followed up on his initial tip that the Cubans wanted to talk. Benes himself had introduced Undersecretary of State for Political Affairs David A. Newsom to Padrón, one of the men who had originally contacted him in Panama. Since May 1978, Cuban and U.S. officials had held secret meetings in New York, Washington, Atlanta, and Cuernavaca, Mexico. The talks were so secret that the chief of the Interests Section in Havana, Wayne Smith, didn't even know about them until the third meeting, in Atlanta, was about to take place in August 1978.

In these meetings U.S. officials emphasized their interest in the withdrawal of Cuban troops from Africa. Zbigniew Brzezinski, Carter's hawkish national security adviser, saw the Cuban presence in Africa as a threat to his plans to try to contain the Soviets' worldwide expansion. Padrón, however, wanted to discuss only the release of political prisoners, which, he insisted, the United States should be ready to accept should the prisoners, once freed, decide not to live in Cuba anymore. The Carter administration agreed and began to work on the logistics of getting the former prisoners out of Cuba and into the United States.

On October 21, 1978, Castro turned over the first forty-six prisoners to a small Miami delegation, headed by Benes, and promised that many more would follow. Benes accompanied the former prisoners and their relatives to Miami. First down the steps of the airplane was Tony Cuesta, who had lost an arm and his eyesight when a bomb exploded in his face during a 1966 undercover operation that Benes had helped finance. Cuesta had been in jail ever since.

From inside the plane, Benes could hear the cheers. As he peeked outside, he saw a sea of tiny Cuban flags fluttering above the multitude. Benes felt lighthearted and giddy. He had finally delivered on his promise: The prisoners were free. He searched for approval on the faces in the crowd. Instead many of the spectators turned away from him; he heard someone call him a traitor. Benes looked around in vain for a single friendly gesture. Confused and afraid, he boarded a bus for the welcoming ceremony at Dade County Auditorium.

About thirty-five hundred fellow exiles waited at the auditorium, ready to engulf the newly released prisoners in tight hugs. Someone began singing the Cuban national anthem, and the whole crowd joined in, their voices already raw from emotion.

When Benes attempted to go inside, eight Dade County police officers in plain clothes surrounded him. There had been threats against his life, they told him, and they had been assigned to protect him. It seemed a small but vocal fraction of the exiled community couldn't understand Benes's motivation. They couldn't see, as plainly as he did, that in order to release the prisoners, he had had to talk to their jailer.

The release of the prisoners, though welcomed by most exiles, helped Castro cleanse up his human-rights record in the eyes of the world. It also contributed to deflate the rhetoric of war that many hard-line exiles still clung to. If Miami Cubans were sitting across the same table from Castro Cubans, who would believe them when they called themselves political exiles? Benes had not been the only exile to talk to Cuban officials, but he was the most visible of all, and so he became the first target of the community's scorn.

But Benes was in too deep now to let anyone derail his plans. He forged ahead, trying to forget the words of the police officers who had warned him about the threats against his life. The following month Benes returned to Cuba as part of a group of seventy-five exiles who traveled to Havana in November and December 1978 to continue the talks, advocating for the release of the prisoners who had remained behind and for the family-reunification program.

Before the group met with Castro, Benes was full of optimism and grandiose visions. He told a *Washington Post* reporter the world was going to change because of the dialogue.

"I think that before this is over, we will see a loosening of the locks on the world's political prisoners," Benes said. "Something major is going to happen."

The first day's talks between Cuban government officials and the exiles lasted five hours. The discussions, held in a small auditorium in the Palace of the Revolution, were described by Cuban and American reporters as "cordial and constructive." Castro, presiding over the meetings from a chair at the center of the table, boasted that the encounter was not due to any international pressure. It's a Cuban matter, he said, one that Cubans have to discuss only among themselves.

The dialogue, much criticized in Miami by die-hard foes of Castro, some of whom believed in bombs and not words, marked the first time that groups of Cubans on both sides of the Straits of Florida had come together officially to discuss the issues that for years had concerned and divided them. By extending a hand to Miami Cubans and demonstrating an inclination to address issues of human rights, Castro was hoping to show the White House that exiles would support the lifting of the U.S. embargo against Cuba and a gradual normalization of relations between the two countries. Instead, anyone paying attention should have realized that the dialogue was about to change Cuban society in ways that almost twenty years of anti-Castro rhetoric and terrorist acts had not managed to accomplish.

IN LESS THAN three months in 1979, more than 3,000 political prisoners were freed throughout the island. In their desire to migrate to the United States, they joined about 5,000 former prisoners who had been released even before there'd been an agreement between Washington and Havana. But "freeing" them was easier than actually getting them out of the country. The U.S. Department of Justice set up such a cumbersome visa process that, although the two governments had agreed that 400 ex-prisoners would travel to the United States each month, no more than 60 a month left Cuba from January to July 1979. The numbers improved later, but the average was 250 per month, still far below the promised quota.

Castro was greatly disturbed by the fact that ex-prisoners were milling about with the general population, sharing their stories of abuse and torture with friends, relatives, and neighbors. The former prisoners themselves were irate at the delay. The way they saw it, the United States owed them. They had suffered years in prison for fighting against a regime that the United States had tried to unseat for years. Many of them, in fact, had cooperated with the CIA and felt they had been forgotten by their trainers and accomplices.

Benes was so upset by Washington's lethargy that he wrote a memo to Phil Wise, the White House appointments secretary, recommending that President Carter himself take action. Among other things, Benes suggested a freedom flotilla." The U.S. or the Cuban American community should send ships to Cuba (prior approval by the Cuban government might be obtained by B.B. [Bernardo Benes]) to bring them to Miami, where President Carter should welcome the first ship," he wrote.

The president would reap some benefits as well, according to Benes's plan. The world did not yet know that the jails of Cuba had been virtually emptied because Castro had been inspired by President Carter's devotion to human rights. "Castro told Benes, on more than one occasion, that he didn't mind President Carter enhancing his human rights stand in taking credit for the atmosphere that he created in the world on this issue. That although it was a unilateral decision of the Cuban government this couldn't have happened under any of the U.S. presidents since 1959," he explained in his memo.

Three days later Wise sent the memo to National Security Council adviser Robert Pastor, Brzezinski's point man on Cuban matters. At the bottom of the memo's cover page, where Wise had asked him for his thoughts, Pastor wrote, "Phil, Great idea. Let's do it."

But Benes never heard from Wise or from Pastor, and the former prisoners continued to languish at home, no longer trapped by iron bars but desperate to escape the prison state that Cuba had become.

THAT SAME YEAR, 1979, more than 100,000 Cuban exiles returned to the island for weeklong visits, bearing gifts and telling stories of prosperity and freedom. Instead of branding returning exiles as traitors, the government baptized them as members of "the Cuban community in the exterior," thereby erasing the political nature of their exile. Families were reunited, and dollars poured into the country. Overnight, returning exiles who for so long had been called *gusanos*, worms, for their abandonment of the revolution, became *mariposas*, butterflies who flew over the Gulf of Mexico to bring beauty and hope to Cuban families.

Suddenly, thanks to the generosity of their relatives, people in Havana looked clean, groomed, and buoyant. Women wore modern clothes and sparkling makeup. Men clad in well-cut pants and clingy polyester shirts walked with an

almost feline swagger. Faces glowed; spirits soared. Levi's jeans fascinated the
young and old alike; Hitachi rice cookers made some women deliriously happy;
Gillette blades brought tears to the eyes of many grown men.

Benes had an inkling of how profound the impact of these visits was when on
one of his trips, as a token of appreciation, he gave a small radio worth $3.50 to
his driver, a man who worked for Castro's security apparatus. The man wept over
the wheel.

You saved my life, man, he told Benes. Next week is my daughter's fifteenth
birthday, and I had no gift to give her.

Up to that point, Benes had believed he was involved in a human-rights mission, bringing families together and freeing prisoners. But as the man greedily
and gratefully took the radio from his hands, Benes began to understand the
scope of the social changes that were quietly taking place in Cuba. If a man weeps
at the sight of a cheap plastic radio, Benes wondered, what would others be willing to do for a late-model car, a carpeted home, a succulent meal? And, he dared
ask himself, what would Cubans be willing to do for freedom?

THREE

Butterflies

A family reunion. From left to right: My father, Orestes; my aunt
Olimpia; my grandmother Teresa (seated); my aunt Oraima; my
Uncle Oswaldo (standing); and the profile of my mother, Mirta.

I STOOD IN FRONT OF my Uncle Oswaldo and wept, remembering the day, eight years before, when I had seen him last.

That day, July 20, 1971, I had refused to accompany him to the airport, where I knew that an airplane would take him much too far from me. For a few weeks that year, while waiting for his Madrid-bound flight, my uncle had lived with us; it was easier to get to the airport from our apartment in Havana than from his house in Las Villas, Cuba's central province. He was eager to begin the journey that would eventually take him to New York, where his pregnant wife and his toddler son awaited him.

Tall and elegant, with a thin black mustache, my uncle looked so much like my father that I sometimes approached one thinking it was the other. Older than my father by only eighteen months, Uncle Oswaldo was my father's best friend and perhaps his most beloved sibling. He was also my godfather, a choice of great significance among Catholics, who believe godparents to be their children's spiritual guides and, if need be, their de facto parents. My uncle took his role seriously, showering me with attention.

Before I had learned to read, he gave me a book titled *Once Upon a Time*, a collection of classic children's stories and poems. The book, with yellowing pages and a worm-size hole that snaked its way from the bottom of the cover page to the top of the last, was obviously secondhand. But I treasured that book, the first one anyone had ever given me. One of the poems was about a playful but unpredictable puppy named Tom. I didn't have a puppy and certainly did not know anyone named Tom, but my uncle read that poem to me every time he visited us, and the poem became a kind of hymn that bonded our special relationship.

Twice I had accompanied him, along with my parents, to the airport, teary-eyed and nervous. Twice the flight had been overbooked and my uncle had been sent back to wait for another flight. We would return home in the afternoons grateful that he was still with us, disappointed that he would have to wait yet another week to leave. Then came the day when I refused to go to the airport and stayed behind with my mother. I could no longer take the emotional seesaw of holding him tight for what we thought would be the last time, only to have him run after us a few minutes later, complaining about the bureaucracy, the government, and the system. On July 20, 1971, the bureaucracy, the government, and the system conspired on my uncle's behalf and against mine. My father came back alone from the airport and gave me a tight hug. Your uncle says he will not forget us, he told me.

And he hadn't.

My uncle had returned, with the government's blessing, to visit us for a week. Standing in front of him, too nervous to move, I savored the moment and began to study him with a certain detachment. He had the same face I remembered, framed by thick, wavy black hair and a now-bushy mustache, sprinkled with gray. He was paler, older, with a potbelly that strained against his too-tight shirt. But his voice, rich and melodious, still flowed out of his mouth like syrup poured slowly over warm pancakes. He was calling my name now, showing me off like a proud father to his two sisters, the aunts I knew only from pictures, who had accompanied him on the trip back. Olimpia and Oraima were exotic names for such normal-looking, kind women with dyed short hair and easy laughs.

My father began to cry. The sound of his sobs loosened my chest, and I could hear my heart as I finally lurched forward, finding refuge in my uncle's extended arms. We hugged in a tight circle. I felt soft and weak, much younger than I was, not at all like a fifteen-year-old going on twenty-seven, as my parents usually described me to their friends. There was so much to say that we said nothing. When the group finally untangled, we looked at each other and smiled, almost shyly. My uncle, rescuing us from sentimentality, took charge. He quickly located a bus that would take us to my grandmother's house in a city called Sagua la Grande, about three hours from Varadero's airport.

It was midnight by the time we were ready to leave. In the bus, dark and air-conditioned, my father and uncle sat whispering the entire trip. Seated behind them, I tried to decipher their words, but I couldn't. Outside, dozens of darkened towns flew by; lightning bugs illuminated the night. My skin felt warm and clammy, despite the air-conditioning. The noise of the engine rumbled through my body, rocking me to a fitful sleep, my head bobbing against the windowpane.

My grandmother was awake when we arrived. She leaped up to greet us, and her tiny body trembled as she hugged all her three returning children at once. My father, pacing back and forth behind them, struggled to control his tears, his shoulders heaving up and down in a way that I had seen previously only when his oldest brother had died the year before.

Daybreak found us sipping steaming hot *café con leche* on my grandmother's porch, talking about the family, avoiding sensitive topics, like the one I was burning to ask them: What do you think about our revolutionary paradise? But I didn't ask anything, deciding it was better to listen to them talk and to pounce on my uncle at the right moment, perhaps when we were alone. My sister and I were eagerly awaiting a signal from the adults to help them unpack. We could not wait to find out what gifts our relatives had brought from abroad.

Though I had always prided myself on maintaining a sense of austerity and contrarian aesthetics—when my friends wore cropped socks, I pulled mine up, all the way to my knees—I was not immune to the lure of a crisp new pair of jeans. During a lull in the adults' conversation, I nudged my sister to ask for our gifts; since she was younger, her indiscretions would be met only with a chuckle.

As it turned out, I didn't get a pair of jeans. My gift was a burgundy pantsuit and high-heel sandals of the same color.

FOR THE WEEK we were together with my uncle and aunts, I concentrated on getting to know them. My uncle was an accountant for General Electric, and after years in New York, he and his family had recently moved to Hialeah, a blue-collar city close to Miami. His sisters lived near him and worked in factories. Their children went to free, public schools. They had cars—but nothing fancy, he hastened to explain.

Contrary to what I had been taught in school about the ways of capitalism, my uncle explained that he had medical insurance, so medicines and visits to the doctor were free or cost very little. If his children earned good grades or were excellent athletes, their university education also would be free. No one told him what to do, except his bosses. And if he didn't like them, he could leave and work elsewhere. He could travel outside the country easily, without having to alert the authorities of his intentions. The neighbors didn't bother him—in fact, he didn't even know most of his neighbors—and he didn't have to work for free on Sundays for the good of the neighborhood. He tended his own garden and made his own repairs at home. He expected nothing from the community but also was not obligated to do anything for anybody, except obey commonsense rules of civility and the laws of the country.

It all sounded so simple it was hard to believe. I kept looking for the contradictions, waiting to catch him in a lie or an exaggeration. My father beamed, though, as if he were telling me without words that he'd been right all along.

I followed my uncle and my aunts everywhere, soaking up information, paying attention to their mannerisms and to the English words they used with each other—words like "party" and "part-time" and "weekend," which to me, hearing them for the first time, sounded festive and light. They were generous and loving, very much like my father. They seemed unchanged by life in a richer world. Before we knew it, the week was over.

On the way back to the airport, my uncle asked my father what his plans were. The same as always, my father responded, lowering his voice, Now is the time. If you can get us out, this is the time.

I heard my father's answer but pretended not to. Through the years I had quietly fought my parents' attempts to get us out of Cuba simply by refusing to engage in their conversations about the lives that awaited us on the other side. I knew that once we started the process to leave the country by requesting a visa, my sister and I could be automatically expelled from school and my father would lose his job. The threat of those punishments would not have been so daunting if I'd known for certain that we would indeed leave. But I knew of many instances in which entire families had effectively withdrawn from society while waiting for a visa that never came.

Before my uncle's visit, I also wasn't sure of what awaited us outside Cuba. The idea of losing my home and my friends was terrifying, but not more so than the thought of living in a society I knew nothing about, except for what my teachers drummed into me and my father immediately refuted. Everything I had grown up believing, I now knew, was at best a half-truth.

IN THE SUMMER OF 1979, the entire country was engaged in a dialogue with our so-called enemies. Former political prisoners, who had been stashed for years in prisons throughout the island, were mingling with us in the breadlines while they waited for their visas to travel to the United States. I met one former prisoner at a friend's house one evening and was aghast at his tales of torture and mistreatment. It was one thing to know, as I already did, about the existence of prisoners, another entirely to hear someone describe how he'd gone naked for months simply because he had refused to follow his jailers' orders to switch from his yellowish khaki uniform with a P on the back to the bright blue uniform worn by common felons. I pelted the man with so many questions that he finally felt compelled to raise his shirt to show me his physical scars, caused by a guard's repeated stabs with a bayonet. The other scars, the ones he carried inside, I could only guess at.

That year more than a hundred thousand Cuban-Americans traveled to the island, adding about $100 million to the government's coffers. Face-to-face with the people who for so long Castro had branded as traitors, many Cubans on the island could not understand why these returning exiles had been allowed to step on Cuban soil again. Perhaps they were never traitors, some concluded, just people who wanted to live their lives elsewhere, outside Castro's grasp. Or perhaps they had been traitors after all, but now that the country needed them economically, they had become useful enemies. As an unexpected reward of their

new privileged status in Cuba, the government opened special stores just for
them, where only dollars were allowed. Some of the family encounters were im-
bued with so much pain and resentment—say, the reunion between a returning
older sister with dollars and a brother who had become a card-carrying member
of the Communist Party but didn't have enough to eat at home—that the whole
country was on edge.

As soon as I returned to Havana I wore my burgundy pantsuit for an outing
with my friend Kathy, who wore an almost identical but beige pantsuit that her
grandmother had brought her from Miami months earlier. I let my long hair loose,
after brushing it one hundred times, and put on a little makeup: chocolate-colored
lipstick and homemade baby blue eyeshadow to highlight my just-plucked eye-
brows. The high heels made me much taller than my five-foot-eight-inch frame,
and I thought I looked sophisticated and older.

On a cool Saturday evening in February, we rode the bus to Vedado, the city's
hangout for hip teenagers, walked all the way down to the sea, and then turned
left on Malecón, Havana's seawall, the sea lapping at our feet as if mocking the
wall's futile effort to hold it back. We walked in the semidarkness until we
reached the crumbling end of the Malecón and then walked back. We talked little. We didn't meet any boys. Nobody whistled at us, in the way Latin men do to
show their approval of beautiful women.

Nothing happened. Nothing needed to happen, really. We were happy. Happier than we had been in a long time.

I HAD TURNED FIFTEEN in February of that year, but we couldn't afford a
birthday party. After five years of depositing coins in a piggy bank, my parents had
managed to save only three hundred pesos, not nearly enough for the traditional
coming-out party given for Latin girls, akin to a sweet sixteen or a debutants' ball. The
money was just enough for a meal for six. And so we decided to go to a nightclub with
Frank, my boyfriend of two years, and his parents. We chose the Copa Room of the
Hotel Riviera, where my parents had honeymooned. I would wear a long, beautiful
dress and new shoes. A hairdresser would do my hair, I would be allowed to wear a
little makeup, and a photographer would capture the moment for posterity.

For a hundred pesos my mother bought the material for the dress—a shiny blue-and-silver cloth more suitable for upholstering a chair with than for dressing a skinny girl like me. Then we went on the search for a pair of shoes. We found them in a small and dirty apartment atop a building in Calzada 10 de Octubre, a wide avenue about ten blocks from our house. For eighty pesos, exactly half my father's monthly salary, the shoemaker we met there promised us a pair of open-toed sandals made of soft leather with a small platform heel so I wouldn't tower over my boyfriend, who was just about my height. My mother left the man's house fuming.

Eighty pesos! she screeched. What is the world coming to?

I suggested we buy cheaper shoes elsewhere, but my mother wouldn't hear of it. She complained, but she was not going to allow the system to win. She would get the best for her first daughter's fifteenth birthday and nothing but the best. The fact that in the government-run stores there were no pretty shoes or long, shiny dresses was not going to deter her from dressing me up on my special day. She had a vision, a sky blue vision of me in white shoes, and she was going to get it no matter what.

My mother spent another eighty pesos on a skintight, long-sleeved, green-and-beige polyester pullover to match a beige skirt she'd made me. For a hundred pesos more, we got a photographer, which took us way over budget. On the day of the celebration, we couldn't afford a taxi. In my floor-length blue-and-silver gown and my blindingly white new sandals, I joined the sweaty crowds on the Route 37 bus that took us to the Riviera. I rode standing up most of the way, my curls unfurling in the heat and my carefully applied makeup running down my face, trickling from my chin to my chest.

Once we got to the Riviera, all worries were forgotten. The photographer took me by the hand and had me pose, placing me next to paintings, marble statues, leather chairs, and Art Deco lamps. Wanting to show my parents that their efforts had paid off, I smiled until my cheeks hurt. We skipped the meal, since we had long run out of money, but the adults drank cold beers and we all danced to the songs of Héctor Tellez, a popular singer then. At the end of the show, he dedicated a song to me.

◆ ◆ ◆

TWO WEEKS LATER I woke up startled by the sound of Frank whistling beneath my window. My parents heard it, too, and opened their own bedroom window to greet him. It was a few minutes past two in the morning. I rarely ever saw Frank anymore. For ten months he'd been away fulfilling his duty to the government in the military service. We saw each other every six weeks or so, whenever his unit came up for leave. He would appear at my house unexpectedly, in his olive green fatigues, dirty and usually feverish from too much work and little sleep. But he had never come to visit in the middle of the night.

What's up? I heard my father ask, sleepily.

I have to talk to Mirtica. To all of you, he answered.

We turned on the lights and invited Frank upstairs. His eyes were red—whether from fatigue or crying, I didn't know. When I hugged him, he held on tighter than usual. He had lost weight but gained muscle. He'd grown a thick beard and seemed older, more serious. The front of his uniform was stained red, from a medicine he'd been taking for a throat infection, he explained.

I've been tapped to go to Angola, Frank said quickly, as if getting the sentence out would appease his fears. We are leaving in a few days.

My mother gasped. My father paled. I personally thought a trip to Africa would be exotic, but I sensed that no one shared my enthusiasm for this adventure.

There is a war in Angola, Frank said, reminding me that for the last four years thousands of Cubans had been fighting in there, helping the Marxist government quash a persistent guerrilla insurgency. Hundreds of Cubans had died fighting a war that wasn't ours, but their bodies were left behind, buried in a foreign land. I knew all this, but somehow I didn't believe it would be Frank's fate. From my readings I knew that although war was brutal, it held infinite romantic possibilities: the letters, the poems, the promises, the good-byes, the tears, the suffering. Already I could see myself standing on the dock waiting for Frank's return, which I imagined would be in a huge warship.

The gravity in Frank's voice brought me back to reality. There was nothing else to say. He needed to go home to get a few things and report to his unit in the morning. My parents hugged him, and I accompanied him to the foot of the stairs, where he promised to write and I swore loyalty. The romance of the war was already kicking in as Frank left in tears, convinced he would not come back alive.

Frank's mother took his departure very badly. A woman who had supported the revolution from the beginning and kept a framed black-and-white eight-by-ten of a baseball-playing Castro in a place of honor on top of her television, she could not understand how the government—indeed how Fidel!—had sent her only child to a faraway continent to fight a war on behalf of people she didn't know or even want to know. The first Sunday without her son, she grabbed the picture from the TV in a fit of fury and threw it out her living room window. It landed in the middle of the street, the glass shattered, the frame bent, but the picture still intact. Because she had once been the president of the neighborhood watchdog committee and because people understood her pain, no one reported her to the police. Her kind neighbors assumed the poor woman had gone crazy, for no one in her right mind would dare throw *el comandante* out a second-story window in broad daylight.

SHORTLY AFTER FRANK LEFT and six months after my uncle and my aunts had returned to Miami, I turned sixteen in the fields of Pinar del Río, an interior province to the west of Havana, where my eleventh-grade class was sent to the country for forty-five days in what was known as *la escuela al campo*, literally "school in the countryside," though no traditional schooling went on. We would spend six weeks planting tobacco, picking tomatoes, or tending to plantain trees, away from our homes and our parents. The work was supposed to make us stronger and teach the all-important lesson that a revolution such as ours required sacrifices, even from its youngest members. Free education and free medicine had a cost, after all; someone had to pull the potatoes from the earth and cut the bananas from the trees. It was also a way to teach children that their loyalties should lie not with their parents but with the revolution and that, when called to prove their devotion, they needed to heed the call.

My parents had briefly toyed with the idea of not sending me to the camp, but everybody knew, though no one actually told us, that children whose parents kept them from field duties were cast aside, sometimes made to repeat a grade as punishment for their lack of accountability and inner strength. The oldest daughter of a couple who lived across the street had been held back because, according to neighborhood gossip, her father had refused to allow her to go away for the forty-five days. They never talked about it, and my parents never asked why their daughter, so smart and well behaved, spent her days on the terrace silently braiding her hair.

I was focused on being the best student I could possibly be, so that when the time came to select the students who could go on to the university, not only would I have a chance to continue my education but I'd also be able to pursue the career I actually aspired to, journalism—a difficult choice, since only a few lucky ones were handpicked every year for that field. Those with poor grades and questionable dispositions were often derailed to some of the practical subjects in fields where the country sorely needed workers, like medicine or teaching, depending on priorities at the time. Not going to the countryside with my class would have certainly made my teachers question my disposition.

But it wasn't fear alone that drove me to embrace these forty-five days of work. I relished the idea of being away from my parents. I thought that, free from their influence, I would somehow become like my friends, happy and buoyant boys and girls who danced at the sound of a drum without worrying what others thought.

Surely none of my friends had fathers who listened to the Voice of America as mine did, his ear pressed to the radio so the neighbors wouldn't hear the distinctive, official-sounding announcer. My friends had parents who worked and volunteered to work some more on Sundays and then went to school in the evenings to improve themselves, to be better for the revolution, to be prepared in case they were called for international duty. My friends didn't have to worry about visas that were never in the mail or spend their time awaiting letters from abroad that came every month stuffed with the promise of life in the United States.

One time, in one of those letters, we received a picture of my uncle smiling at the camera as someone behind him rummaged through a refrigerator. My uncle looked fine, as always, but we weren't interested in him—we were looking at what was in the refrigerator. Is that orange juice, that yellow liquid? The red can we knew to be coffee, because once my uncle had sent us a three-dimensional almanac with the picture of a little girl holding a yellow-and-red can and a sign that said, IN MY HOUSE, WE DRINK BUSTELO. By then most people we knew in Havana were grinding chickpeas to make coffee, so the sight of a beautiful, gleaming can containing that precious staple of the Cuban diet left my parents speechless and left me wondering why the little girl in the picture would tell the world what coffee her parents brewed.

IN THE WINTER OF 1975, when I was eleven, I was sent to a camp for the first time. The week before that first trip, my classmates and I were each handed a thick cotton shirt, work pants, a straw hat, and a pair of black work boots. I was lucky that my boots were only a size larger than I actually needed; some of my friends ended up with shoes so large they couldn't wear them.

Unlike other city girls, who had never been outside Havana, I was familiar with the country, because both of my parents had been born in remote small towns in Las Villas, without electricity and very little, if any, working plumbing in their homes. Every summer I visited my grandparents, who still lived in the same houses where my parents had been born. I was used to the red clay that clung to my shoes and my clothes, even my underwear. I had learned to tolerate the mosquitoes, and I could cope with the heat fairly well. I knew how to urinate in a bowl and take it outside in the morning to dump it in the hole inside the outhouse. I could find my way in total darkness, and I had learned to hold a flashlight under my chin so that I could read at night. I was an expert at climbing trees to reach a juicy mango, and I could spot the ripest guava in a tree, even from afar.

Nothing like that awaited me at camp, a desolate place on the outskirts of Havana, in a speck of a town where it rained nonstop. It was so cold and humid that in the mornings my teeth hurt and felt loose because I'd been clenching them so hard in my sleep. I slept with my legs folded all the way up to my chin and a pillow covering my face. The two buildings that housed us and the mess hall were long and narrow, with crudely poured cement floors and completely devoid of any human touch. A low roof made out of dry palm leaves hung over our heads. Wall openings let in air and sun, since there were no fans. A lone lightbulb shone weakly over the beds where more than a hundred girls slept.

There was no space to put our personal belongings, no drawers or cubicles, so our suitcases, perilously perched between the bunk beds, functioned as our closets, medicine cabinets, and pantries. We wrote letters in the afternoons using the tops of our wooden suitcases as desks. In the evenings, we used them to drum out a rumba and pass the time with some measure of joy. There was a row of cement sinks in which to wash our clothes and clean our faces in the morning, and a row of cubicles with holes on the floor where toilets should have been. Most girls hid behind the bushes when they needed to go, though. No one could stand the stench that emanated from those barren cubicles.

In the mornings the camp leaders would wake us at a quarter to six with a loud yell: On your feet! I used to sleep in my work clothes so that I could stay in bed a few minutes more. Then I'd rush to the mess hall for breakfast: a piece of dry bread and powdered milk, which left lumps of powder on the roof of my mouth, down my throat, between my teeth. I couldn't swallow it and soon learned to prepare my own breakfast: two fingers of condensed milk, a spoonful of chocolate powder, and as much water as I could stand to make the precious condensed milk last. I got the milk and the chocolate from my parents when they visited on Sundays. If I disciplined myself, I could make my supplies from home last for an entire week. Food was my biggest preoccupation in the camp, because there was never enough, it was often bad, and everyone was always hungry. Lunch and dinner seldom varied: a boiled dry root vegetable, a spoonful of greenish-looking rice, and, if we were lucky, a hunk of meat of indeterminate provenance. Sometimes the cook would prepare a tasty stew. But most days I gave my food away to children whose parents didn't visit or didn't bring them enough.

The work was hard, but I didn't take it seriously. I did what I could and took many breaks. My friends did the same. We wondered aloud why anyone would think that girls like us, spoiled girls who couldn't even make our beds right or comb through the knots in our hair without crying, could actually help the country's bottom line. That first year we planted, seeded, weeded, transplanted, and irrigated tobacco. I came to know tobacco intimately. My fingers were yellowish and always sticky from the constant handling of tobacco leaves.

My father often came to visit in his truck, taking a short detour from his delivery route in towns nearby. I never knew when he would show up. I could be knee-deep in water irrigating tiny tobacco plants when, all of a sudden, out of the corner of my eye, I would see his green truck barreling down the dirt road, a trail of dust in its wake. I always dropped what I was doing and ran after the truck until he saw me, amid the dust, in his rearview mirror. I relished his hugs, his presence, his words of encouragement. When he asked how I was, I told him I was fine. And in some way this was true. Despite the hard work, hunger, and exhaustion, I enjoyed being with my friends, singing in the fields and making up stories to entertain each other. We told jokes, we described in detail movies we'd seen and books we'd read. We pretended we were actresses in a play. We did everything but talk about the reality of those endless days.

In the evenings we took showers in a roofless room with wooden partitions and no curtains, bathed in moonlight. The water, spouting in a thick gush from a faucet, was so cold that it hurt when it hit our backs. Sometimes, if many girls were bathing at once, the gush became a pitiful trickle, not enough to wash my matted hair. More than once I left the shower stall sticky with soap and shivering with cold.

Christmas came and went, but no one noticed because beginning in 1969 the government had abolished that holiday. Fidel had dictated that the country had more serious things to worry about—mainly, that year, an unreachable goal to cut enough sugarcane to produce 10 million tons of sugar. The twenty-fourth and twenty-fifth of December were days like any others for us; New Year's Eve was different, because the country celebrated not only the end of the year but also the end of Batista's dictatorship and Fidel's triumph on January 1, 1959. In the camps we celebrated the near end of our yearly labors by treating ourselves to a banquet patched together from the leftover food at the bottoms of our suitcases.

＊ ＊ ＊

I TURNED SIXTEEN on Sunday, February 10, 1980. My parents and sister had a terrible time that day finding transportation to the camp, which was inappropriately named Felicidad—Happiness. Felicidad was about six hours from Havana by bus. Loaded with food and clean clothes for me, they arrived late in the afternoon, at an hour when most parents were leaving. I was relieved to see them—I'd been waiting all day, fearing they wouldn't come—but anxious knowing that they would have to leave in less than an hour to make it back to Havana before nightfall, when transportation all but stopped in this part of the island.

In an orange grove adjacent to the camp, we ate my mother's beer-soaked yellow rice and chicken, my favorite. With dark clouds approaching, my mother hastily unwrapped the cake she'd baked. Pink frosting, made with sugar, butter, and food coloring, covered a hard concoction of eggs and flour. Peanuts served as decoration. As my father prepared to light the sixteen candles, it started to rain, and the wind and raindrops blew out the candles before I could. Angry, my father, a man incapable of violence or a harsh word, punched a tree and cursed.

I understood my father's frustration when he punched the tree. He was a truck driver who worked long hours to earn 163 pesos a month; who chased chickens with his large truck to offer his family a treat; who saved for his children every piece of candy, every sandwich, every slice of pizza he managed to buy in the streets. A grown man who hid in his bedroom when the members of the Committee for the Defense of the Revolution knocked on the door to recruit him for projects he deemed worthless; sent his wife to the balcony to lie for him, to say to whoever came looking for him that he was not available—he'd gone to visit his sick mother or was sick himself, in the hospital, delirious—anything to avoid marching with a wooden stick slung over his shoulder as if it were a rifle, pretending to defend the revolution against a U.S. invasion that he knew would never come. And here he was, at forty, still in Cuba, stuck in mud, hitting a tree, trapped in a revolution he never supported, desperate to get out.

My father, however, would never have done anything without the support of his family. For a long time he had known, without ever having asked me, that I did not want to leave my country. He wasn't looking for my obedience; he knew he had that. What he wanted was my unconditional support, even willingness to leave, the same kind he knew he had from my mother and my sister, who, at eleven, was too young to contradict him and too sheltered by all of us to have formulated her own political thoughts. And so that day at the foot of the tree, I finally uttered the words he'd been aching to hear. Okay, arrange the papers for the visa, I said. Do what you have to do! I yelled, and I ran to my dorm, crying. Because even after I told my father to get us out of Cuba, I was not sure I would.

FOUR

Héctor Sanyustiz:
A Way Out

Aerial view of the March of the Combatant People, a
government-organized show of repudiation against the
more than 10,000 people who sought asylum in the
Peruvian embassy in Havana, April 1980.

HÉCTOR SANYUSTIZ rode his red motorcycle at forty miles per hour, the speed limit. He knew that if he drove too fast now, the police might assume he was running from something or somebody. Too slow and they would deduce he was casing the area. Either way they might stop him, a possibility he desperately wanted to avoid. He would rather die than face jail time or remain in Cuba, which to him was one and the same.

It was the spring of 1980 and Sanyustiz, like thousands of Cubans who had been rattled by the exiles' visits the previous year, was looking for a way out. He felt like a lab rat trapped in an experiment: blindly running through a maze and bumping into walls. For the past several months, Cubans had begun escaping the country in stolen or hijacked boats, knowing that Washington would welcome refugees from communist regimes—or at least not return them to the island. Each time the Cuban government had asked the United States to prosecute the hijackers, the Carter administration had turned a deaf ear. But for Sanyustiz, who liked to maintain a sense of control, the waters of the Gulf of Mexico were too unpredictable. What if the Americans changed their minds and sent him to jail? What if the boat sank?

He drove down Havana's Fifth Avenue, passed the church of San Antonio de Padua, a modern building of yellow bricks with a sole tower occupying the corner facing the ocean. From where he was, Sanyustiz could smell the sea. Fifth Avenue, in Miramar, was the city's most elegant address. Though Sanyustiz had been a bus driver for a long time, his route had never taken him here, and he had rarely needed to come to this neighborhood before. But since his resolve to find a way to leave

Cuba had sharpened, getting to know Fifth Avenue had become a crucial part of his escape plan. He would ride up and down the avenue, meandering through some of the side streets to study the movement of the area's security personnel: guards coming in and out of embassies, officers in boxy Soviet-made cars being driven in and out of their homes, soldiers manning important-looking offices, mansions partly hidden from view by the Spanish moss that hung off the city's old oak and silk-cotton trees. He was searching for an inviting embassy, one whose layout would make it easy for him to ram a city bus against its chain-link fence. Sanyustiz had come to the conclusion that for him this was the only way out.

Since the previous fall, about eighty-five Cubans had sought refuge in several Latin American embassies, where, as per international treaties, protection was offered to those fleeing persecution. Sanyustiz was intrigued by the Peruvian embassy, which at times seemed unguarded. In his weeks of observation, he had never seen more than three guards at its perimeter.

But for now the Peruvian embassy was out of the question. On January 17, 1980, twelve people intent on obtaining political asylum had crashed a minibus against its gates. The Peruvian ambassador, Edgardo de Habich, a professed admirer of the Cuban revolution, sent the gatecrashers back to their homes without authorization from his government. Five days later *Granma*, the official newspaper of the Communist Party, published a statement by de Habich asserting that his country was not prepared to give asylum to anyone who forced his way into the embassy.

Sanyustiz kept searching.

Barely thirty-one years old, Sanyustiz, a thin man with a droopy mustache and deeply set brown eyes, was tired of his life. He was unemployed, restless, and besieged by the Committee for the Defense of the Revolution, the block-by-block watchdog organization that kept an eye on everyone, but especially on people like him—people with a police record, no job, a bad attitude, a questionable source of income, and a weak commitment to the revolution. Such people were thought of as lazy bums, and there were laws to punish them.

Though the laws were not always applied, Sanyustiz knew that they could be, and the arbitrariness of the system kept him on edge. As far as he was concerned, there was only one way to live in Cuba: in fear and expecting the worst. "Inside the revolution, all is possible; outside, nothing," Fidel had said once to a group of intellectuals. Sanyustiz was no intellectual but he had no doubt that with his record he would always be considered to be standing squarely *outside* the revolution. Take a false step and people who held power over him—his supervisors, his block's leaders—could make his life miserable; a slipup could cost him jail time.

SANYUSTIZ'S MOST RECENT encounter with the capricious way in which power was exercised in Cuba had begun more than two years earlier, a warm February afternoon in 1978. He was driving the Route 54 bus, on his usual shift down Infanta Street, in the center of Havana, making a right onto San Rafael Street, when suddenly a pregnant yellow dog crossed his path. To avoid hitting the dog, he stepped hard on the brakes. The passengers lurched forward. Some cursed him, but most clapped when the dog emerged unscathed from under the bus and went on its way, tail wagging.

Among the passengers, though, there was a young black man, dressed in a suit and tie, unusual attire at the time in Havana's sweltering climate. The man angrily confronted Sanyustiz.

You could have killed us, the man admonished him.

Sanyustiz, who had a short fuse and no tolerance for arrogance, took a deep breath and slowly tried to explain himself. *Compañero*, he started, I didn't want to kill a pregnant dog. Understand?

The man didn't like Sanyustiz's condescending tone. Do you know who I am? he asked.

No, and I don't care, Sanyustiz retorted, turning back to the wheel.

The man attempted to show him an identification card, but Sanyustiz wouldn't look.

The man persisted. Here, take a look. I'm a prosecutor, he said, spitting out the words.

Sanyustiz made a dismissive gesture with his hand and drove on in silence.

Two stops later the man in the suit got off the bus, and as he crossed the street in front of it, Sanyustiz yelled from his window, *¡Vaya fiscalito!* mocking the prosecutor with a belittling form of his title. The man stopped for a moment, shook his head in disbelief, and walked on.

Sanyustiz shrugged off the incident and kept driving. When he finished his shift and took the bus back to the garage, two police officers were waiting for him. Behind them was the young prosecutor, who pointed at Sanyustiz. The officers grabbed him and told him he was under arrest. Sanyustiz thought the whole thing was a charade but avoided the prosecutor's eyes just in case.

You should have looked at my ID! the prosecutor yelled at Sanyustiz as he was being led away. I promise you, you are never going to drive a bus again!

Sanyustiz was angry, but he wasn't scared. Trouble had been the one constant in his life.

HE WAS BORN in his parents' home in La Torcasa, a small town in Oriente, on September 27, 1949. When his mother developed a fever after delivery, the midwife thought it was best to take her to the hospital; Héctor's twin sister, Hilda, was born there the next day. Little Héctor was a free-spirited boy. He climbed on trees and rode horses; he milked cows and helped to slaughter pigs. When he was about six, his mother thought her children would receive a well-rounded education in the capital and moved the family to Jesús del Monte, a poor barrio of Havana. From the start the city did not suit Héctor. He was one of the few white boys in a mostly black neighborhood and the only one who'd been born in the country, which made him the target of taunts and sneers. He disliked wearing a uniform and shoes to school; in fact, he abhorred going to school. He missed the ripe mangos he used to pluck from the trees and the river where he bathed in the afternoons.

Héctor had never played with toys in the country. He was used to fashioning playthings from tree branches, like a bat or a stick. One day, as he was returning home from school holding his sister's hand, he noticed a boy who seemed to be gliding on the sidewalk. When the boy got close, Héctor could see he was wearing some sort of rolling shoes. Héctor stared at the boy openmouthed, which must have annoyed the boy, because he took off one of his roller skates and hit Héctor hard on the head, splitting open his forehead. Héctor and his sister ran home.

Stitched up and bandaged, Héctor began to plan his revenge.

Remembering how his cousins had sharpened branches to build traps for pigeons in the fields of Oriente, he shaved down the wood casing of a pencil without exposing the lead and kept his weapon with him everywhere he went. When he saw the boy approaching on his shiny skates one morning, Héctor positioned himself next to the porch of a house and stuck his leg out. The boy tripped and fell. In a second, Héctor attacked, plunging the sharpened pencil as far as it would go into the boy's shoulder. The boy screamed in agony, and had to be taken to the hospital. To avoid conflict in the neighborhood, the Sanyustiz family moved to San Miguel del Padrón, another marginal barrio.

That year Héctor stopped going to school. In the afternoons he would copy his friends' lessons so his mother wouldn't find blank pages in his notebooks. He began to smoke, picking up the half-chewed cigars adults left behind, and drink the rum his parents kept stashed in the kitchen. When Héctor got caught, his father punished him by forcing him to kneel on rice grains or by ordering him to stay under his bed for days, where his mother would bring him food. None of the punishments worked; Héctor pretended to go back to school but spent his time selling newspapers and shining shoes in the wide and shady sidewalks of Havana. To earn more money, he ran errands for neighborhood prostitutes who paid him fifty cents to bring them cigarettes or a quart of milk; for a three-dollar tip, he carried water up three flights of stairs for an old lady who couldn't walk. In the evenings he enjoyed strolling in front of the other kids in the barrio, jiggling the money in his pocket. When he was feeling particularly generous, he invited some of his friends to the movies to while away summer afternoons. By the time he was ten, Héctor had realized that what made him happiest was his independence, not having anyone tell him what to do.

When, in January 1959, Castro and his cadre made their triumphal entrance into Havana, Héctor was told that the revolution was meant for children like him: poor, misguided kids who needed to be schooled. Instead Héctor saw how the revolution eroded, one by one, the small freedoms he treasured. His odd jobs disappeared as Castro eliminated private enterprise and prostitution. No one gave money for errands anymore because all revolutionary boys were expected to be polite and helpful, not to charge for a favor.

In 1964, when he was fifteen, Sanyustiz got a job as a trainee in the canine unit of the Ministry of the Interior, through an older brother who worked there. When a dog died under his care and he was accused of killing the animal, Héctor was sent to patrol the beaches of Havana at night, to protect the country against outside enemies and prevent deserters from rowing away toward the United States. Though he never captured anyone, he witnessed many thwarted attempts to leave. Because he felt sorry for the shivering and scared men and women detained at sea and brought back to shore, he sometimes offered to call their families for them, even though he knew that to show any kindness toward a counterrevolutionary could cost him his assignment. Soon enough he was caught taking a piece of paper with a telephone number from one of the detainees, and was summarily and dishonorably dismissed from his first important job.

At seventeen Sanyustiz was drafted for obligatory military service. By twenty-one he was married, had a daughter, and had already been jailed twice for a total of ten months: once for accidentally ramming a friend's truck against a bodega when he was sixteen and again, at nineteen, for punching a military superior so hard in the face that he dislocated the lieutenant's jaw.

When he was twenty-four, divorced and remarried, Sanyustiz began to drive a bus, the only skill he had mastered while in the military. He had dreamed of being behind a wheel ever since he was a child and used to stand on the sidewalk of his neighborhood admiring the American cars that rolled down the streets of Havana: the red Cadillacs with their silver fins and the two-toned Chevrolets with their shiny hubcaps. Being a practical man, he also enjoyed the limited freedoms the job of bus driver afforded him in a totalitarian country where neighbors watched each other and where even teachers and doctors might secretly work for the Ministry of the Interior, collecting information, dissecting your life, forcing you to become a person you no longer recognized.

And now a yellow dog and an overzealous prosecutor had landed Sanyustiz at the mercy of the government he longed to keep at a distance.

As he stood before the judge, under the stern eye of the prosecutor, Sanyustiz's usual bravado abandoned him. His mouth was dry, his mind empty of words. All he could think was to do whatever was necessary to leave that place and ride home on his motorcycle. He responded to the judge's questions with barely audible monosyllables. When his time came to explain his actions, he was deeply apologetic, but the prosecutor was not satisfied. He accused Sanyustiz of racism and ordered him to explain to his coworkers what had happened and how he'd had to apologize for his disrespect of Cuba's legal system. The judge agreed. The punishment struck Sanyustiz as laughable, a sign that the prosecutor didn't have much on him; if he had, the sentence would have been a lot worse. Sanyustiz was released in a few hours.

The next day Sanyustiz went back to work, explained to his supervisor what had happened, but didn't call a meeting with his peers. From that day on, the prosecutor boarded Sanyustiz's bus every day and sat in the seat he had occupied the day of the incident with the dog, behind the driver. After a couple of days, Sanyustiz had memorized the stop where the man would board, and his back would tense as he approached the stop, for fear of running a red light or doing anything else that could give the prosecutor an excuse to haul him off to jail again.

Two months after the prosecutor began to ride the bus every day, Sanyustiz was caught smoking marijuana with a friend in a car. He was arrested, tried, and sentenced to nine months in jail. On the eve of the feast day of San Lázaro, December 17, the saint to whom he turned when he was desperate, Sanyustiz was released. He had bargained with the saint that very day, promising that if San Lázaro somehow was able to get him out of jail, he would walk to El Rincón, the sanctuary where a life-size statue of the saint was kept. Sanyustiz interpreted his early release as a miracle. But when he got out, a fifteen-hour walk to thank a plaster statue suddenly seemed absurd. Instead Sanyustiz went home and had a beer. Then another. His promise was soon forgotten.

THE DAY SANYUSTIZ RETURNED to work, the prosecutor climbed aboard his bus and whispered in his ear, I heard you were in jail. Then he smiled and took his usual seat. Sanyustiz understood then, clearly and with great force, that he could no longer bear the sight of that man. At the end of his shift, he resigned from his job, a good position that officially paid him a little over two hundred pesos a month but unofficially made him much more money, even rich by Cuban standards. For years, at the end of his daily shift, a coworker who had a master key to open the coin deposit box of every bus would split the take of the day with Sanyustiz—anywhere from twenty to twenty-six pesos each, a considerable sum at a time when beer was 80 centavos, an ice cream cone was fifteen centavos, and a bus ride cost five centavos.

Aside from the money, the job gave Sanyustiz status and freedom. He had regular riders who became friends, and although he was married and had a four-year-old son, he kept an assortment of girlfriends at various stops throughout the city, who cooked lunch for him and sometimes even offered a chance for romance in the middle of a hot afternoon. Sanyustiz was an excellent driver. He reveled in the praise he received from riders and the camaraderie among coworkers who respected his years of experience. Giving up his job was heartbreaking.

Sanyustiz had to find another job, and quick. The government offered him two choices: gravedigger or crocodile hunter in the Zapata swamps, far from home. He rejected them both, aware that by doing so he could be arrested under the dubious, all-encompassing charge that a lazy person was a dangerous one.

Sanyustiz began to live like a fugitive. He kept his motorcycle in the kitchen so nobody would notice when he was home. When he spotted a police car cruising by, he retreated from the windows and turned off the lights. He had instructed his wife to tell the police, should they come by, that he was in another province visiting relatives. Sanyustiz, who had never seriously thought that he should attempt to make a life outside Cuba, began to contemplate leaving his country.

ON MARCH 28, Sanyustiz set out to take his wife to work at a pizzeria at the intersection of Prado and San Rafael, in the center of Havana. On the way there, his motorcycle faltered in the middle of the street. He urged his wife to board a bus, or she would be late for work. They kissed good-bye, and she ran off after a bus he had flagged down. Sanyustiz set astride his motorcycle, trying to figure out what to do. He couldn't just leave it in the street and run to get a mechanic. He had paid thirty-five hundred pesos for it—the equivalent of a doctor's yearly salary—and knew that it would be stolen the moment he took his hands off it.

Before he'd made up his mind, the decision was made for him. Sanyustiz felt a large presence behind him and heard the screeching sound of brakes careening out of control. From the corner of his eye, he saw that a bus was about to hit him. There was nothing he could do but duck. The impact sent him soaring in the air, somersaulting above the motorcycle. When he landed, about twelve feet from the crash, half his body was under the wheels of a truck. He heard people screaming, assuming he'd been killed.

Sanyustiz carefully moved his legs and arms and rolled his neck. Nothing hurt, so he got up and walked back to his motorcycle, attempting to pull it from under the wheels of the bus. People gasped and urged him not to move. Blood was streaming from a scratch on his right leg. Soon the press arrived to record the details of the three-car crash. Dozens were badly hurt; Sanyustiz became the miracle victim. A newspaper photographer took his picture holding on to the handles of the motorcycle and wearing a broad-brimmed hat, his rail-thin body standing erect, not looking at all like a man who had nearly died. Sanyustiz wanted to get away from the scene as soon as possible. The last thing he needed was his picture and his name in the newspapers. He took a deep breath, smiled faintly to the well-wishers who surrounded him, and went home. The next day both his picture and his name appeared in the newspaper.

Sanyustiz understood that it was time to go.

Two days later Radamés Gómez, a twenty-five-year-old neighborhood chum who had heard about the accident, went to see him. Radamés was as eager as Sanyustiz to leave. The year before, two events had rocked his world with such force that Radamés could no longer think of a reason to stay in Cuba. First, he had been unnerved by visits from the members of the so-called Cuban community in the exterior. He couldn't understand why returning exiles, who hadn't sacrificed for the revolution, were given the privilege of shopping in special stores that he, a model worker in an optical store, couldn't even get into. Then, just as he was beginning to sense he had become a second-class citizen in his own country, his mother died of pancreatic cancer, which severed his last tie to home. With no family in the United States or anywhere else outside Cuba, he had no possibility of ever getting a visa. He was depressed and desperate, and, just like Sanyustiz, he felt trapped.

Gómez's visit to Sanyustiz wasn't just a worried call to an injured friend; he had some rather urgent news. A driver whom they both knew had crashed his bus against the fence of the Peruvian embassy on Friday, the same day Sanyustiz had had his accident. The man had risked his life because a friend who worked at the embassy had told him that the position of the Peruvian government regarding refugees had changed. The old ambassador, Edgardo de Habich, had been forced to readmit to the embassy the twelve asylum seekers he'd refused to accept back in January, and he had been called back to his country to account for his actions. His replacement, a young man named Ernesto Pinto, had been ordered to give asylum to those who merited it, in accordance with international agreements. What's more, Radamés said, there was a rumor in the streets that the driver and others who were already in the embassy would be traveling to Lima on Wednesday, April 2.

Sanyustiz, who had already concluded that the Peruvian embassy would be easy to penetrate, got up from his chair, grabbed a shirt, and told his friend, We are leaving with them. The two hatched a plan to somehow make it to the embassy the first day of April, only two days away, so that Peruvian officials would be forced to take them on the Wednesday flight.

That night Sanyustiz and Radamés drove past the embassy to get a sense of the place. It was dark, and they couldn't see too well, so they resolved to come back in the morning. They did not yet have a bus, but that didn't bother Sanyustiz; he was sure that someone, any one of his former coworkers with access to buses, would be eager to join them. They needed a reliable bus that wouldn't leave them stranded steps away from the embassy and that would be sturdy enough to protect them from the shower of bullets they would surely face.

On Monday morning Sanyustiz left Radamés at a café to avoid attracting the attention of the guards and, alone, drove by the embassy looking for a marker, a way to identify the building before he actually saw its façade. He needed to know the precise moment he could begin turning the wheel of the bus. If he turned too soon, he could miss the embassy by a foot or two. Armed police officers would arrest him before he could call for help. If he turned too late, he ran the risk of getting too close to the security detail. He would be killed before he could step off the bus.

The embassy was immediately ahead, on Seventy-second Street, to his right. He craned his neck, forcing his memory to capture every detail of the grounds. There was no obvious marker; oversize branches obscured the view. He did notice that the best access to the gardens stood exactly between the third and fourth trees at the end of a block, where there was only one other house. If he could remember that, he thought, he would be okay.

He focused on the building. The two-story corner structure with a faded, red-tiled roof occupied almost an entire city block. He studied the gardens, the gate, the entryway, the fence, the movement of the security personnel. He noticed, with alarm, that security had been increased. Where before there seemed to be only three guards, now there were six. Maybe even more in the back.

Sanyustiz's scrutiny of the embassy took less than a minute, but the palms of his hands were clammy and his heart was racing. He feared that even from across the street the guards could detect his anxiety and read his intentions. Large circles of sweat began to form under his arms. He sped on, making sure the feel of the avenue—the way certain tree roots stuck out, as well as the colors and shapes of the bushes—stayed with him.

On April 1, the last day on which they could possibly seek asylum to make it on the expected Wednesday flight, Radamés remembered a young man who lived near his house and drove a bus on Route 79, the same one that passed in front of the embassy several times a day, every day.

His name was Francisco Raúl Díaz Molina, and he was just twenty-seven years old, recently married, and living with his wife, mother, and stepfather in a small apartment in Lawton, a working-class neighborhood of Havana. Sanyustiz knew him as Raúl; they had worked together in the same garage before he had resigned the year before. He remembered Raúl as a prankster whose nickname was "El

Títere," the puppet, for his affable and malleable personality. When Raúl got into trouble for not showing up for work, Sanyustiz covered for him. Now Radamés was asking him to put his cherished plan, his one chance of leaving Cuba, in the hands of a young man who seemed always to be in need of protection. Sanyustiz didn't think Raúl would agree to breaking into an embassy, but he went along with Radamés because he couldn't think of anybody else with a bus who might just be crazy enough to follow them.

When Sanyustiz and Radamés arrived at Raúl's house, he was resting after his first driving shift. His mother roused him from the couch. The three men went outside to speak. If Raúl was surprised, he didn't show it.

When? That was the only question he asked.

Today, Radamés told him. Sanyustiz stood quietly to the side.

Okay, but I have no idea where the embassy is, Raúl said quickly, struggling to keep his voice even.

Don't worry. I know, Sanyustiz said.

They agreed to ride together in Raúl's bus that afternoon. It was understood that Sanyustiz, the more experienced driver, would take the wheel. After dropping off the last passengers of Raúl's shift, they would drive to the embassy and crash it.

Raúl had lunch with his wife as if nothing had happened and took her to the bus stop for her ride to work. He kissed her, as he always did, but this time he had a hard time letting go. Then he went back home and put on his uniform with special care: navy pants, white shirt, and a blue tie. He hugged his mother good-bye for a long time. She hugged him back unquestioningly.

Sanyustiz, too, had been going through the rituals of his daily life, trying desperately not to cry. He hated the idea of being separated from his little boy. The night before, he had told his wife of his plans. But because he was always talking about leaving, she hardly worried. Just in case he really did do it this time, she asked him to take along her seventeen-year-old son from a previous marriage. If he didn't leave the country then, he was sure to get drafted for military service, running the risk of being sent to the war in Angola.

That morning, Sanyustiz had taken his son to day care. He told the boy that he was leaving that day for a long trip, to fight against bad men in an international mission that would bring honor to the family and to Cuba. He promised to be back soon.

After leaving Raúl's house, Sanyustiz drove home, showered, put on his old uniform, and went to have lunch at the house of one of his girlfriends, María Antonia, a single mother of an eleven-year-old son, who lived next door to the garage where Raúl parked his bus. It was agreed that Raúl would pick them up in front of her house. Toñita, as she was called, told Sanyustiz that she and her boy were going with him, wherever he might be headed and however he was going to get there.

When Raúl stopped the empty bus at Toñita's, the group quickly boarded and spread out to find seats without speaking to each other. Sanyustiz perched behind the driver's seat. He had never before been in that type of bus, a modern, three-door, thirty-foot-long Japanese model assembled in Cuba. Unlike the buses Sanyustiz was used to, this one had a stick shift off to the right side, placed at such an angle that an inexperienced person would have had to look down and to the side to switch speeds. At the moment of the break-in, Sanyustiz couldn't afford to waste precious seconds eyeing the stick shift. He needed to be able to operate the bus as if he'd been born in its driver's seat.

At the first stop, at about a quarter past one, Raúl handed the wheel over to Sanyustiz, who pretended to be a driver in training. Sanyustiz felt the wheel slide smoothly under his practiced fingers. He checked the brakes and the gas pedal. He was testing for acceleration power. He was afraid to get stuck on the grass before at least one of the doors was on the Peruvian side of the gate. If he failed— if the door jammed or if bullets or tree roots stopped the bus in its tracks—Sanyustiz knew that the guards would kill them, or, if they lived, they would be sent to jail for at least thirty years, maybe even for life, or be executed by a firing squad for betraying the revolution.

On the way back from the first round of his test drive, Sanyustiz once again cruised past the embassy. This time the building was on his right, exactly the way he knew it would be when the time came to break in. One. Two. Three. He counted three guards. Where were the others? he asked under his breath. It looked too easy. Raúl, who sat behind him in a passenger's seat, urged him to forgo the initial plan and crash the gate now. Get in, get in, get in, he whispered with urgency. Sanyustiz shook his head, No. He knew he couldn't risk the lives of the passengers in the bus. If one of them died, Sanyustiz would be branded as a murderer, and no country would give him asylum. He was angry with Raúl for even suggesting such a thing.

A few stops before the end of the run, Sanyustiz got up from the driver's seat, thanked Raúl for the "training," and got out of the bus. That was the cue for the other four—Sanyustiz's stepson, Radamés, and Toñita and her son—to follow him. Raúl would pick them up an hour and a half later for the last leg of the trip.

Once the bus had left, Sanyustiz told Radamés that Raúl had just risked the entire operation with his big mouth.

Forget it, then, Radamés said, thinking that Raúl would be too angry at Sanyustiz's reaction to come back for them.

Oh, yes. He is coming back, Sanyustiz answered. He didn't know why, but he was sure that if Raúl had gone this far, he was not going to back away. Sanyustiz instructed the group to disperse once again, to avoid attracting the attention of patrolling police officers.

While they waited, Sanyustiz put his thoughts in order. He went over the details of the driving in his head. He could almost feel the wheel in his callused hands as he rehearsed the right turn to the embassy grounds. He knew the steps: After the big house on the right, count three trees. Between the third and fourth trees, foot on the brakes, big turn of the wheel to the left, and then release the brakes, quickly turn to the right, and shift to third. He was ready. He could do this.

Before he knew it, Raúl's bus returned as promised, with a few passengers on board. Raúl put on the emergency brake and came down the steps to join the expectant group. He reached into his shirt and pulled out a gold medallion of Our Lady of Charity, Cuba's patron saint, who according to legend had saved the lives of three fishermen in a storm. Raúl kissed the image, and, one by one, Sanyustiz and the others did the same. They all boarded and found seats, except for Sanyustiz, who stood in the front, still playing the role of apprentice.

He leaned over and told Raúl to stop near Coney Island—a once-famous park in Havana, remnant of prerevolutionary times when U.S. landmarks were reproduced in Cuba—and announce to the passengers that the tires were low on air and he needed to call for help. Raúl did as he had instructed. But just as the last passenger was disembarking, a uniformed bus inspector came running toward them.

Can you give me a lift? the man pleaded, out of breath.

Raúl looked at Sanyustiz, who returned his stare, steely-eyed. Raúl glanced at his watch. It was 4:35. They were running out of time. If he didn't call the garage soon, the route inspector was bound to notice his absence and report him. Someone might come searching for them. If so, there was no way they could get into the embassy today.

We are just going to the telephone to call for help, Raúl said, a little too curtly.

That's okay. I'll go to the telephone with you, and then we'll see what we all do, the inspector replied, assuming perhaps that Raúl would be ordered back to the garage so he could give him a lift.

Raúl nodded. Sanyustiz made eye contact with Radamés and the others who were standing on the sidewalk. *We'll be back*, he desperately wanted to tell them, but he couldn't. He hoped they would stay put. Raúl, Sanyustiz, and the inspector got in the bus and drove in silence until they located a phone a few blocks away. Raúl called the garage, explained that he had had a flat tire, and was instructed to return without passengers, just as he had hoped. Sanyustiz used the phone to call his wife at work.

I'm going to have to say good-bye now, he told her, trying to swallow the lump in his throat and keep his voice even. She couldn't say anything for fear that interrogators would later insist that she had to have known about her husband's plan because her coworkers had overheard her wishing him good luck minutes before he'd crashed the bus. *Adiós*, she said simply, and hung up.

Back in the bus, Raúl lied to the inspector.

We've been told to wait for help, he said. We have to stay put.

The inspector, accustomed to the capricious ways of the transportation system, shrugged and went running behind another bus that had just stopped nearby. Raúl and Sanyustiz watched him disappear into the crowd. He had stolen a few precious minutes of their plan; it was time to get the others. Once they had picked up the rest of the group, Sanyustiz took the wheel and ordered everybody to lie on the floor toward the back. He knew that the guards would aim to kill the driver, not the passengers. Still, he was afraid a bullet might ricochet and hurt some of his friends or even the children. Radamés stubbornly refused to lie down. He sat behind Sanyustiz.

Get in the back, Sanyustiz ordered him.

No, I want to see what you see, Radamés insisted.

ALONE AT LAST, with wide Fifth Avenue empty ahead of him, Sanyustiz pressed the gas pedal and quickly reached forty miles an hour, about ten miles above the normal speed for a bus that size in a neighborhood like Miramar. There were no traffic lights between Ninety-sixth Street and Seventy-second Street, where the embassy stood. He grabbed the wheel hard and held his breath. Before he expected it, he saw the house. Then the trees. One, two, three. Now! every nerve in his body seemed to scream at him. Now! He stepped on the brake pedal, making a loud screeching sound that he was sure would attract the attention of the guards in the back. With all his might, he veered hard to the left and then sharply to the right, knowing that the weight of the bus might cause it to tumble over. If that happened, he figured, the trees would cushion the fall and the bus would right itself.

He went over the grassy hump with ease and plowed through the gates, bringing them down as if the fence were made of butter sticks. But Sanyustiz had miscalculated two things: how wide the fourth tree was and how fast the guards could run. He felt a tree trunk crush into his side of the bus; the metal of the bus pressed against his left leg. The guards knelt down in front of the bus, shooting from one knee. He stepped on the gas and shifted to second gear. If they're shooting, I'll have to run them over, he decided. It was his last coherent thought. He was one with the machine now. The bus led the way, and Sanyustiz followed.

When the bus finally came to a halt, more than a third of it was inside the embassy grounds and a portion of the fence lay beneath its wheels. The shooting stopped, and Sanyustiz opened the front door, the only one he was sure was completely inside Peruvian territory. Radamés was bleeding from the head and the back. A guard was down. Sanyustiz's left leg pained him as he limped out. Noises, loud and distant, were attacking his senses. The heat was unbearable. He was achy and thirsty, but he was on the other side now, the safe side.

Sanyustiz lay on the ground and for a moment closed his eyes.

FIVE

Ernesto Pinto:
An Embassy Under Siege

A demonstrator screams her support for Fidel Castro
during a massive rally in Havana, on April 19, 1980,
to denounce the Cubans who were seeking refuge
in the Peruvian embassy.

ERNESTO PINTO, chargé d'affaires at the Peruvian embassy, leaned against his car in his crisp, white *guayabera*—a pleated linen shirt with four pockets—and dark glasses. An April breeze, warm and moist, tousled his black hair. He was relaxed but pensive, facing the ocean and discussing his take on Peruvian-Cuban relations with another diplomat. While in Havana, Pinto always went somewhere near the water to talk about delicate matters. The sand, pristine and soft, was the only place he knew where the Cuban security apparatus could not possibly install microphones.

He had been in Cuba for only two months, and already he was troubled by the number of people seeking asylum at the Peruvian embassy. There had been two break-ins since January. The most recent one, under his watch, had occurred just four days before, on March 28; thirty-two people were hidden in the embassy's garage at the moment. Among them were a police officer who had jumped the fence, a man who appeared to be mentally ill, and a prostitute who had made it clear that she wanted to marry a Peruvian. Pinto had not yet been instructed what to do with them. He knew there were rampant rumors in Havana that the refugees would soon be sent to Lima, but the truth was that his superiors, busy with domestic matters, were paying no attention to Pinto's turf.

A few days earlier, he had asked the Cuban Ministry of Foreign Relations for formal authorization to move the embassy from its virtually unprotected, open site to the twenty-third floor of a secure building downtown, but his request had not yet been approved. He was pondering the significance of this delay with his colleague when he heard the shots—first two, then too many to count. Pinto knew instinctively that they had come either from his embassy, about a mile away, or from the nearby Venezuelan compound. It was 5:00 P.M. on April 1, and the sun was beginning its long descent into the Atlantic.

Let's go, he said, and the two men jumped in Pinto's car, a 1979 Camaro with a seven-liter engine that he'd had shipped to Cuba from New York. If he floored the gas pedal, the car could reach 130 miles per hour within seconds. He didn't have to. Even at half that speed, he reached Miramar's Fifth Avenue in less than two minutes; the embassy was in sight.

PINTO'S TAKE on the delayed authorization to move the Peruvian embassy downtown, which he would have shared with his colleague if the shots had not stopped him, was that the Cuban government had facilitated the embassy break-ins or even instigated them, in order to test the loyalty of Peru's military government.

The president of Peru, General Francisco Morales Bermúdez, who had ousted General Juan Velasco Alvarado in a bloodless coup in 1975, had kept Castro at arm's length. The two countries had cordial relations, but not excessively so. Two years before, in 1978, a right-wing faction of the Peruvian military had bombed two Cuban ships anchored at Callao, Peru's main port. The incident led to the withdrawal of Cuba's ambassador from Peru and to a nine-month period of tense relations. Pinto had then been sent to Cuba to try to repair the standoff between the two countries. After six weeks and a long conversation with Castro, Pinto had left Cuba satisfied with his diplomatic efforts. An investigation into the bombing had not yet revealed the culprit, however.

Now Pinto, a brash young lawyer with a sharp mind and European reserve, was in Havana once again to mend the damage from the diplomatic nightmare his predecessor, Edgardo de Habich, had instigated by denying refuge to Cubans who had entered the embassy by force back in January. Pinto was the perfect man for the job. In addition to his successful negotiating stint in 1978, he'd been sent to Havana in 1979 to substitute for de Habich for a short period, and in New York, as a Peruvian envoy, he had worked on several United Nations committees alongside Ricardo Alarcón, Cuba's ambassador to the UN. Pinto believed that he understood the Cuban mind or, rather, the scheming minds of the men in charge.

Pinto relished both his new job and living in Cuba. An admirer of beautiful women and old cars, in Havana he felt like a boy in a toy store at Christmastime. Though he was married and had two small sons, he was seeing a Cuban ballet dancer and generally enjoying both the perks of power and his own sense of importance. Though he was only thirty-three—young for someone in diplomatic circles—his government had placed him in positions of increasing responsibility, negotiating delicate deals with a world leader of the stature of Fidel Castro. The excitement and challenges of his new job, the sense that in Cuba trouble always seemed to loom ahead, energized him.

GIVEN HIS NEW POSITION, Pinto thought it wise to be cautious. Even with the ballerina, Pinto kept a wary emotional distance. He knew that she could be an emissary of the Cuban government ordered to spy on him. Or that she could simply be a desperate young woman eager to get out of the country, who had calculated that her chances for a visa would increase by dating a diplomat. Either way Pinto sensed that her feelings for him had nothing to do with love or even with his tanned good looks and red Camaro.

After the most recent bus had barreled through the Peruvian embassy's main gate in the last week of March, the officer in charge of the Cuban soldiers who guarded the embassy came up with a plan to step up security at the building's perimeter. He had heavy rocks delivered and arranged so as to create a barrier inside the fence; then he brought in more guards, positioning them one behind the other. Pinto thought that was a dangerous arrangement, and he told the man as much.

If someone does break in, you could end up shooting your own people, Pinto warned.

You don't interfere with my job and I won't interfere with yours, the officer brusquely responded.

Pinto let it go.

Forty-eight hours later, Pinto's warning proved to be on target.

◆ ◆ ◆

WHEN PINTO ARRIVED from the beach, the first thing he noticed was the
iron fence. A portion of it was down, crushed like a country fence after a cattle
stampede. A battered red bus was wedged between two old trees. A Cuban guard
whom he knew by the last name of Ortiz lay bleeding on the ground. Another
guard was aiming his AK rifle at the walls of the embassy.

Sons of bitches! the guard yelled at Pinto, and he opened fire randomly, emp-
tying his rifle. You are at fault for this!

Pinto had no idea what he was being blamed for, but he didn't have time to find
out. Two men from his security detail pushed him to the ground and covered him
with their bodies. From his position Pinto saw several men—at least two of them
wounded—and a woman and child getting out of the bus. One of the injured
men was Héctor Sanyustiz, who walked with a limp; the other, Radamés Gómez,
was bleeding from a shot that had grazed his head. A Cuban guard approached
his colleague with the AK rifle, and a brief struggle ensued as he attempted to dis-
arm him. Pinto could hear police sirens in the distance. He noticed the stunned
face of his wife, Lily Barandiarán, who was standing at the door of the ambassador's residence. Their children, two boys aged four and seven months, had been
watching cartoons in a room off the front yard. They were unhurt, but the outside
wall of that room was pockmarked with bullets. Everything was happening both
too fast and in slow motion. Now Pinto could see that Ortiz was bleeding pro-
fusely from the chest. The other soldiers picked him up and carried him to a waiting ambulance. Suddenly Pinto realized he was the highest-ranking person there.
He was in charge, but he was facedown on the ground.

Quickly he shook himself free of the bodyguards, stood up, and instructed his
chief of security to take the bus passengers and the driver to the house. Soon after, General José Abrantes, head of Cuba's much-feared State Security, dressed as
a civilian and hiding his eyes behind dark Ray-Ban sunglasses, arrived on the
scene and approached Pinto. An armed bodyguard followed close behind him.

I'm General Abrantes, and I want you to hand over the assassins to me, he
said curtly.

Who died? Pinto asked, angry at the general's menacing tone. Who killed whom? Is the guard dead?

Pinto had not yet been told that twenty-seven-year-old Pedro Ortiz Cabrera had died of a chest wound. It was not known whether one of his own bullets had ricocheted off the bus and killed him or whether a stray bullet from another guard had struck him.

Those sons of bitches in there! Abrantes shouted, pointing his finger first to the embassy and then to Pinto's face. The ones you are protecting. They killed him!

Pinto was used to analyzing things in a different way. The son of a German mother and a Peruvian father, a scientist, Pinto was an uncommonly serious, mature man. His first language was German, but he spoke Spanish flawlessly. He was punctual, organized, and he thought carefully before he spoke. He had a sharp, mathematical mind that rarely failed him.

And right now he needed more time to think. He considered asking the general to join him inside the embassy so they could have a civilized conversation in private, not shouting at each other in a yard strewn with the detritus of the crash and stained with blood. But he didn't know Abrantes well and assumed he was armed. Pinto decided that the conversation would be outside and that it would be short.

The first thing we need to do is determine if in fact someone died, then wait for the results of the autopsy and a ballistics test to know who shot him, Pinto said in his most lawyerly voice.

With your permission or without it, I'm going in to get those men, Abrantes retorted, and he began walking toward the embassy building.

Then I have nothing to discuss with you, Pinto responded, raising his voice but staying put. This is a political matter. If you take a false step, I won't follow.

The word "political" stopped Abrantes in his tracks. He came back and, out of earshot of his bodyguard, once again tried to convince Pinto to turn over to him the people from the bus. Pinto refused. General Abrantes left in a huff.

Pinto turned his attention to the people inside the embassy. Members of the security detail had searched them and found that none carried weapons. He learned that Sanyustiz had been wounded in the right buttock and that Gómez had a bullet in his back, a mere half inch from a vertebra. Pinto asked the embassy personnel to take the wounded to a military hospital and instructed his staff not to leave the men alone; from that moment on, they were the responsibility of Peru, protected by international treaties.

Pinto didn't know whom he had just vowed to protect, nor did he approve of the violent way these people had sought asylum, but he knew what it was like to feel trapped in a country one was eager to flee.

ERNESTO PINTO-BAZURCO RITTLER was born in Germany in 1946, right after World War II. His father, also named Ernesto Pinto-Bazurco, was a middle-class Peruvian who had moved to Munich twenty years earlier to study medicine. There he fell in love with a German woman and decided to stay, finding work in a hospital after graduation. When the Nazis seized power and war broke out, Ernesto saw no reason to leave. He was grateful to Germany for giving him a career, a good-paying job, a wife he loved, and a lifestyle he cherished. He and his wife were not political, so they figured they would be left alone. But then Peru declared war against Germany, the first country of the Americas to follow Washington's lead. Pinto's grandfather, Moisés Pinto-Bazurco, was a highly regarded Peruvian navy officer. Because Moisés's son, Ernesto, bore the same compound last name, the Germans thought he was the same man and promptly arrested him. For three months in 1941, while the Nazis investigated his identity, Ernesto was detained in a concentration camp in the south of Germany, where he worked as a doctor.

By the time Pinto was born, Germany had lost the war and Munich was a city in ruins. Pinto's earliest memories were of playing in the rubble of what once had been grand houses. The American occupation, far from bringing relief to his family, brought headaches and hardships. The soldiers, rude and inexperienced, made crude jokes and terrorized the neighborhood. Once, when he was about three years old, Pinto found his mother crying in the backyard. American soldiers had unearthed four eggs she had hidden under the ruins and used them to play a silly game of baseball. Fearing that the Americans would never leave and that the rebuilding of Munich would take decades, the Pinto family boarded the *Rimac*, a

Peruvian ship loaded with five hundred other Latin American expatriates, and headed home in September 1950. Five weeks later they arrived in Lima as refugees.

Pinto was raised in the jungles of Peru, where his father researched the curative powers of native plants, and, when the time came, chose diplomacy as a career because he knew that, far from bringing solutions, war wreaked mostly pain and destruction. He understood why the Americans had fought the Germans, but he still despised what the Americans had had to do to win the war, and he especially distrusted anyone who wore a military uniform. He viewed diplomacy as the only way to end conflicts without having to bomb entire cities.

When he was sent to Cuba to substitute for de Habich, Pinto knew that his mandate was to reestablish credibility to an embassy his superiors felt had been disgraced by de Habich's obvious diplomatic faux pas and barely disguised ideological identification with the Cuban revolution. Pinto's other purpose was to avoid embarrassing his government in a time of transition.

After twelve years of military governments, the general in charge, Morales Bermúdez, was intent on setting Peru on a democratic track. He had called for elections to be held in the spring of 1980 and had promised to relinquish control of the government to the newly elected president on July 28. At the time of Sanyustiz's embassy break-in, President Morales Bermúdez's priority was to prevent a crisis that might interrupt, delay, or simply cast a shadow over Peru's transition to democracy.

Pinto knew that it would be in Castro's best interest to find a solution to their mutual problem before the elections. There was no harm if Castro antagonized a Peruvian president on his way out. But to poison a relationship with a newly elected president—a possible ally—was another matter entirely. Castro, too, would be cautious. Or so Pinto hoped.

Without waiting for instructions from the minister of foreign relations, Arturo García-García—an experienced diplomat Morales Bermúdez had brought out of retirement to help him manage the transition—Pinto decided to visit his old friend Alarcón, now vice minister in the Ministry of Foreign Relations. He wanted to make sure that the Cuban government, in its zeal to get its hands on the gate-crashers, wouldn't dare to attack the embassy to take the asylum seekers by force. For the next two days, Pinto held several meetings a day with Alarcón. One of the meetings took place at 2:30 A.M. on April 4, Good Friday, but the fact that it was a holiday hardly mattered, because Cuba had abolished religious holidays a decade earlier. At that late hour, exhausted after two days of tension and scant sleep, Alarcón assured Pinto with the phrase he was hoping to hear: All's going well.

Pinto believed him and went to sleep.

Early the next day, Pinto was taking a shower when he heard a rumbling noise, like a large tractor burrowing its way into the embassy's front yard. He peeked from his bathroom window and saw that two diesel-powered bulldozers had demolished the cement sentry boxes beside the front gates and were hauling away the debris. Another bulldozer was removing the boulders in the driveways meant to protect the embassy from further bus crashes, leaving the entire perimeter wide open. Once the area was clear, the Cuban guards simply walked away from their posts. Pinto rushed to his office and ordered his staff to scatter throughout the embassy the thirty-six Cuban asylum seekers hidden in the garage. He feared that the Cuban government had cleared the fences in order to attack the embassy and take the refugees by force. He sent an urgent cable to Lima asking for instructions, and then went outside.

Had the Cuban newspaper been delivered that day at 6:00 A.M. as it usually was, Pinto would have read it before his shower and perhaps he would have understood that the plan the Cuban government had just set in motion was far more sophisticated and sinister than a simple military assault against an embassy. But the paper was delivered at 8:00 A.M. that day, at the exact time workers were demolishing the last barrier of separation between Peru and Cuba.

What the paper stated, in a front-page editorial signed by the Revolutionary Government of Cuba—which meant Fidel Castro himself—was that Cuba had decided to stop protecting the Peruvian embassy from those who wanted to leave the country. This decision had been reached, according to the editorial, because Peruvian diplomats, refusing to cooperate with Cuban authorities, had decided to tolerate the intrusion of social misfits and delinquent men and women onto the premises of their embassy. The editorial accused Peruvian diplomats of siding with the United States' campaign of terror against Cuba and also declared that not one of the people who had tried to obtain a visa by breaking into an embassy would ever be allowed to leave Cuba.

Pinto reread the editorial and thought of the implications. He feared for the lives of the asylum seekers and of the employees under his charge. Did this mean that anyone who wished could walk into the embassy and expect asylum? Was that what Cuba wanted? The editorial read like a declaration of war, with Pinto himself cast as the enemy. But simply because the government had decreed these roles, that didn't mean he had to follow them: Pinto decided he would act as he always had, as the diplomat who seeks solutions through dialogue. He grabbed the phone and dialed Alarcón's number. He wasn't in, just as Pinto had expected.

Pinto then called all the ambassadors he knew in Havana and asked them to come to the embassy at 9:00 A.M. for an urgent meeting. When they had all gathered in his office, Pinto asked for their cooperation. He wanted the whole world to know that the Cuban government no longer guaranteed the safety of the representatives of Peru on its territory. This could have happened to any of you, he told them.

Forty-five minutes later, the embassy was swarming with reporters from several international news agencies. Certain that as long as the press was at his front door, no one would dare to invade his home and office, Pinto drove over to the Ministry of Foreign Relations. The only person who would see him there was the chief of protocol, who, through a series of exaggerated hand gestures, led Pinto to believe that their conversation was being taped. He didn't seem to know what was going on anyway.

BY THE TIME PINTO returned to the embassy, dozens of Cubans were standing quietly on the lawn, in small groups. Peru's security personnel had searched the first thirty who walked in at five minutes past eight. The chief of security told Pinto he was sure the thirty were members of the State Security apparatus, sent to monitor and report on the embassy's activities. They had walked in soon after the guards had left, they were well dressed, and their hair was neatly combed. Besides, one of them had the recent mark of a pistol holster on his ankle. Pinto surmised that part of their mission, too, must be to encourage others to follow them to the embassy, with the intention of creating chaos. The chief of security had decided to send them to a different part of the embassy, away from the original thirty-six Cubans inside the building and far from the newer and expanding number of people clamoring for asylum and protection in the front yard. The grounds of the embassy measured twenty-five hundred square meters. Quickly doing the math, Pinto calculated that a thousand, maybe even fifteen hundred Cubans could seek refuge there.

As word spread through the country, hundreds of people began to flock to the embassy. By nightfall it was obvious that Pinto had miscalculated. Thousands of Cubans stood on the grounds: women, children, old couples, students, doctors, thugs, police officers in uniform, even soldiers—who shed their jackets before joining the crowd—and members of the Communist Party, who tore up their red identification cards and threw them on the sidewalk. Some, who had gone to the embassy just to have a look, were pushed or encouraged to get inside. Soon all of Fifth Avenue seemed to be a never-ending parade leading to one final destination: the Peruvian embassy.

Pinto was eager to talk to Castro and kept calling various contacts to ask them to arrange such a meeting. Sometime around eight in the evening, a Russian Zil limousine cruised slowly down the street in front of the embassy. Pinto's wife recognized it as Castro's car and dashed to it. She stood in front and waved her arms as the vehicle came to a stop. Pinto rushed after her.

I think it's time we talked, Pinto said, opening the back door.

Get in. I'm not going to get out, Castro said.

Why not? Pinto was surprised. He didn't think Castro was afraid.

I don't want to see all those worms inside, Castro said.

Pinto thought for a moment about how he should proceed. His wife, who'd had some experience in diplomacy, had urged him earlier not to negotiate alone, without friendly witnesses. But Pinto had few options. He knew that if Cuban troops attacked the embassy, hundreds of unarmed people would be killed. He abhorred the thought of such violence occurring on Peruvian territory under his watch. All day he'd been trying to reach the man in charge, and now the man was in front of him. Pinto quickly made up his mind to accept Castro's invitation.

Before stepping into the car, though, Pinto removed the revolver he'd been carrying holstered to his waist since that morning and gave it to his chief of security. Castro revealed his own weapon, as if indicating that Pinto should keep his. But Pinto disregarded the gesture. He squeezed his wife's hand and bent his head to slide into the car, unarmed.

The car took off without any particular destination. For about an hour and a half, the two talked. Castro insisted that the United States was behind Peru's reluctance to return the gate-crashers. Pinto reminded him that he was no fan of the Americans and told Castro about his childhood in Munich, a city devastated by the Allies.

Pinto took the lead in the conversation by trying to establish his neutrality on Cuban issues: Look, Fidel, you either frighten or charm people. But I'm neither charmed nor frightened by you. What we have to find here is a solution that suits us both.

Castro listened attentively to Pinto. But he wasn't alone; he was accompanied by Manuel Piñeiro, one of the most respected members of his inner circle, nicknamed "Barba Roja," because of his red beard.

All we have to do, Piñeiro interrupted Pinto, is shoot a few rounds, and you'll see how all of them leave the embassy hopping like bunnies.

Pinto shifted his attention from Fidel's face, which he'd been studying for clues, and focused on Piñeiro. Pinto had never seen the man before, but his reputation preceded him: Piñeiro was the person in charge of fomenting and aiding revolutions in Latin America. All matters related to Latin America were to be discussed, cleared, and decided by him—in agreement with Castro, of course. To Pinto, Piñeiro seemed like an angry little man with nothing of the revolutionary aura that he felt emanate from Fidel.

Piñeiro extended a sheet of paper to him. Pinto glanced at it without picking it up.

You must sign this, Piñeiro said. If you don't, we cannot be responsible for anything that might happen.

The document was a request to Cuban authorities, on Pinto's behalf, to help him rid the embassy of the hordes of people who were camping there. In essence it was an abdication of Peru's jurisdiction over its embassy, as well as an admission that it had lost control of its grounds.

Pinto didn't know it, but at that moment, barely two miles away, about two hundred highly trained soldiers from a military division called the Special

Troops, akin to the U.S. Army's Delta Force, were getting ready to launch an attack against the embassy. They had been ordered to evacuate the building at any cost, but without using weapons. Dressed as civilians, the men waited in their barracks for Castro's go-ahead.

Sensing a trap, Pinto refused to sign the document. He didn't even touch it for fear of leaving his fingerprints on a piece of paper that could doom hundreds of people. Instead he offered Piñeiro a threat of his own.

The moment one of those people dies, I'm getting on a plane and returning to Lima, and then this is your problem. If you can't guarantee their safety, there is no point in continuing these negotiations, Pinto said, barely containing his anger.

Emboldened by Castro's silence, Pinto went on: I'm willing to negotiate in whatever terms you want, except death. My methods are peaceful. I'm a diplomat, not a revolutionary.

Because Piñeiro and Pinto had reached an impasse after about forty-five minutes of conversation, Castro ordered the driver to return to the embassy and told Pinto that he would prefer to speak with General Morales Bermúdez. Pinto asked for time to arrange the presidential meeting and told Castro to return for him in about an hour.

Sometime around 10:00 P.M., Castro's limo returned and began circling the embassy again. This time Castro was alone. Pinto thought it was odd that Castro wanted to speak without witnesses, in the darkness of his car instead of in his office, where he was freer to move and could attempt to impress a junior ambassador.

As soon as Pinto got into the car the second time, Castro's bodyguard, who had been sitting in front, next to the driver, moved to the back. But Castro quickly put Pinto at ease by asking him about his wife.

I would have liked to talk to her, he said, and suggested they return for her.

With Pinto's wife in the car, Castro was polite and even flirtatious. He asked her what she thought about the storming of the embassy. She told him that there were dozens, if not hundreds, of children there and she was concerned for their well-being.

I want you to know that the revolution has nothing against you or your family. This is not personal, Castro assured them, looking her in the eye.

Pinto felt somewhat uncomfortable with the personal nature of the conversation and tried to get Castro's attention by reporting that his president was willing to talk, but only if there was a concrete proposal to discuss. Peru was not interested in prolonging the situation. The country, which at the time had an average per capita income of eight hundred dollars, had no budget or willingness to feed thousands of people for an indefinite period of time. A solution had to be found as soon as possible.

But for now all Pinto wanted was assurance that there would be no bloodshed, and nothing short of a commitment from Castro would do. The tone of the newspaper editorial still echoed in his ears. The last line had warned, "If the objective is to use diplomatic immunity to legalize crime, protect criminals, violate our laws, and foment an insecure climate for the foreign representatives in our country, we will adopt all necessary measures at any price to put an end to it." The way Pinto saw it, the situation was grave: thousands of people ready to die and a government he suspected was ready to kill. It was like placing a lit match atop a pile of dry wood, he thought.

Castro nodded at Pinto's interruption but resumed his conversation with Lily, as everyone called Pinto's wife.

We know you are worried about the children and also about your own children, he told her. We also know that your children are not here anymore. We know where they are and that they are safe, he said.

Pinto and his wife were speechless. That afternoon they had brought their children to the home of the Canadian ambassador. They took Castro's comment not as a reassurance but as a veiled threat and an assertion of the omnipotence and omnipresence of the Cuban government.

Finally, after a pause, Castro offered the message that Pinto had sought all along: Not a single shot will be fired, Castro told him.

That was enough for Pinto.

You have to trust me just like I'm trusting you, Pinto said, grabbing his wife's hand as he exited the car.

He felt relieved but also physically and mentally exhausted. His back hurt, and his eyes were burning. For tonight someone else could deal with the logistics of what to do with so many people. Soon, perhaps the next day, he would have to fly to Peru to arrange the meeting between Castro and Morales Bermúdez. But there was something else Pinto needed to do that night.

He went to a balcony on the second floor and took a look at the garden. Thousands of people had trained their eyes on him, he knew, but in the darkness he could see only those who were closest to him. A hush came over the embassy as the Cubans gathered there realized that someone important was about to address them.

I have just talked to Fidel, Pinto said, using Castro's first name, as he knew all Cubans did. And he has assured me that your safety is guaranteed.

At this there were cheers from the crowd.

Many of them had grown up with the revolution, and the only leader they had ever known was Fidel. When in the past Fidel had told them that hardships would come, sure enough, butter disappeared from bodegas and no meat could be found in the butcher shops. When Fidel had warned them that many sacrifices should be expected, volunteer brigades had cropped up all over the island seemingly overnight to cut sugarcane on the weekends. And when Fidel had once asked rhetorically in an early speech, "What do we need elections for?" he had made good on his word and eradicated all vestiges of democracy on the island. The Cubans whom Pinto spoke to that night had every reason to want to escape Castro's oppressive regime, but also every reason to trust his word.

I can assure you, Pinto continued, that I'm doing everything in my power to find a quick solution to your predicament.

He kept his speech short and refused to answer questions, but he advised the crowd to avoid any kind of provocation from the outside. Already, even after Castro's assurance that the people in the embassy would be safe, an angry and accusatory mob had begun to form across the street.

LISTENING ATTENTIVELY FROM her perch under a mango tree was Mercedes Alvarez, a twenty-two-year-old nurse who was five months pregnant and had her three small children—aged five, two, and one—with her. Mercedes, who had followed her husband inside the embassy just three hours before, was scared.

On her lap her youngest children slept, exhausted after crying in vain for milk. She had left her house in such a rush that she'd not had the time to pack diapers or milk for her baby.

Mercedes woke up on the morning of April 4 with no other plan than to make sure her eldest son had a fun fifth-birthday party that afternoon. In the morning she went to the bakery to buy the cake every family was entitled to for birthday parties, weddings, and Mother's Day. The cake—plain white, with a colored ribbon of frosting around its outer edge—was just like all the others for sale. Mercedes tried to make it look more festive by putting a pair of old plastic Tom and Jerry toys on top. In the early afternoon, she secured rationed candies and sodas, also doled out on children's birthdays, as well as some balloons and a piñata in the shape of a swan.

Just as she was done with the last details of the party—ironing a checkered tablecloth, setting out the candles for the cake, and stuffing bags with candy for the guests—her husband, Filiberto, rushed in to tell her that the Peruvian embassy was open to asylum seekers.

Let's go, he said, racing to the bedroom to prepare a bag before Mercedes had a chance to answer.

No, no, no. I'm not leaving, she finally managed to say, thinking of her mother and her siblings and the danger in which she would be putting her own children.

Okay, then I'll take the children and send you a visa so you can join us later, her husband said. Mercedes just looked at him, eyes wide with disbelief.

There was no way that Mercedes would accept a separation from her children. Abandoned by her father when she was three, she knew what it was like to grow up poor and with only one overworked, overwhelmed parent. Her mother was always so tired at the end of the day that she had no time for hugs or endearing words for her children. When Mercedes became a mother herself, at eighteen, a year after marrying Filiberto, she vowed never to be apart from her own children. She was determined they would never go to bed without a kiss from her.

Right before the guests were due to arrive at the party, Mercedes's husband began packing for her, trying to get the children on his side. He told them he was going to take them on an outing they would never forget, but only if their mother joined them. The older children began to cry and beg their mother to join them.

Mercedes stared at her husband, who stood at the door with the bags. A taxi he had called earlier honked its horn outside. Filiberto pleaded with his eyes, but Mercedes realized he was going to leave with or without her. She grabbed the birthday cake, dropped it in a plastic bag, and followed her husband and her children out the door. In the cab, when it was too late, she remembered that she hadn't yet taken a shower that day.

When they approached the embassy, there were so many people in the streets carrying bags of clothing and food and lugging heavy suitcases that the driver couldn't go on. He stopped the car and abandoned it on the side of the road, joining Mercedes and her family as they immersed themselves in the sea of people who silently marched toward the embassy. Mercedes had never been part of such a quiet crowd. Not even at a funeral.

It took the family about an hour to find a place where they felt they could squeeze into the crowd and safely spend the night. Mercedes held tightly to her children's hands, fearing to lose them in the multitude. When they cried for milk, she gave them pieces of the crumbled cake and rocked them to sleep one after the other. Surrounded by their tiny bodies, she began to think of the consequences of what she had done.

It occurred to her that this might be a trap, that the government might send them all to jail. She was so nervous she couldn't concentrate; her thoughts were flapping around in her head like birds trying to escape a cage. She was calmed somewhat by the realization that if anything happened to her, the government would still provide for her children's health care and education. This paradox— that the same government she was trying to flee was also the one that she knew would take care of her children—made her question why she really wanted to leave her country. After all, the Cuban government had helped her mother get an education so that she no longer had to work ironing other people's shirts, and it had allowed Mercedes to enroll in nursing school—a privilege that had been financially out of reach for most black women before the revolution.

Still, what she wanted for her children was something she had never experienced herself and knew she would never be able to provide for them in Cuba: freedom. That's it, she thought with certain relief. In her despair and fear, she needed to find a powerful reason to justify putting her family at risk. Freedom would be her gift to her children.

The authoritative voice of a man speaking from a balcony above her cut through the fog of Mercedes's thoughts. He said he was in charge at the embassy and that Fidel had promised that nothing would happen to them this night. Mercedes made a mental note of the limited nature of Fidel's assurance of safety, and for a moment she worried about what would happen the next night and the one after. At last, lulled by the murmuring voices of the thousands of people who surrounded her, Mercedes fell sleep, her children by her side.

AT TWO IN THE MORNING of Saturday, April 5, about three hundred members of the Special Troops that had been assembled since 5:00 P.M. the previous day finally received Castro's order to move. But their mission had changed. They were no longer charged with clearing out the embassy. By then about 10,000 people were already inside the compound. Dressed in full combat attire—olive green uniform, a gun in a hip holster, and above-the-ankle black boots—the men were driven to the embassy in twelve matching olive green Russian trucks and eight jeeps. All they had to do was show up, they were told. Their mere presence, the implied threat of their power, would prevent anyone else from even approaching the building and intimidate those already inside so they understood they were not yet fully beyond the grasp of the Cuban government. As they parked their vehicles, the crowd fell silent. Nobody moved, expecting an attack that never came. Only two officers approached the fence but said nothing as they simply and quietly eyed the crowd before going back to their jeeps.

When the show of force was over, the men, the majority of whom had never revealed their faces or even peeked outside the trucks, drove away. But as soon as they left, members of the security apparatus, in civilian dress, joined uniformed police officers and block leaders to cordon off the neighborhood around the embassy for a distance of two to four blocks, preventing anyone from crossing in either direction without an official pass. Dozens of people, perhaps even hundreds, still managed to get in during the next forty-eight hours, but the blockade managed to accomplish what the government had promised in the editorial not to do: to police the embassy once again, preventing any more Cubans from asserting their right to political asylum.

Less than twenty-four hours after Castro had for the first time in twenty-one years relinquished his hold over his people, he'd had to seize it back.

ON SATURDAY MORNING the Foreign Ministry called a meeting with all diplomats in Havana and announced that the government did not oppose the travel of the asylum seekers at the Peruvian embassy to Peru or any other country that authorized it. Diplomats were perplexed that Castro had so grossly miscalculated his own people's reaction to an open gate. He may have reacted out of anger, many concluded. One of Castro's aides told Wayne Smith, the chief of the U.S. Interests Section, that when informed of the guard's death at the embassy, Castro had turned deep red. "I have never seen him so angry," the aide said. Castro's judgment may have been clouded by a series of personal problems, as well as by a host of internal and international pressures that had plagued him since the year before.

In 1979 the country's economy had taken a dive. Job absenteeism and lack of motivation among the workers had lowered production levels, to the point that Castro had felt obliged to address food and housing shortages in a speech on December 27: "[Cuba is] sailing in a sea of difficulties," he said. "We have been in this sea for some time, and we will continue in this sea, sometimes more stormy and other times more calm, but the shore is far away."

Castro was also embarrassed that month by the Soviet Union's invasion of Afghanistan. It did not bode well for his worldwide reputation that his strongest allies had invaded one of the founding countries of the Non-Aligned Movement without consulting or informing him, the chairman of the movement. And he was troubled by the exiles' visits, which had fomented much restlessness among the citizens, as well as suspicion of the United States' foot-dragging in granting visas to former political prisoners. To top it all off, in January 1980, Castro's secretary and confidante, Celia Sánchez, had died. Those closest to him knew that Castro had lost not only a friend and ally, but also his own personal compass.

After the guards were removed from the embassy, one Cuban official, surely echoing Castro's certainty, had bet Smith five pesos that not more than a few hundred people would seek asylum.

BY SATURDAY EVENING the beautiful lawns of the embassy were quickly disappearing under the constant shuffling of thousands of feet. The refugees had by now formed a central committee to communicate their needs to embassy personnel. The committee included, among others, a convicted car thief, a furloughed convict, a third-year law student, a surgeon, a Seventh-day Adventist, and a truck driver. But not even a committee could solve the most pressing issue: lack of space. There were so many people on the embassy grounds that each person had a mere ten inches of space. Some used the thighs of strangers as pillows or slept precariously balanced on the branches of the mango trees.

Shirtless men stood on the roof of the building and stomped angrily; others hung from tree branches and made obscene gestures to the police in the street, feeling free for the first time in their lives.

That night a government van with a loudspeaker on top parked in front of the embassy. A disembodied voice proclaimed that the Foreign Ministry was prepared to give exit permits to all Cubans who had entered the embassy after Tuesday, clearly differentiating between Sanyustiz and his friends, who entered by force, and the thousands who had entered with the tacit approval and encouragement of the Cuban government.

TWO DAYS LATER, on April 7, Castro visited the embassy. He wanted to reassure everyone they would be allowed to leave the country. Nobody said a word, and Castro kept his visit short. In a front-page editorial that morning, the government had for the first time publicly acknowledged the events at the embassy. The unsigned editorial, which began and ended with the words "This is Cuba's stance," accused Peru of protecting common criminals. As examples of the kinds of people in the embassy, the editorial cited homosexuals, gamblers, and drug users. "Throw them out!" the editorial exhorted.

That same day, Pinto flew back to Peru to negotiate the terms of the meeting between Morales Bermúdez and Castro and to place his family out of harm's way. Pinto was convinced there was nothing more he could do for the men and women in his embassy. Diplomacy would take its course, he believed. The Cubans would eventually leave the island. All everyone had to do was wait.

DAY AND NIGHT, government-controlled radio stations droned over loud-speakers, urging the refugees to return to their homes, since Peru couldn't do anything for them; they had to trust the Cuban government to provide them with exit documents to leave the country. Some people stuffed cigarette butts in their ears to drawn out the noise. Others, less patient, yelled back at the loud-speakers, *Mentira, mentira, mentira*. Lies, lies, lies.

As the days wore on in the embassy, a baby boy was born and an old woman died. Portable bathrooms were installed around the perimeter of the compound, but some refugees refused to use them for fear they would not be allowed to get back inside the grounds, preferring to relieve themselves in plain sight of other refugees. The garden soon became a fetid caldron where it was difficult to walk and impossible to lie down.

Around the fifth day, Mercedes moved inside the embassy building and had her first bite of food. For five days her husband had been able to gather only yo-gurt and milk for the children. For the first three days, Mercedes had sat in the same spot without moving, lest she lose her place. When she felt the urge to go to the bathroom, she held it and waited until her children fell sleep so that she could get up and arrange their legs in such a position that no one would be able to take her spot next to them.

The Cuban government distributed food, handing boxes of yellow rice with pork or ribs and sometimes even fish and rice and beans over the fence—but not nearly enough for everyone. The Peruvian embassy didn't have the resources or the personnel to prepare food for so many people. Sometimes rations for 2,500 were doled out to a crowd of almost 11,000 people. Fights erupted, and women and children often lost, even though the food was intended mainly for them. Mothers bore the marks of their desperation: bleeding arms from the scratches produced by the spiky ends of the fence as they extended their hands over it to try to grab food for their children. The number of rations was kept low intentionally to create chaos, to demonstrate to the world that the people inside the embassy were dangerous.

Rumors circulated that someone had boiled and eaten the ambassador's cat. People were tearing leaves from the trees and eating them—the mangoes had long been gobbled up. Some made soup from fish bones and drank warm water seasoned with salt to alleviate their hunger. Most people, especially the children, began suffering from dehydration, sunstroke, and gastroenteritis. The international press congregated in Havana, and the pictures beamed to the world sent a devastating message: The people of Cuba would rather suffer inhumane conditions, eating pets and shrubbery to survive, than live in a communist paradise.

Embarrassed, perhaps as he had never been before, Castro devised a smear campaign against the people in the embassy, calling them *escoria*, or social misfits, a term later explained at length in the newspaper *Granma*: "Social misfits are those who are lazy parasites, delinquents or predelinquents, people with vices." The image was fueled in part by the way people were positioned at the embassy. Women and children were kept inside the building while the men—mostly young, angry, and hungry—camped outside. When the cameras panned their way, they rallied, asking for help. What the lens transmitted across the globe was an unruly mob of desperate men.

Feeling international pressure to take care of the refugees humanely, the government sent buses to the embassy and offered safe-conduct passes to those who agreed to return to their homes to await their time to leave Cuba. At first few took the offer, fearing a trap, but after several days more than a thousand had gone home. The government then called on its citizens to show the "scum" what true revolutionaries were made of. Those who took the government's offer and left the embassy had to walk a gauntlet of about three hundred people who shoved, cursed, and sometimes punched them. But that was not enough. As they arrived in their neighborhoods, holding their safe-conduct passes, they were viciously attacked with clubs and fists by neighbors and former coworkers, who had been meticulously instructed and organized by their leaders. The police, for the most part, stood by as men and women were bloodied in front of their homes and their families for having the temerity to want to flee.

IN LIMA, Arturo García-García, the Peruvian foreign minister, pleaded for international help, explaining to his friends in the diplomatic community that Peru could not possibly take care of so many people on its own. Peru offered to receive up to 1,000 refugees. The United Nations high commissioner for refugees stepped forward, and so did the International Red Cross, as well as countries like Spain, Costa Rica, Ecuador, and Canada, which offered to take 500, 300, 200, and 300 refugees, respectively. Belgium asked for 150, and Venezuela 500. Though those offers did not cover all refugees, García-García remained confident that other countries would eventually heed his call.

Granma began to run stories pointing out that Lima, twenty-five hundred miles to the south, was too far for the refugees to travel. A place closer to Havana was needed—what better place than Florida, just ninety miles due north? the Cuban government suggested. Castro had surely been irked by a comment made by President Carter early in the crisis, when he told a group of businessmen at a reception in Washington on April 9, "We see the hunger of people on that island to escape. Our hearts go out to the ten thousand freedom-loving Cubans who took the opportunity to enter an open gate." Five days after that comment, the Carter administration pledged to accept up to 3,500 refugees, offering Costa Rica, only seven hundred miles west of Havana in Central America, as a refugee-processing center.

Initially Cuba accepted, and daily flights to San José, the capital of Costa Rica, began on April 16. Two days later, when only 676 had been flown to Costa Rica, Castro halted the flights, claiming that there was really no need to use a temporary processing station; it would be much more efficient for all if the refugees flew directly to their country of destination. Out of the earshot of the press, however,

Cuban officials were openly fuming at the spectacle of the refugees arriving in Costa Rica. Many kissed the ground the moment they stepped off the plane and used Costa Rica's free press to criticize the regime they'd just left behind. Castro needed to come up with another solution to the embassy crisis, one that would take the problem out of his hands and place it fully in the hands of his enemies.

On April 17 the government began to promote a massive demonstration, that would take place two days later in front of the embassy, designed to repudiate those who had given the country a black eye; a million Cubans were expected to march. For the event to impress the international news media, there had to be a significant crowd left in the embassy. The demonstration wouldn't succeed if the people who had thrown the country into such turmoil were hundreds of miles away eating steak and fries and drinking beer while revolutionary Cubans hurled insults against an empty, ruined building. For now, Castro had to keep the embassy refugees in the country—and the world watching.

SIX

Unwanted

The day I turned fifteen, in the fields of Pinar del Río,
with my father and my sister, Mabel, then ten.

T HE MORNING OF the April 19 march found my family huddled in the bedroom, peering at the busy streets through the wooden slats of the windows above my parents' bed. Our neighbors knocked on the door, but my father hushed us, pressing his index finger to his pursed lips. We were not to make a sound. In the silence of our small apartment, we could hear the neighbors' loud voices outside, debating what to do next. If they couldn't find us, our block wouldn't have a full participation in the demonstration.

We hadn't seen the newspaper that morning because we hadn't dared leave the house, but the day before, *Granma* had carried a huge banner headline urging Cubans not to miss the march: EVERYONE TOMORROW TO THE MARCH OF THE COMBATANT PEOPLE! Detailed instructions followed: Attend the march with your block; don't leave until you are told to do so, as the flow of people in front of the embassy must be constant and unbroken; be disciplined, focused, and patriotic. Each block in every neighborhood of Havana and its surrounding provincial towns had to show its revolutionary zeal and commitment to the government by marching. A block without 100 percent participation would reflect badly on the ability of its leaders to rally foot soldiers for the revolution. The idea that four people might be hiding in a bedroom, as we were, was intolerable to our exasperated neighbors.

Orestes! Mirta! Are you there? they yelled one last time, perhaps because they suspected we were home and it rankled them that we would dare to upset their perfect-attendance goal; or perhaps none of them really cared about the march or the goal and were only faking their ire so the others in the group would think they were true revolutionaries.

It was impossible to decipher their intentions because after two decades most Cubans had become adept at hiding their true feelings and motivations. We lived submerged in a world of shadows. Everyone wore a mask in public, sometimes even at home, and you never really knew who your friends were. You had to listen and say little, go with the flow, lest the friend turn out to be the enemy who could ruin your life. The smallest of disagreements, the most trivial of conversations, the slightest wavering of thought could be fodder for anyone intent on advancing his career by destroying someone else's. The events at the Peruvian embassy had exacerbated everybody's fears and insecurities. People in Havana crossed the street or averted their eyes to avoid talking to someone they suspected was an informant or, worse, someone about whom one would have to inform. No one was exempt.

We stayed on the bed so as not to make noises that our downstairs neighbors could detect. When we heard the dry click of their door lock, we knew that they, too, had left for the march. From the bedroom windows we saw them walk toward the waiting crowd and turn right, on their way to the designated stop, where the bus picked them up and rumbled off, leaving a cloud of dark smoke behind. And then silence. The streets were empty.

Stepping off the bed, we swatted away chips of white paint that stuck stubbornly to our foreheads and noses after so many minutes of pressing our faces against the old window, and moved cautiously, as if the neighbors could still hear us. My sister and I sat quietly, playing checkers. No one thought of turning on the television. My mother went to the kitchen to cook a stew.

FOR MORE THAN two months, ever since my sixteenth birthday, when we had talked of leaving for the United States, I had been slowly letting go of my life and my city. Certain that we would leave soon, my parents allowed me more freedom than ever. They also let me splurge, since it no longer made sense to save money that was worthless outside Cuba. With my friends from school and my little sister in tow, I went to all the places I had always wanted to visit: to the beach in winter, a treat that my parents would never have permitted before; to the theater to see a hilariously funny Cinderella spoof; to the famed Cuban National Ballet; to the Napoleonic museum; to José Martí's birthplace; to the National Library to browse large-format art books; to the cathedral in Old Havana; and to the restaurant famous for being one of Ernest Hemingway's haunts, La Bodeguita del Medio, to eat with my friends and follow the custom of leaving our signatures on the walls.

At the restaurant a waiter pointed to a chair hanging from the ceiling and reverently told us the chair had belonged to Hemingway himself. We picked the table right under it. When the time came to sign our names on the wall, instead of my own, I scrawled "Holden Caulfield" in large block letters. I had just finished reading *The Catcher in the Rye* and felt that Holden Caulfield was a kindred soul; his alienation from the world mirrored the isolation I was beginning to feel from everything I'd once held so dear, including my former certainty that the government was *not* intent on making our lives miserable.

There was a grand plan for the revolution, I had always believed, and that plan had not yet completely excluded my family, for we had never really strayed form the path our leaders had set out for us. The problem was that in the last few years the path had narrowed in ways we had never anticipated, until, by the time of the march on April 19, there was nowhere for us to stand.

IN LATE FEBRUARY my parents had received a telegram from Las Villas. Come get your prize, it read, a message my father understood to mean that my mother's brother had finally slaughtered the pig he'd set aside for us the year before.

Transporting a dead pig across the island was no minor feat. The sale and consumption of food was strictly controlled by the state. With the exception of small farmers, who had special agreements with the government to farm their own small plots of land and raise their own animals to eat, people were allowed to consume only what they could purchase with government-rationed coupons in government markets. If by the end of the month a family had run out of rice or beans or even soap, they had to do without. Most Cubans, however, skirted the

law and survived using a kind of primitive barter system that allowed them to exchange their government-issued cigarettes for, say, a pound of rice. It was risky
business. One could go to jail for buying goods on the black market.

The news, therefore, that a forty-pound pig awaited us at my uncle's house
was an occasion to rejoice and fear.

My parents planned their trip carefully and traveled alone to Las Villas as if
making a short, routine visit to their relatives. My sister and I stayed with our
friend and neighbor Maricusa, a welcome treat for us because we each got to
sleep in a real bedroom and in real beds, instead of pressed against each other on
the old living room couch.

For the trip back, my parents wrapped the pig in heavy plastic and placed it
inside the small wooden suitcase I used to take to my forty-five-day stay in the
fields every year. The trip was long: the bus made all its usual unscheduled stops
and also broke down for a few hours halfway to Havana. When they arrived at
the terminal, the heat and humidity of the depot finally got to the pig. By the
time it was wheeled out in front of my awaiting parents, the suitcase was leaking
blood. Some of the passengers, especially those whose luggage had been bloodied, began to yell at the attendant.

My father pushed his hand deep inside his pants pocket and pulled out a fistful of change and wrinkled bills. *¡Compañero!* he yelled at the attendant, leaning
over the railing and waving the hand holding the money. That wooden suitcase
below the blue one—it's mine. I need it now!

The suitcase instantly materialized in front of him. My father grabbed it with
both hands and quickly gestured to my mother to follow him. They ran toward
the exit and took a taxi before anyone could stop them, leaving a trail of blood on
the granite floor of the terminal.

My sister and I heard this story when our parents woke us up at about 2:00
A.M. to take us home. We were exhilarated with the tale of the chase, but I immediately understood that my parents had risked jail simply to put food on our table.

NOT EVERYONE IN Cuba had to smuggle food like my parents. Although
"elite" was a concept that was supposed to have disappeared with the advent of

the revolution, the revolutionary leaders of the last twenty years lived in a separate, privileged world. I never actually met any of them, but I knew they existed because some of my friends had had brief encounters with that world and had come back with stories of lavish parties and sumptuous meals. The children of government officials had access to the country's top schools, such as the Lenin School, and went to military country clubs to swim laps in large pristine pools that were nothing like the crowded public pools where my mother would never let me dip a toe.

The children of the elite wore trendy clothes—jeans, tight polyester shirts, and John Lennon–type eyeglasses—while I wore whatever my mother could make from remnants of the cloth she'd used for her clients. My clothes were often two-tone: green plaid on the front of a blouse with a solid green of a different hue on the back; pants that were blue down to my knees with bell-bottoms that opened in a pattern of wild pink flowers. My glasses had frames of a thick, muddy-colored gray plastic; I was so miserable wearing them that my father took pity on me and, for the first and only time in his life, wrote a letter to his brother in the United States asking him to send me a pair of modern, thin, gold frames. The new glasses arrived promptly, folded in a leather case and accompanied by a letter of warning: Take good care of them, my uncle wrote. They were very expensive. Less than a week later, a boy asked me if he could borrow them. I refused at first, but he insisted, and I finally gave in, afraid to be labeled by my more popular peers as uncool and selfish. I never saw my glasses again.

I knew that the children of government ministers didn't have to worry about stolen prescription glasses; their fathers or mothers could always bring them another pair from any of the countries they visited on missions abroad. When they were hungry, all they had to do was open the refrigerator or ask to be taken to a fancy restaurant. My family went to restaurants several times a year; it was the only luxury my parents had preserved from their pre-Fidel lives, but we tended to go to those where my father knew the maître d' so we wouldn't have to stand in line, since few restaurants took reservations from the general public.

To be able to eat at Mónaco, our favorite Italian restaurant, where we didn't know anybody, we concocted a plan with our neighbor, a retired Spaniard named Aquilino Canal Cabazas. Some Saturdays, while my father worked, Aquilino

would stand in line for hours in front of Mónaco and save a place for us until we
showed up about an hour before dinner. We would then hold his place while he
went home to take a shower and change into his frayed, blue-gray suit. He would
return with his date—a widow named Rosaura—after we were seated at a table
for six but just before the lasagna arrived. Together we would return home after
the meal, stuffed and tired and dragging Rosaura, who always had too much ver-
mouth to drink, but happy that once again we'd managed to squeeze some sweet-
ness into our lives.

My father began to sour on eating out after he became convinced that even at
restaurants political influence determined who ate well and who didn't. One year,
on Father's Day, he took us to a restaurant well known for its stuffed-rabbit dish.
When we were finally seated in the posh dining area, he asked the waiter for orange sodas for my sister and me. We ran out, the waiter said, and my father, accustomed to such responses, didn't press the point. We opted for water. A few
minutes later, we saw another waiter carry a trayful of sodas to a curtained-off
area to the side of the main dining room. Puzzled, my father called our waiter
back and asked him to explain how come his girls didn't have soda but whoever
was behind the curtain did. Oh, the waiter said, that was a special order. That
was for el compañero Fernández. And he walked away, as if my father would of
course understand that José Ramón Fernández, the minister of education, and
his guests had every right to drink sodas but we did not. We ate in silence. When
we left, I was certain we would never again eat at another fancy restaurant.

IN EARLY 1980 OUR departure from Cuba seemed only months, or perhaps
even weeks, away. I knew that once my father had taken the steps to obtain our
visas, nothing would hold us back. If Spain didn't authorize our travel, another
country would. My father would find a way. I didn't want any change of behavior
on my part to reveal my family's plan. At school I acted as if nothing were happening, as if I weren't shedding my old skin and readying myself to leave Cuba.

Staying on course was tricky, because at the age of sixteen came another
government-dictated rite of passage: the invitation to join the national communist youth group. I was in eleventh grade and taking college courses at the Uni-

versity of Havana in the two subjects I excelled at, chemistry and literature. I was an A student, with a perfect attendance record and a disposition that made me, I'd been told by young communist leaders, a natural recruit for their organization. The problem was that I had no intention of becoming part of a group whose ideals I no longer shared; yet if I were tapped to join, there was no way I could refuse, for denying such recognition of my potential would be out of character for me and a sure signal to all that my politics had changed.

The day of the meeting for new recruits, I was greeted by an unexpected surprise. A girl with whom I'd had several heated arguments over silly things I no longer remembered got up and stated, in a voice that clearly defined her as the leader of our group, that she was unwilling to second my nomination because I had not demonstrated true commitment to the revolution. As an example she mentioned that I had not dedicated enough time to political activities, such as going to the public square where Fidel spoke, joining demonstrations, or participating in a welcoming committee to greet one of the dozens of communist leaders who visited us every year from the Soviet-bloc countries or from the Third World.

Ordinarily, competition and pride would have compelled me to defend myself, but this time I couldn't have been happier to concede. A huge load had been lifted from my shoulders.

I understand her position, I said when my time came to speak. And I thank her for forcing me to realize my misguided ways.

I kept my speech short. I wanted to confound, not enlighten them. At long last I, too, had learned to wear a mask.

The smartest among my friends knew that I was harboring a secret. They didn't tell me, but I could see it in their eyes. Nevertheless, they applauded with the rest of the group, and when the meeting was over and we walked home together, no one said a word. It was as if the meeting had never happened.

THE DAY AFTER the Peruvian embassy break-in, a friend of my father's came to visit with his wife and children. In the darkness of a blackout, the adults talked on the terrace. With little information coming from the government, rumors had

begun to roll through the streets of Havana like marbles on a steep incline: Anybody who gets to Miramar can just walk through the fence. People are coming
from the interior provinces on foot, dragging their suitcases and pleading for
rides. Children are being impulsively handed over the fence to friends and relatives while their parents go home to pack. All will be jailed. They'll be sent to
Peru. They'll disappear quietly in the night, never to be seen again. They're all
spies. It's all a ploy of the *americanos*.

My father and his friend contemplated joining the crowd at the embassy but
decided that it would be too dangerous for the children. They thought it impossible that so many who had dared to express their dissatisfaction with the Cuban
government would be allowed to leave without harm. My father suggested that
the whole thing was a plot designed by Castro to root out the source of the dis-
content that was sweeping the island. It would end badly, perhaps even that
night, he concluded. We stayed put.

The next few days at school were confusing and tense. Teachers were distracted, and students were somber. Everybody knew somebody who had jumped
the fence. The term "jumping the fence" became an immediate synonym for betrayal and abandonment. If a student missed school, a contingent of his peers
was sent to his house to search for him; the thought was that he, too, had decided
to jump the fence. No one assumed a family problem or an illness. The result was
that the entire student body was intimidated but punctual. No one dared miss a
class or utter a thought that wasn't perfectly aligned with the messages we received from our leaders.

The newspapers were full of stories about Héctor Sanyustiz and Pedro Ortiz
Cabrera. Sanyustiz was portrayed as a wife beater and marijuana-smoking bum
who roamed the streets of his neighborhood in a motorcycle and trafficked in
stolen goods. Ortiz, on the other hand, was described as a hero, the son of farmers from a remote town who always had a kind word or gesture for his coworkers. He had been a model pioneer and a hardworking cane cutter who had
unfailingly said yes when the revolution had needed him. Just before he died, he'd
shared a cigarette with a friend.

Caricatures of the ugly and unruly crowd at the embassy ran in the paper
every day. *Granma*'s cartoonist depicted the men and women in the embassy as

dirty flies escaping from trash cans. Letters of support for the Cuban government poured in from other communist countries, while friendly worldwide organizations sided with the hardworking and decent people of Cuba who never wanted to abandon Fidel. I had already grown used to the worm label, but the depiction of those who wanted to leave as dirty dross began to make me feel as if my family's two-decades-old resolve to join our relatives in the United States had been tainted by the events of the embassy. My father told me not to believe a word of what I was reading and began to keep the paper from me.

Soon it became evident that the government was instigating, or at least facilitating, acts of violence against the fence jumpers. Television news showed men in civilian clothes punching and clubbing people who dared leave the embassy with a supposedly safe pass. I was outraged that Cubans would turn with such viciousness against their countrymen.

One evening as I was walking home with a group of my friends, we began to talk, tentatively, about the events of the week. Sergito, a small but strong boy who had earned a black belt in karate, talked, and we listened. His father was a member of the national militia; we all knew that. What we didn't know was that Sergito, so sweet and apparently harmless, would want to follow in his father's footsteps.

I went to the embassy yesterday to beat the shit out of those delinquents, Sergito said suddenly.

I stopped cold and gasped for breath. Sergito was like a little brother to me, the only boy I could trust with my crushes on various professors and the only boy who visited my house regularly since my boyfriend had been sent to Angola. We shared notebooks and sometimes worked on our homework together. We were friends.

How could you? I finally managed to say, turning beet red.

How could I what? he answered, puzzled.

How could you hurt people who haven't done anything to you, people who only want to leave the country? They have done no harm, I said.

Some of our friends, realizing the tone of the conversation, kept walking without looking back. Others stayed and tried to pull me by the arm, indicating that this was dangerous territory. Sergito was livid.

How can you say that? They have damaged our international reputation! he cried. They are traitors! Don't you know that? What's the matter with you?

Nearby a woman opened her front door and let her dog out. It began to bark fiercely, and a few onlookers surrounded us.

Traitors to what? I pressed on, finding words I didn't know I had in me. Traitors because they want to eat better, because they crave freedom?

At this, some people I didn't know began to hoot, siding with Sergito. She is one of them! someone yelled. The woman with the dog threw a bucket of water on her tiled porch, intentionally splashing us, perhaps to get us away from the front of her house. We didn't move.

Why don't you join them, then? Sergito said, emboldened by the mob.

Maybe I will, I retorted. If that would get me away from people like you.

The woman, who had stopped pretending to clean her porch, approached me and asked me, gently, to leave. It's for your own good, she said.

I looked up and realized we had been arguing in front of that block's watchdog committee. I broke away from the group and began running alone down a steep hill to catch the bus that would take me home. The world was askew, I thought. We all seemed to have lost our footing, especially people like me, who had grown up with two separate and distinct allegiances—to the revolution and to our families.

ON APRIL 19, Fidel Castro led the march of the combatant people, driving past the embassy in a jeep. Behind him a million people marched all day long, chanting *¡Que se vayan! ¡Que se vayan!* Good riddance! They held posters depicting worms in all kinds of ridiculous poses: worms flying with tattered suitcases, worms dressed as gangsters, worms being flushed down the toilet, worms warmly embraced by President Carter.

As the sun was setting, our neighbors returned home. The comfortable sounds of our street came with them: children crying, doors slamming, a man whistling, the woman across the way yelling at her husband. Once again we huddled in the bedroom and turned off the lights. My sister and I fell asleep in our parents' bed, our faces rubbing against the fuzzy pink chenille bedspread. Sometime during the night, my father must have carried us to the sofa bed in the living room. I woke up there early the next morning, my brain muddled by the events of the day before. I kept my eyes shut, trying to still my mind. Out of the confusion and fear I felt, only one thought managed to rise above all others: a fervent wish to sprout wings and fly away.

SEVEN

Napoleón Vilaboa:
The Golden Door

Napoleón Vilaboa (center) in Cuba in the years he
was negotiating the release of the Bay of Pigs prisoners.

NAPOLEÓN VILABOA, rotund and balding, with piercing blue eyes and a frown on his unlined face, stood outside the Peruvian embassy's fence, overwhelmed by the sight of so many people defying the government for a shot at freedom. But he was not surprised.

From the first time he had traveled to Cuba for the 1978 dialogue to help negotiate the freedom of political prisoners, Vilaboa had understood that the presence of exiles on the island would transform Cuban society. Looking at the people hanging on to the fence of the embassy, clamoring for attention, he remembered the story of a Miami carpenter who had returned to visit his family the year before and had discovered that he was immensely richer than his brother, a medical doctor who'd remained in Cuba. After years of medical school and sleepless nights tending to the sick and dying, the doctor lived in a crowded apartment with his in-laws, had no car, and scrambled to put food on the table, while the carpenter owned a house, ate meat and vegetables every day, and drove the latest-model car of his choice. When he heard that story, Vilaboa came to the conclusion that Castro's regime would not be able to resist the onslaught of hundreds of such stories of riches filtering in from Miami.

And here was proof: more than 10,000 people looking for a way out. Vilaboa, who had been able to approach the now heavily protected embassy because, as a member of the dialogue group, he was a special guest of the Cuban government, shook some of the outstretched hands over the fence. The young men and women inside were eager for information, and their eyes searched Vilaboa's broad

face for clues to his thoughts. Yes, he was from Miami, he said, but he had no
news for them. Instead he listened to the refugees and learned much from them
in a few minutes. None had any intention of going to Peru; Miami was their destination. Many of them seemed to be about half his age, which was forty-three;
some were much older. He calculated the average age to be twenty-six or so.

The children of the revolution, Vilaboa muttered to himself. Dazed by the
scene, he asked to be driven back to the Riviera, the hotel where he stayed on his
frequent trips to Cuba.

From the large corner balcony of his oceanfront room, Vilaboa scrutinized the
dark waters of the Atlantic just across the street. On the other side of that darkness, more than three hundred miles north, was Miami, where his wife and six
children awaited him, as did his job as a car salesman, which he had all but abandoned ever since he'd started traveling to Cuba a year and a half before. He had
come as a returning exile with a mission: to find a way to liberate the eight men
still in prison for participating in the Bay of Pigs invasion nineteen years earlier.
He had already managed to wrangle five from the clutches of the government;
three remained. They would have to stay there a while longer, he thought. With
the Peruvian embassy attracting the world's attention, Castro had more pressing
problems.

That night Vilaboa couldn't sleep well, his mind searching for a way to help
the people in the embassy before he was due to return to Miami. By breakfast
time he had a plan, and he went to share it with his old friend René Rodríguez,
a top government official in charge of relations with the people of other countries, including the United States. Rodríguez and Vilaboa had met as journalists
in Havana in the 1950s; Vilaboa was a writer and Rodríguez a cameraman.
Both had fought against Batista and joined Castro's army, Vilaboa in 1959 and
Rodríguez much earlier. On more than one occasion, in the early years of Castro's government, when Vilaboa had dared express his doubts about how communism was encroaching on the revolution, Rodríguez, fearing for his friend's
safety, had helped to rein him in. Eventually Vilaboa had left the country; Rodríguez had stayed, but the friendship had endured the years of silence and
separation.

Now, sitting across from Rodríguez in his air-conditioned office with photographs of Fidel Castro and his brother Raúl looking down from the walls, Vilaboa began to reveal his plan.

Look, he told his friend, you have a problem because the United States won't take these people, and I have the solution.

Keep talking, Rodríguez encouraged him, leaning forward on his desk.

Vilaboa's plan was simple: He was sure that Cubans from South Florida would be willing to come to the island to transport the thousands of embassy refugees back to the United States, but only if—and this was a crucial if—the government permitted them to retrieve their own relatives as well. Vilaboa envisioned the plan as a fifty-fifty proposition: For each relative you take, you must also take an embassy refugee. He imagined that at the end of the operation no more than 22,000 Cubans would travel to Miami. The city could certainly tolerate that number. In fact, it would welcome them.

We Cubans are like the Chinese, Vilaboa told Rodriguez. We'll do anything for family. It could work like Camarioca.

Vilaboa surmised that Cubans in Miami were ready for another Camarioca. After years of enjoying prosperity in South Florida, most Cubans would be willing to spend part of their savings chartering boats to Cuba, he thought. Nothing—not the laws of the United States, not a lack of funds, not the dangers of the sea—would keep Cubans away if they were convinced that they could rescue their impoverished relatives and take them home to America.

Indeed, anticommunist sentiment was running high among the exile community in Miami. Early in April, drivers in the streets of Hialeah and Little Havana, two of the most populated Cuban enclaves in South Florida, had continuously honked their horns in support of the embassy break-in. Homemade anti-Castro signs started to appear on lampposts and phone booths throughout the city, and massive street demonstrations were held despite torrential rains. Young and old alike shouted, War! War! War! on street corners, eager to discuss the fate of the "Havana 10,000," as the press baptized those at the embassy.

Hoping that the crisis at the embassy could trigger the much-desired beginning of the end for the Castro regime, many Miami Cubans who for years had shunned politics and concentrated solely on making a living now rushed to join belligerent local anti-Castro organizations and to demand help from the United

States to invade Cuba. Some ran to army-surplus stores to buy combat gear and supplies. Local radio stations held food drives and fund-raisers to send goods to Cuba. In the span of forty-eight hours, one station collected fifty thousand dollars and enough food and clothes to fill six cargo planes.

All of this, Vilaboa knew, had happened despite Washington's decision to distance itself from the crisis. The State Department had dismissed the entire matter as being "up to the Peruvian embassy." No one in Miami seemed to agree. Even religious and elected officials publicly stated that Miami could not possibly stand idly by while Cubans risked their lives for freedom.

WHEN VILABOA FINISHED explaining his idea, Rodríguez remained silent for a moment. Then he got up from his chair and patted Vilaboa on the back. As he accompanied his friend to the door, he told him that he needed to consult with his superiors. Vilaboa understood that could only mean Fidel Castro. But Rodríguez surely knew that Castro would approve of the idea: It was one that Castro himself had already voiced.

For months, ever since the Carter administration had chosen to ignore Cuba's demands that it prosecute the Cuban hijackers who in late 1979 and early 1980 had stolen boats to travel to the United States, Castro—first through emissaries in private conversations and later publicly in a speech—had threatened to unleash a mass exodus the magnitude of which Washington couldn't begin to imagine. Only a month earlier, in March, he had even reminded the Americans of Camarioca. "We hope they will adopt measures so they will not encourage the illegal departures from the country, because we might also have to take our own measures. We did it once," Castro had warned.

Two days after their initial conversation, Rodríguez went looking for Vilaboa at the Hotel Riviera.

Oye, Napo, he said, using Vilaboa's nickname. I talked to number one, and he is interested. He wants to talk to you.

Vilaboa didn't have to ask who "number one" was.

Though circumstances had changed and Vilaboa now called Castro "Doctor"—not only in deference to his Juris Doctor degree but also because Vilaboa

couldn't bring himself to call him "President" or even "Commander in Chief"—
the two went back a long time. They had never been friends, though. Vilaboa was
convinced that leaders don't have friends—they have followers. For almost a
decade in the 1950s, he, too, had been a follower.

THE FIRST TIME Vilaboa saw Fidel, he was about fourteen and already a
member of the youth branch of the Orthodox Party, one of the principal parties
on the island's political scene in the 1940s and into the early 1950s. Castro was
twenty-five, a former student leader vying for the candidacy of a congressional
seat in the Orthodox Party. The party's founder was the widely admired Eduardo
Chibás, a muckraking senator with a popular radio program. In August 1951,
Chibás, who'd led a crusade against the government of Carlos Prío Socarrás, shot
himself in the stomach at the end of his weekly radio talk because he had failed
to deliver to his audience, as promised, proof that the then minister of education
was stealing public funds. He died of his wounds ten days later.

Vilaboa went to the funeral at the University of Havana, a tumultuous event
that drew more than three hundred thousand people. Castro was both a speaker
and a member of the honor guard standing next to the casket. He also managed
to be the center of attention by proposing during the eulogy that the entire group
march toward the presidential palace to demand the resignation of the president.
Cooler heads prevailed, and the group marched toward the cemetery instead.
Young Vilaboa was struck by Castro's ability to turn any occasion, even a burial,
into a platform for his ideas and ambitions.

Vilaboa wasn't a stranger to political ideas and ambition. He grew up in a
family where politics was stressed and militarism was exalted. His own name
was a testament to his parents' grandiose plans for him. At birth he had been
named Manuel, and his family had called him Manolito until he was about a
week old and an uncle returned from a trip to France. Enamored of Napoleon's
legendary conquests, the uncle declared, We should name the child Napoleón.
The uncle even gave the family a medallion bearing a picture of baby Napoleon
Bonaparte, who he swore looked just like their own little Napoleón: bald and
cherubic, with a lone blond curl on top of his head.

Napoleón Vilaboa learned to read at three, under the tutelage of his mother, a teacher. By the time he started school, he'd read all the magazines he could reach from his uncle's library, among them *Bohemias* and *Carteles*, beautifully designed and widely read weeklies that devoted much of their column space to politics and to corruption exposés. At dinnertime his family often discussed the same ideas he'd read about in the magazines. Napoleón's father owned a prosperous marble business, right across from Havana's main cemetery. As a typical hardworking Spanish immigrant who had come to Cuba from Galicia, he was often the first person to arrive at his shop every morning, don an apron, grab a hammer, and set to work chiseling and sculpting marble. Vilaboa's mother played piano and violin. The boy was so smart and curious that his father often asked him to recite the world's capitals in front of his friends. Little Napoleón happily obliged.

Both his parents called themselves "Batistianos," followers of Fulgencio Batista, the army colonel who had been democratically elected president in 1940. Napoleón, on the other hand, declared himself a fan of the Authentic Party—of nationalistic and New Deal Democrat tendencies—perhaps because he wanted to demonstrate to his family that he had a mind of his own, or maybe because the headquarters of the Authentics was so close to his home that he would often go to their meetings to pass the time after school. The party's leader, Ramón Grau San Martín, noticing the child in the crowd during a speech one day, called him to the podium and introduced him as the party's youngest member. Napoleón was seven.

In his adolescence Napoleón dreamed of enlisting in the military; he wanted to enter the Cuban naval academy at Mariel, a harbor about twenty-seven miles west of Havana. His parents would take him occasionally to the town of Mariel, where he would look up at the white, castlelike building of the academy perched on a hill and crave the life of the military: the power, the uniforms, the rituals. But on March 10, 1952, when Batista, who had left the presidency in 1944, enacted his coup d'état, the democratic process came to a halt, and so did Vilaboa's military aspirations.

The day of the coup, Vilaboa joined a massive protest against the new dictator. He was promptly arrested, taken to the local police station, and beaten.

Seventy-two hours later his mother managed to get him released, arguing that her bloodied son was only fourteen years old. Vilaboa continued his political activism, though, which led to about thirty detentions in seven years. Eventually he decided to study journalism, one of the surest ways then to influence public opinion in Cuba. He also joined a succession of organizations that worked to unseat Batista and promote independence and democracy in the Americas. In 1955 Vilaboa was one of the founders of a committee that sought the freedom of Pedro Albizu Campos, the *independentista* Puerto Rican leader jailed in the United States. That same year he flew to Costa Rica with a dozen Cuban revolutionaries to fight invading Nicaraguan troops aiming to overthrow the government of José Figueres, a democratically elected social democrat. The invasion was squelched within a few days, and Vilaboa returned home, an eighteen-year-old branded by war and invigorated by the joys of a quick victory. He started smoking cigars and carrying a gun under his shirt.

About that time, Vilaboa began writing for a small newspaper and hosting an hourlong program on one of the radio stations that opposed Batista. Although Vilaboa was a firm anti-Batistiano, he felt restless with Castro's style of leadership. Castro behaved as if he were the indisputable leader of the entire opposition movement. Even while he was in jail for leading the attack against the Moncada military barracks in 1953, nothing could be done without Castro's approval, and those who attempted otherwise met his wrath.

Vilaboa felt it firsthand one day in 1955, shortly after Castro's release from prison. Castro had published an essay that Vilaboa wanted him to read on his radio show. After failing to locate Castro in his usual Havana haunts, Vilaboa asked a comrade, an unassuming young man named Ñico López, to read it on the air. Toward the end of the broadcast, at half past noon, Castro kicked open the door to the studio and, with a wild look in his eyes, confronted López, who still held the essay in his hands.

How dare you? he yelled at López, yanking the paper from him. This can only be read by me, me, me!

Castro punctuated each word by pounding his fist on the table and went on to curse López, who babbled an apology. Vilaboa wanted to disappear into the wall paneling. When Castro left, López, pale and teary-eyed, behaved like a child, blaming himself for the transgression and apologizing on behalf of his boss. Vilaboa was in shock. What kind of man, what kind of leader, has the power and the will to reduce a trusted subordinate to such tears and acts of contrition?

Shortly after this event, Vilaboa resigned from Castro's 26 of July movement but continued fighting in the underground movement against Batista. When Batista fled three years later and Castro assumed control of the government, Vilaboa, though he'd never forgotten Castro's tirade against López, was ready to serve the new revolutionary government in any capacity. He figured that Fidel was the embodiment of the ideals he'd fought for since he was a teenager. What did it matter if he had a bad temper?

Vilaboa joined Castro's army with the rank of captain and was assigned for duty at La Cabaña, a former Spanish fortress–turned–prison, where he and others were charged with conducting summary trials and, often, summary executions against the so-called enemies of the revolution. Vilaboa managed to avoid participating in the executions, and he skirted the trials, which were a mockery of the judicial system. Neither Vilaboa nor the majority of the other men assigned the role of judge and jury had had any experience or training in the law. The men and women brought before them were not given any access to a defense attorney.

Vilaboa began to wonder about the path the new revolution seemed to be taking, closer to communism than to the nationalism he had hoped for. He hadn't fought for a revolution all those years to have Cuba end up as a satellite of the Soviet Union, a fatal misstep in his view, since he was against any doctrine in which there was little room for nationalistic feelings and no place for God. Vilaboa's hierarchy of beliefs was country, God, and family, in that order.

Disenchanted, he started to look for a way out. He couldn't just go into exile, for after all, he wasn't a Batistiano. He couldn't fight the regime from the inside, because there was not yet an organized inside opposition movement to join. With no easy options, he did the only thing he'd been trained to do: He pledged himself to another revolution. In April 1959 he joined a group of revolutionaries who thought they could help liberate the rest of Latin America, just as Cuba had been liberated from a U.S.-backed military government, and prepared an invasion of Panama to dethrone the government of Enrique de la Guardia, a puppet leader controlled by the country's army.

The group, including Vilaboa, was arrested soon after landing and deported to Cuba. The Cuban government, which had looked the other way during the invasion, chastised Vilaboa and the others for placing the reputation of the Cuban revolution at risk. Vilaboa was demoted and given a job patrolling the streets of Havana as a police officer, a position he disliked even more than the previous one.

Early in 1960 he quit and began to work selling Citroën cars. Through friends who were connected with the underground movement that was beginning to take shape against Castro, Vilaboa heard that some Cubans in the United States were preparing to invade the island. Intrigued, he started to look for a way to join any outside effort aimed at unseating Castro's government. A short time later, when Citroën opened a factory in Mexico, Vilaboa managed to get a visa to Mexico with the pretext of checking out the new plant's operation. On June 4, 1960, he boarded a plane to Mexico City, leaving his ex-wife and one-year-old daughter behind. He was only twenty-three years old.

Cubans from all points on the political spectrum were in Mexico that year. Some were there for the long haul: Exiles who from the early days of the revolution had realized the true nature of the regime and decided to escape. A few were there temporarily, waiting for what they were sure was the only possible solution: Washington's intervention. Still others, like Vilaboa, harbored no illusions about the United States but were certain that Cubans on the island, aided by a trained army from abroad, would rise against Castro and reclaim the revolution they had fought for. Flare-ups were common between these different sects of exiles, each group blaming another for squandering a precious opportunity to return democracy to the island. Batista was bad, and so was Castro, they all agreed. But who was to blame?

On July 26, Vilaboa attended a meeting in which Batista followers criticized the Cuban revolution and accused all revolutionaries of being pro–Soviet Union communists. Vilaboa was outraged. He took the floor and argued at length that, despite what Castro was doing, the revolution that had taken him to power was nationalistic and democratic and that he, Vilaboa, repudiated both the Soviet and American empires.

Listening attentively in the crowd was an American consul in Mexico. At the end of the meeting, he approached Vilaboa and congratulated him on his speech. The American asked him to visit him at the consulate sometime, extending his hand and a business card. Soon after, Vilaboa went to the consulate to ask for a visa to travel to Miami, where, he'd heard, a group of men were training to invade Cuba. A man who spoke flawless Spanish greeted him and seemed to know who he was.

You'll go to a training camp, but not in Florida, the man said, and Vilaboa knew that he'd finally found the contact he longed for.

TWO DAYS LATER, Vilaboa was on a small plane landing in the jungle of Guatemala. Under the tutelage of the Americans, he was trained as a member of what came to be known as Brigade 2506. On April 15, 1961, the Bay of Pigs invasion was launched. Forty-eight hours later Vilaboa's battalion disembarked at Playa Larga, off the Zapata swamp on the southern coast of the province of Matanzas. The plan was to take over the area and declare it free territory, a place where a government of returning exiles could be established. Initially the invading brigade seemed to have the upper hand. But when the air support promised by the United States never came, the brigade was abandoned on the swampy beaches of southern Cuba without supplies, at the mercy of Castro's better-equipped and more numerous troops.

Vilaboa somehow ended up alone, with little food and no radio communication, in an area where the rocks were so sharp that they could cut at a man's legs just like dog's teeth. Hiding inside a small, deserted wooden house with a straw roof, he found temporary relief: a cot and a baby bottle full of sugary water, which he promptly drank. He also found a Cuban army uniform that happened to fit him. Vilaboa set out toward the road, any road away from the beach, walking at night and sleeping during the day, hoping to avoid detection by the victorious Cuban forces. He drank filthy water from ponds, taking care to neutralize microbes by using the pills provided by his trainers, and ate whatever animals crossed his path, including a woodpecker, some lizards, and a hen. On the eighth day, Vilaboa woke up from his afternoon slumber with a gun pressed against his temple.

Don't move, a soldier ordered.

Vilaboa's stolen uniform had not fooled the Cuban army. He'd neglected one detail: His boots were brown, whereas the boots of the Cuban army were black. He was quickly disarmed.

Vilaboa, then twenty-four, and others arrested that day were taken to jail and told they would be sentenced to death. But, in fact, in a summary trial similar to those conducted at La Cabaña in the early days of the revolution, he was sentenced to thirty years in prison. In total the invading brigade lost about 120 men; 1,180 were captured and sent to prison.

President Kennedy assumed responsibility for the failure of the invasion, and the two antagonistic governments began to negotiate the release of the prisoners in exchange for tractors, credits, medicines, or cash. The Cuban government set the price for the freedom of each soldier. Vilaboa's was priced at $100,000, one-fifth of the $500,000 Cuba demanded for each of the invasion's three top leaders. In the end, the exchange netted Cuba $62 million in medical supplies and food as well as a victory so significant that it consolidated Castro's power over the island and gave his government an enduring reputation as the first country of the Americas to defeat the colossal power of the north.

Vilaboa left his prison cell on Christmas Day, 1962, but nine of his peers remained behind, made to pay for crimes the Cuban government said they had committed against the people of Cuba prior to the invasion. As he was getting ready to leave, one of those men, a friend, whispered from his cell's window, Vilaboa, don't forget me.

AFTER HIS RELEASE from jail, Vilaboa was in Miami long enough to hear President Kennedy promise that he would one day return the brigade's flag to a free and democratic Cuba. Vilaboa believed him and joined the U.S. Marines.

For two years he bounced from base to base, training for what he still thought was his mission in life: to rescue the Cuban revolution from the traitors who governed in its name. But soon after Kennedy's death, Vilaboa saw clearly that the U.S. government no longer had a plan for Cuba. In 1965 he left the marines and moved to Miami with his new family, a Mexican-American wife and their three children.

Vilaboa shelved his dreams of military action and got a job selling cars to support his family. Instead of a rifle, he began to wield a pen. Writing in a series of local exile newspapers, he bitterly criticized U.S. policy toward Cuba, including the abandonment of the soldiers on the beaches of Playa Girón during the invasion and, moreover, the way Washington had so conveniently allowed Castro to remain in power to take advantage of his failures as a lesson for Latin American countries flirting with socialism. The future of Cuba, Vilaboa wrote often, addressing the exile community, depends on us.

By 1968, Vilaboa had reached the conclusion that the only way to influence politics inside Cuba was to get closer to the people who surrounded Castro. Plain folk, he reasoned, would never be able to topple an entrenched regime, but the army could. And to get to the army, he told himself, one must first get to Cuba. Not quite sure of how to proceed, Vilaboa began to search for ways to get closer to Cuba and to his former friends on the island.

In the fall of 1977, Vilaboa got his wish.

DO YOU KNOW who this is? a distinctly familiar voice said when Vilaboa picked up the phone in the living room of his home in Kendall, a suburb of Miami where houses have deep, well-tended backyards and children play baseball in cul-de-sacs.

What's up, Tony? Vilaboa replied, taken aback, as always, by the ease with which Castro's emissaries moved through Miami.

Vilaboa knew Antonio "Tony" de la Guardia and his twin brother, Patricio, from their days in the urban guerrilla movement against Batista. They would often meet at the posh hangouts of Cuba's privileged class, tennis and yacht clubs where no one would have suspected that a bunch of young men were planning a revolution. Unlike Vilaboa, the de la Guardia brothers had stayed on Castro's side, steadily rising through the ranks. Tony de la Guardia—who had sandy blond hair and a mischievous smile and was a true bon vivant—had reached the rank of lieutenant colonel in the Ministry of the Interior, handling Castro's most delicate missions abroad.

Over the years they had met in Miami for occasional chats. De la Guardia seemed intrigued by Vilaboa's unusual position. He was an exile who refused to become an American citizen. He was against communism but not against Fidel. He claimed to be a revolutionary, yet he openly called for the Cuban army to oust the communists from the island, conveniently overlooking the fact that the leader of the Communist Party in Cuba was Fidel Castro. It was enough to confuse even a deft agent like de la Guardia, who thrived on ambiguity. When de la Guardia came to Miami on business, before he called anybody else, he called the FBI to register his presence as an agent of a foreign country and to deliver bottles of Cuban rum to his friends in the Bureau.

The day de la Guardia called, Vilaboa invited him to his house that same afternoon. If he was going to talk to the enemy, he thought it was best to do it in the privacy of his home, where no one could see him shaking the hand of one of Castro's top men. In the late 1970s, what Vilaboa was about to do was dangerous. From 1973 to 1976, the FBI investigated 103 bombing attempts in Miami, and two men had already been killed by right-wing fanatics for advocating the need to open a dialogue with the Cuban government.

De la Guardia arrived punctually, accompanied by a man Vilaboa had never seen before. The three sat in the darkened living room, which was sparsely decorated with used, unmatched furniture and lacked any lamps or ceiling lights. Vilaboa wore his dire economic situation almost as a badge of honor. What better way to show Cubans from the island that he was still a struggling revolutionary than to invite them to his simple home? Though he had a job selling cars, Vilaboa worked on commissions and hardly made any money because he was seldom at work. Cuba—already his passion—had also become his work.

Would you be willing to participate in negotiations for the freedom of the prisoners in Cuba? de la Guardia asked him in the offhand way of a man who already knows the answer to his question.

In exchange for what? Vilaboa replied cautiously. There was nothing he wanted more than to bring home the last remaining prisoners from the Bay of Pigs invasion, but he wasn't about to show his eagerness.

Nothing, de la Guardia answered dryly. You have nothing we want.

De la Guardia also told him that many other Cuban exiles were interested in participating in the negotiations and that several had already committed to the task. Vilaboa said he needed to think about it and asked de la Guardia to call him in a week or so. But he didn't have to think very long to reach the conclusion that, in order to fulfill the promise he'd made not to forget the prisoners he had left behind, he would be willing to talk to the devil himself.

Months went by, and Vilaboa heard nothing more from de la Guardia. Then one day he got a call at home from Bernardo Benes, a man he knew as one of the city's movers and shakers, one of the few who had penetrated the Anglo establishment. Vilaboa didn't say anything about his conversation with de la Guardia, allowing Benes to make his pitch for talks with Castro.

IN NOVEMBER 1978, Vilaboa traveled to Cuba with seventy-four other exiles for the first of two encounters with Cuban officials. For Vilaboa the discussions served to open a door to a past he had thought long closed. In Havana he reconnected with relatives and old friends, many of whom held important positions in the government, including René Rodríguez. Now that years had passed, there was no animosity between them for choosing such different paths; there were only the good memories of a shared past. Vilaboa got along so well with his old comrades that he was approached to become an agent of the country's intelligence services, but he declined. As long as he wasn't on anybody's payroll, Vilaboa figured, he was free to collaborate with those who shared his goals to remove Cuba from the Soviet orbit. Besides, the kind of comfortable relationship he was developing with Cuban officials—their exchange of information and their similar disdain for the United States—already made him, in the eyes of Cuba's power elite and of the exile community, a Castro agent or, at the very least, an eager collaborator.

Thus it was only appropriate that when Vilaboa thought he had devised a plan to help Castro get rid of the 10,000 refugees at the Peruvian embassy, he would turn to his good friend Rodríguez for guidance.

FOR FOUR HOURS in April 1980, Vilaboa had been pacing back and forth, back and forth, in his carpeted hotel suite, watching the hands of the clock move slowly. Rodríguez had told him not to leave his room. The commander in chief would call on him when he was ready.

Vilaboa glanced at the telephone, willing it to ring, but it remained silent. He browsed through some books he'd picked up earlier that day in a bookstore at Twenty-third and L, the nerve center of Vedado, the most cosmopolitan neighborhood in Havana. Bored with the books, he decided to listen to the radio, almost falling sleep to the voices on Radio Reloj, an all-news station where announcers read sixty-second headlines accompanied by the sound of a ticking clock. *Clock Radio gives you the time: 10:58.*

The telephone next to the bed rang, and Vilaboa leaped up from his chair by the window to pick it up on the second ring.

Señor Napoleón Vilaboa? a commanding voice resonated on the line.

Yes, who is it? he asked, though he knew.

The commander in chief will see you now, the man on the phone said. Go to your door, and two *compañeros* will escort you to him.

Vilaboa hung up and ran his long fingers through his hair. A knock sounded at the door. Two men dressed in loose, safari-type shirts greeted him and escorted him in an elevator to an office on the twentieth floor that was apparently used by members of the secret police.

Castro had not yet arrived. Vilaboa was ushered in by another man, who offered him a Chivas Regal mixed with water. He let his eyes take in the room: a well-worn red carpet and faded red wallpaper, a black sofa on one side of the room, two overstuffed chairs and a low wooden table in the center. Half an hour later, several uniformed guards entered the room without knocking, quickly stepping aside in perfectly coordinated movements to allow the commander in chief to come in. Vilaboa got up and extended his hand, but Castro waved him off.

Give me a hug, *chico*, he said, and the two embraced.

Vilaboa winced. Castro was smoking a cigar, and the aroma of the tobacco, which Vilaboa enjoyed, was mixed with the odor of rancid sweat, cognac, and old coffee. Castro kept his olive green cap on, and Vilaboa noticed that it was sweaty and stained. Vilaboa wondered how long he had been wearing the same uniform. How long since he had taken a nap, or a bath?

Vilaboa sat in a chair to the side of Castro so that the two were almost touching knees. Castro seemed worried and angry. He said he'd been to the Peruvian embassy and didn't like what he'd seen. Vilaboa told him he, too, had been there, and then he repeated to Castro what he'd told Rodríguez. Vilaboa knew that his plan echoed Castro's repeated threat over the years to launch another Camarioca, but he went through the motions of explaining why he thought Cubans in Miami would not pass up an opportunity to come to the island to retrieve their relatives. Castro listened, chewing on his cigar. When Vilaboa finished, Castro got up and told him to come back the following day.

The next evening Vilaboa was ordered once again to stay in his room until Castro was ready to receive him. For seven hours Vilaboa waited, too wired to take a nap. At 1:00 A.M. the call came and he was taken to the same office on the twentieth floor. This time Castro was accompanied by Rodríguez, de la Guardia, and José Abrantes. For two hours the five men debated the details of the operation. Castro discarded Camarioca as the chosen port but didn't explain why. He wondered about issues of safety and cost—and, moreover, he asked, who could convince the Miami Cubans to cross the waters for their relatives?

Leave that to me, Vilaboa said.

The next day, April 14, the same day President Carter announced that the United States was prepared to welcome up to 3,500 refugees from the embassy, Vilaboa returned to Miami to await further instructions.

At the airport in Miami, journalists approached him, eager to know what was happening in Havana. He told them he thought the refugees would not want to go to Peru. There's only one place they want to go to, and that's Miami, he said, laying the ground for what he knew would soon follow. With that phrase Vilaboa became in effect, if not in fact, an agent of Castro's interests in Miami.

Two days later the owner of a travel agency that booked trips to Cuba—one of several that had sprung up since the year before—called Vilaboa at home and asked him to meet at his office in Hialeah right away. Vilaboa didn't ask why. He jumped into his car and, battling evening rush-hour traffic, made it to the man's office in about an hour. Tony de la Guardia was waiting for him.

The plan you discussed with number one has been approved, and the port has been decided, de la Guardia said. It's Mariel. Can you arrange it all so we can begin quickly?

Don't worry about it, Vilaboa said, sipping the Black Label whiskey he'd been served. From now on, Mariel is my problem.

THE NEXT MORNING Vilaboa called Jorge Luis Hernández, the news director of Miami's most-listened-to radio station in any language, WQBA–La Cubanísima, a ratings phenomenon that appealed to the most politically conservative exiles and set the city's agenda regarding Cuba. Hernández, who had a 6:00–10:00 P.M. talk show, was the station's most recognized voice. Vilaboa knew that if his friend backed him, he would have no problems spearheading a flotilla to sail for Cuba in less than twenty-four hours.

Hernández was used to friends and foes alike suggesting unusual propositions, asking special favors, and even proffering questionable deals. In the Miami of 1980, when Cuban exiles had few agencies they could go to for help, Spanish-language radio had become their main link within the community and to the rest of the world as well. Cuban exiles turned to the radio for news about Miami, news from Cuba, information about social services, and access to local politicians, who were often guests on the talk shows, especially while campaigning for office. In the spring of 1980, a politician who sought the Cuban vote had to spend 100 percent of his advertising budget in Spanish-language radio, most of it at WQBA.

Hernández, who had come from Cuba in 1960 at the age of seventeen, was not immune to the local obsession. He, too, thought that Cuba should be the focus of the station's programming, and he was staunchly anti-Castro and anticommunist. But Hernández was also a practical man; he had studied political science in the United States and had a deep understanding of politics, particularly Cuban politics.

His father, Facundo Hernández, had been a congressman in the years that Batista ruled over Cuba. As such he had been the leader of the Authentic Party, and he'd just been elected to the senate when Castro seized control of the congress in 1959. Hernández understood the reticence of exiles to become involved in U.S. politics, but he fought it. With his microphone he waged a daily campaign to convince his listeners it was time for Cuban exiles to participate fully in the political processes of the United States—becoming citizens, casting their votes, supporting candidates, and even running for office. Those were not signs that exiles were forgetting Cuba or becoming soft on Castro, he told his listeners. On the contrary, if exiles elected Cuban leaders in Miami, their fight to remove Castro from power, known in Miami as *la causa*, would move from the privacy of the home and the enclaves in Little Havana and Hialeah to the broader agenda of the city and the county, maybe even the state and beyond.

Hernández could tell that his words were already making an impression, because the tone of the calls he'd been receiving that year was changing. Callers to his talk show were still primarily concerned with Cuba, but they were starting to talk about local issues as well and to identify who among them could best represent them. Already the deputy mayor and a commissioner in the city of Miami were Cubans, and two other Cubans—César Odio and Sergio Pereira—were assistant city and county managers, respectively.

Nevertheless, this straying from *la causa*, albeit slightly, was beginning to cost the station listeners. A month before Vilaboa called him, Hernández had had a rather tense lunch with his boss. The station manager, a so-called Miami Anglo who understood well the nature of exile and the needs of his audience, rarely told Hernández what to do. His role was merely to cash in on the profits as the station expanded his influence and advertisers clamored for thirty-second spots. But at that lunch the station manager surprised Hernández with the news that ratings were slipping.

You better come up with something dramatic soon, his boss told him.

Thereafter Hernández had been thinking about what he could possibly do to bring the ratings back to their former level. Hernández was worried about his audience. Ever since the 1978 dialogues, Miami Cubans had been traveling to the island every week. As the trips grew more popular, the men and women brokering them and securing visas for the travelers had become influential figures in the community. Their power derived from the dull ache Cubans had carried deep in their hearts for two decades. The opportunity to see their relatives had unleashed all that pain and turned it into a desperate quest for visas. People who struggled to keep up with their monthly bills were paying exorbitant fees to unscrupulous brokers. Hernández saw the rising importance of the Cuban travel business as an erosion of his own personal clout.

Hernández had more than one weak flank. Listener surveys revealed that younger Cubans were seeking out bilingual programming or all-English stations. His bread-and-butter audience—men and women who were too old to learn English or too set in their ways to make the switch to other stations—remained loyal, but they were either beginning to die of old age or entering an age group at which, demographically, they weren't attractive to national advertisers, the station's most-sought-after accounts. He needed new blood: young Cubans he could turn into faithful listeners.

Still, when Vilaboa called Hernández and asked for help in whipping up enthusiasm for exiles to join him in a flotilla to sail to Cuba, Hernández reacted not with his cool business head but with his Cuban heart.

Are you crazy? he barked at Vilaboa. You are playing right into Castro's hands.

Hernández believed any activity coordinated with the Cuban government to be tainted by ill intentions. He also thought that Castro wanted to promote a boatlift to get rid of malcontents while circumventing the laws of the United States. Why help build a bridge to the tyrant? Hernández tried to reason with Vilaboa. Let the dissidents stay and foment a revolution from within, he argued.

In the end Vilaboa told Hernández that the flotilla was going to take place with or without his help. He would simply take his pitch elsewhere. Hernández became irate and told Vilaboa that if he went ahead with his plans, Hernández would use his microphone to discredit the operation and make sure that no one in Miami followed Vilaboa's lead. After all, he had done it before when he called for a boycott of Bernardo Benes's bank because of Benes's role as one of the in-

stigators of the dialogue with Castro. Hernández hung up in a huff and rushed
to the station for his daily program.

Driving to the station, Hernández wondered what would happen if Vilaboa
carried out his threat and went to another station. Hernández already knew that
there was nothing more important to Cubans in Miami than to be able to embrace again an elderly mother or a son left behind. He also knew that a flotilla, if
handled well, could be a high-profile event, one that would immediately increase
the ratings of any station that backed it. A lesson from his years as a student of
political science arose in his mind: To change a system, any system, he remembered hearing a professor lecture, you first have to alter the status quo. A flotilla
might just alter the status quo in Cuba.

By the time Hernández got to the station, he was picturing himself engaged in
a chess match with Fidel Castro. All he had was a microphone that delivered his
voice to thousands of homes every evening during the week. Castro, on the other
hand, had an army and the vast resources of the country at his disposal to either
promote an activity or quickly bring it to a halt. But what if the whole thing got
out of hand? Would the Cuban army really intervene and side with Castro?
Would they kill civilians simply for trying to board an unarmed vessel? The more
he thought about it, the more he relished the idea of upping Castro's ante.

For months Castro had claimed that the United States, not he, was keeping
Cubans from its shores. He was willing to let anybody go, he'd said time and time
again, but the United States offered few visas. Many more wanted to leave, yet no
country seemed to want them. Well, Hernández thought, smiling to himself,
what if I prove him wrong? What if I fill the harbor with thousands of boats and
he has to let everybody go? When Hernández called Vilaboa back the next day,
he had already developed a slogan for his campaign: "Let my people come," which
was, in fact, perfectly aligned with Castro's current battle cry: "Let them go!"

Vilaboa attended Hernández's show on the evening of April 17, 1980, and the
two began to whip Miami into a frenzy. In a matter of hours, it seemed that
everyone who didn't already have a boat was looking for one. Cubans sped to the
Miami River and to the beach, carrying thousands of dollars in their pockets to
entice reluctant boat captains to take them to Cuba. Hundreds of captains were

persuaded by the open wallets and the abundant tears of pleading grandmothers and grown men.

TWO DAYS LATER, on April 19, as 1 million Cubans marched past the Peruvian embassy to show their repudiation of the asylum seekers and to commemorate the nineteenth anniversary of the Bay of Pigs victory, Vilaboa left for Cuba on another sort of invasion. At the southernmost point of Miami Beach, he boarded a forty-one-foot recreational yacht named the *Ochún* after the Afro-Cuban deity of love. Forty-one boats followed the *Ochún*'s lead. No one alerted U.S. authorities, but Vilaboa called his Havana contact with the news: Mariel was on.

EIGHT

Leaving Cuba

Some two hundred refugees reach Key West aboard the
shrimp boat *Big Baby* at dawn on the second day of the boatlift.

M Y FATHER WALKED INTO the house clutching a newspaper to his chest and in four long strides stood next to my mother, whose back was bent over the sewing machine. He had moved so fast—from the front door, through the small living room, and past the bedroom door—that she hadn't had time to react. When she looked up, he was by her side, pressing a wrinkled copy of the daily newspaper into her hand.

Read, he said, forgoing the chaste kiss on the forehead that was his mode of greeting her.

Startled, my mother tried to focus on the paper. There was a story on the front page of *Granma* about an event that night commemorating the 110th anniversary of Lenin's birth. Another article was about a photo exhibit on Lenin's life. Those wouldn't have motivated my father to urge her to read, she was sure. She scanned the paper for more. A three-paragraph note to the left of the page announced that the day before, April 21, two boats had left the port of Mariel headed toward the United States. The boats, which had arrived from Florida, had taken with them 48 "social misfits," meaning only a few of the more than 10,000 who had sought asylum at the Peruvian embassy earlier that month, as well as "some relatives of U.S. residents." The paper also said that eleven other boats, already at the port, were scheduled to depart carrying a total of 300 people. By the tone of the story, it was clear that more were expected. "We have withdrawn our custody of Florida's waters," the story concluded, a somewhat subtle way to acknowledge that the Cuban government was not going to deter people from arriving in Cuba and taking a boatful of relatives back to Miami with them.

This is it, my father said when he thought she had finished reading. This is our opportunity.

My mother began to tremble; her hands shook so much that she dropped the newspaper.

The afternoon was brilliant and clear, not a cloud in the sky, she noticed. A breeze wafted through the open window over her old Singer sewing machine. Everything had seemed so perfect just a moment before. She'd been making a green dress for one of her clients. She was going to charge the woman fifteen pesos; with the money she hoped to buy milk on the black market to make us one of our favorite desserts: *dulce de leche,* a creamy concoction loaded with calories that could be served at any hour of the day with a piece of bread. She looked at the clock: 3:00 P.M. My sister and I would soon be home from school.

What could she say to my father? What could she do? She tried to smile, but instead tears ran down her face. She tried to talk, but sobs choked her words. She had lived for so long with the idea that she would one day leave Cuba that the longing and the waiting had become deeply imbedded in her daily routines. Wanting to leave, but never actually doing it, was an important part of who she was. The possibility of leaving now seemed like an upsetting disruption in the careful order of her life.

We have to call Oswaldo and ask him to come for us, my father said, rescuing my mother from the fog of her thoughts. We'll call him tonight.

The conversation was cut short when my sister arrived home. I walked in minutes later. The rest of the afternoon and early evening were uneventful. My parents didn't tell us anything, and I had no idea what was happening at a port twenty-seven miles west of Havana because I had not yet read the paper that day. I'd had an appointment with the ophthalmologist in the early afternoon to get a new prescription for eyeglasses, since my modern American glasses had been stolen by a classmate. The doctor had dilated my pupils and ordered me to continue to dilate them that night with the drops he gave me and to return to him in the morning.

With my pupils dilated, I could hardly see, so I went to bed early, without watching the news on television. My parents tucked us in to bed and told us they were going downtown to the former telephone company to place a call to my Uncle Oswaldo in Miami.

Why? I asked, puzzled that they would leave us alone on a school night.

Oh, we haven't heard from him in a long time, my father said quickly.

I shrugged and turned to face my sister, who was already asleep next to me.

BY THE TIME my parents arrived at the building that housed the city's only bank of telephones for operator-assisted international calls, there was a long line of Cubans clutching their copies of the newspaper, like my father. My parents settled into the rhythms of the line, shuffling a bit every five minutes or so, thankful that it wasn't summer yet and that a breeze made the wait tolerable. When my father's turn came, a few minutes before midnight, nobody answered the telephone at my uncle's house. My father then called one of his sisters, Olimpia.

The reason you can't reach him, she said, is because he has already left to get you.

My father hung up and turned to my mother, beaming.

He's on his way, he said, and they hugged, not so much out of excitement but because they didn't know what else to do. Quickly calculating the distance a boat had to cover from Miami to Mariel, my parents were sure that in two days we would all wake up in the United States.

MY AUNT WAS MISTAKEN, though. My Uncle Oswaldo had not yet left Miami. He didn't own a boat, nor did he know anybody who had a boat. In fact, he rarely went near the water and at age forty-two had yet to learn to swim. But on April 21, when he saw a news report about some Miami Cubans who had taken two boats to Cuba and returned that day bringing dozens of their relatives with them, he remembered the promise he'd made to my father in Havana the year before. The opportunity to get you out of here will come, and I'll take it when it comes, he'd whispered in my father's ear as they hugged good-bye. The opportunity was here; all he needed was a way to grab it.

Two days later, one of his neighbors, also eager to get his relatives out of Cuba, called him at work. He'd found someone who could take them to Cuba, he said. He had a contact who worked on the Miami River who knew somebody who charged a thousand dollars for every refugee he brought back and required a 50 percent deposit before leaving. No guarantees or returns allowed. It was a good deal, he insisted. Others were charging fifteen hundred per relative, or more than fifteen thousand dollars for the rental of the boat.

My uncle left work—in the accounting office of a real state developer—and rushed home to Hialeah. He packed a bag with two sets of extra clothes, fruit, canned sardines, and crackers and kissed his wife and children good-bye. Without thinking of consequences or possible dangers, without even calling work to let his boss know that he wouldn't be in the next day, he drove with his neighbor toward the Miami River.

At the river, Cubans were desperately waving wads of cash at anybody who had anything that even remotely resembled a boat. Some captains were reluctant, wary of any plan that had Castro's approval; others worried about the U.S. government. No word had come from Washington. Was this legal? they wondered. The more experienced captains were concerned about the trip itself. The waters of the Straits of Florida were notoriously unpredictable. One moment you could be looking out at a placid sea and a cloudless sky, and then, in a matter of minutes, the sun would hide behind a suddenly dark cloud and a torrential downpour could leave you soaked to the bone and battling angry, five-foot-high waves. Miami was full of stories like that.

But few captains could resist the lure of cash; others couldn't stand to see men and women cry for their children and grandchildren waiting for them on the other side. Exiles who couldn't find willing captains simply rented the boats without crews and set to sea themselves. People who couldn't differentiate between stern and bow became instant mariners on their way to Cuba.

Within minutes my uncle and his neighbor had found their contact and joined ten others on a sixty-foot boat called the *Valley Chief*, which for nearly thirteen of its twenty-three years had been used to fish for shrimp in the waters off Nicaragua. The captain was an old Cuban man who understood the plight of his people and had a weakness for cash. The *Valley Chief* left the Miami River at

5:00 P.M. on Wednesday, April 23. The same day, alarmed U.S. Coast Guard officials patrolling the waters of South Florida reported seeing at least a thousand vessels of all shapes and sizes—from fourteen-foot outboards to ninety-foot pleasure craft—heading south.

A MAN OF FEW interests other than his family and gardening, my uncle led a sedentary, secure life. He had two young children and a stable job. In just under nine years in the United States, he had built the life he'd dreamed about in Cuba. He drove the right car, lived in a beautiful house, and vacationed all over the country. But none of it—the marriage, the house, the job, his contentment—none of it had come without sacrifices.

Born, like my father, in a house with wooden walls and no electricity, he had managed to escape an all-but-certain future as a farmer, thanks to a scholarship to attend a boarding school in the city for middle- and high-school children. When graduation approached, his father, my grandfather, sensing that his third son was not made for farmwork, urged him to continue his education and offered to pay his college tuition.

But in November 1956, just as my uncle was starting his studies, my grandfather died at age sixty-two, of a heart attack. Committed to his course, my uncle returned to the city after the funeral, and began to work in a jewelry store to pay his own way through school. Five years later he graduated with a degree in accounting. By then he had fallen in love with Tere, a dark-haired beauty he'd met in college and who was just as determined as he was to make a life different from her parents'.

Like the majority of Cubans, my uncle had great hopes for the government of Fidel Castro, but he was never a fan of the man. During the years of the struggle against Batista, he'd concentrated on his education and his job and had had no time to join a demonstration or to help transport weapons to the rebels in the Sierra Maestra Mountains, as other men of his generation did. Like my father, he tended to see the world as the sum total of the efforts of individuals working to improve their own lot. He had no interest in collective endeavors and disdained all rhetoric that attempted to divest the individual of his or her uniqueness. It is our individualities, he thought, that make us human. Our similarities only turn us into herds, cows following the leader down a mountain in search of an ever-fresher patch of grass.

Still, with the revolution entrenched in the country, my uncle tolerated the slogans and the volunteer work and the intimidation of colleagues who de-manded total loyalty to the regime—or else. A year after graduation, he went to work as director of the statistics department of the newly created Paper Consor-tium in Old Havana. For a while he lived with my parents. When I was born, in February 1964, he was still there, sleeping in the living room and having dinner with us every evening. He read me fairy tales, but never at bedtime; he thought children should be alert to fully appreciate the wonders of books.

In January 1966 he and Tere married and moved to a neighborhood to the east of Havana. Two months later they applied for visas to the United States. When my uncle told his supervisors at work of his intention to leave the coun-try, he was fired. Despite his aversion to farmwork, my unemployed uncle was forced to move with his new bride back to the country, to live with her family. He helped his in-laws tend to the animals and harvest the vegetables, rice, and beans the family depended on for food.

Two years later, five months after his first son was born, my uncle received a telegram from the local police precinct ordering him to show up at the station with his bags packed. He was sent to a camp, one of dozens that dotted the is-land, to work on a collective farm as punishment for wanting to leave Cuba.

His timing couldn't have been worse. In the late 1960s, Castro set an impos-sibly high quota for the entire country: By the end of the sugar harvest in 1970, Cuba had to produce 10 million tons of sugar. The entire country was mobi-lized to meet the goal, but forced laborers, like my uncle, who had no choice but to work as ordered if they wanted to be approved for an exit visa, carried the brunt of the work. For three years, from 1968 to 1971, he worked ten hours a day planting, tending, and eventually cutting sugarcane. For lunch he would often eat just a mango and swallow a fistful of sugar to boost his energy. Evening meals in the mess hall usually consisted of watery soup made from cow bones that hung from the kitchen's ceiling and were recycled night after night. Sometimes there would be a boiled yam in the soup, on rare occasions a potato. He was allowed to go home on the weekends to see his wife and son, take a hot bath, wash his clothes, and eat a proper meal. But come Monday morning he had to report back to the camp.

His hands, used to shuffling papers and operating calculators, became first swollen and tender, then callused and rough. His face reddened, peeled and darkened under the relentless sun. If he quit, he would lose his chance to leave the country. If he got sick, he might be excused from hard labor, but only if a camp nurse certified the nature of his illness. If it rained, he still had to work in the mud until the end of his shift. Some of his campmates quit, but my uncle had a powerful reason to stay: In December 1970, his pregnant wife and three-year-old son had left the country on one of the freedom flights arranged after the Camarioca boatlift. He remained behind, devastated, but certain that if he continued doing what was asked of him, when his time came, the government would have no choice but to allow him to join his family abroad. He aimed to be a model worker.

His visa was granted in June 1971. The next month he left for Spain. From New York his wife sent him money until he found a job in construction and rented a small room in an apartment right across from Madrid's Royal Palace, a privileged neighborhood of impressive monuments and narrow streets that did much good for my uncle's bruised soul. Once again he reveled in the beauty and order of city life. Hot chocolate and *churros* tasted like heaven to him; the lights flashing from street signs at night seemed like stars twinkling in a vast new sky of possibilities. Six months later my uncle arrived at Kennedy International Airport, where his wife and sons waited to meet him. His second son was already four months old.

Exactly two weeks after his arrival, he began to work in the mailroom of General Electric headquarters in Stamford, Connecticut. He took English classes after work with a private tutor and in four months managed to get transferred to the accounting department, where he made $125 a week. His wife soon joined him at the same company as a keypunch operator. In the evenings the two cleaned offices to supplement their salaries.

By 1979, they had saved $25,000, enough to move to Florida and put a down payment on a house in Hialeah that was selling for $39,000. Later that same year,

Oswaldo cast aside the bad memories from the labor camps and the fears of being separated from his family to return to Cuba with his sisters for a short visit. Already used to the abundance, order, and cleanliness of the United States, my uncle was horrified by conditions on the island: the rundown buildings, the dirty and often out-of-order public bathrooms, the dilapidated state of the interstate roads, the lack of food, the relentless flies, the garbage piled up on street corners, and the utter destruction of a country that had once been vibrant and modern, a leader in commerce and technology for all of Latin America.

When he returned to Miami he began the cumbersome and lengthy process of getting us out of Cuba through the newly revived family-reunification program. But before he could file the papers for our visas, Castro opened the port of Mariel, forcing my uncle once again to return to the country he had twice before thought he'd left for good.

I WOKE UP AT DAWN on Wednesday, April 23, to the sounds of my aunt's sobs at the foot of my bed.

What's going on? I asked in a panic, knowing that she wouldn't have come from her house in Guanabacoa, across the narrow Bay of Havana for a casual visit. It was still dark out.

You are going to *el norte*, my aunt sobbed. My mother joined her by my bed, and she, too, began to cry.

I could hear them, but I couldn't see them clearly with my still hugely dilated pupils. I leaned back against the wall, speechless, and closed my eyes. My mother then told me about making the call to Uncle Oswaldo during the night and about going to get her sister so she could see us one last time and pick up some precious items my mother knew she wouldn't be allowed to take with her, like her wedding ring and our baby pictures.

Today is the day I leave Cuba, I thought, and immediately I threw myself into action, because I knew that if I didn't, if I cried or hesitated or somehow crumbled under the ache of leaving, I might not go at all.

My sister and I stayed home from school that day, and my father did not go to work. We were sure we would leave within hours and wanted to be close to home to avoid delays and confusion and, especially, the separation of our family. I entertained myself by dividing up my possessions to give to friends whom I thought would miss me as much as I was already beginning to miss them. I labeled paper bags with their names and began to fill them with everything I held dear: Most of my clothes and a diary we had shared in eighth grade went to Maytée who was my same height; my books I divided between Odalys and Annette, both serious readers who had often hunted Havana bookstores with me, looking for new titles; my makeup and my pictures went to Alina, the oldest of my friends and the most sentimental. Then I stored the bags under the bed and thought about how and when I would distribute them.

My father had cautioned us not to say anything about our impending departure, in case something had happened and the boat hadn't left Miami after all, or on the chance that the boat arrived but the government wouldn't let us go. In that event we would have to return to school and face our classmates and teachers as traitors. My sister and I were too young to have our lives tainted as our parents' had been. No, my father told us, best not to say a word until we are on the other side.

With nothing else to do, I decided I ought to fix my hair. If I was going to Miami, I might as well look good. My mother was going out to run some errands, and since we had no telephone, I asked her to stop by the house of my friend Kathy and tell her that I needed help setting my hair in rollers. In less than half an hour, Kathy was at the door. With our birthdays only two months apart, it seemed as if Kathy had always been a presence in my life. From kindergarten on, we had attended the same schools, often sitting side by side. Now that we were teenagers, we studied for tests together, went out together, and walked to school and home together every day. On more than one occasion during final exams, her father had been our math tutor.

And yet when I opened the door and greeted her, Kathy didn't ask, nor did I offer to tell her, why my eyes were red or why I wanted my hair set—something I never did—or even why my mother looked so nervous. She simply offered to wash my hair in the cement sink on the patio. I bent over the edge of the sink while she burrowed her fingernails into my scalp. Carefully she wrapped my hair with a towel and asked, Do you want it wavy or straight? I said straight, so she used the big rollers, which we had fashioned from toilet-paper tubes.

She didn't say a word as she worked, and I didn't either, but we both knew what the other was thinking. Our complicity unfolded like a symphony of unspoken words—one thought chasing the other through the silence, never uttered but always acknowledged. Even at sixteen we both knew that some things were best left unsaid. If we didn't speak about it, she could never be forced to tell; people could ask, but she would have nothing to say. She left early in the evening just as she had arrived, without questions and without sentimentality. We hugged, but we didn't say good-bye.

Evening came, and then nightfall, and we were still in Cuba and alone in our home. We had not heard from my uncle. It was clear that we were not going to leave that day.

THE DAYS OF MARIEL were the first time the country had turned against itself since the beginning of Castro's regime in 1959. The government encouraged violence against those who were leaving, a widening of its policy of repudiation toward the embassy refugees. Enraged mobs prowled the neighborhoods of Havana day and night, armed with sticks, rotten eggs, and tomatoes. When they discovered that a family was leaving, they would plant themselves outside the house shouting epithets and insults for hours or even days. More often than not, the targets of the mob's scorn hid under their bed until the fury outside subsided or was diverted elsewhere.

Sometimes windows were shattered and doors kicked in during scuffles. Some people were killed, hit on the head with clubs or stones. Others killed themselves when they could no longer stand the wrath of their neighbors and the ongoing entrapment in their homes. There were rumors that a student from the Lenin School had been dragged by her classmates for about two blocks in her school uniform as punishment for daring to soil the school's reputation with her attempt to leave the country.

With the entire island engaged in a de facto civil war, we had to tread carefully. As the days wore on, we could not tell anyone we were leaving or change our behavior in any way. We could not take part in the acts of repudiation, because it was against our nature and because we so easily could be targeted for them ourselves. Yet we could not criticize them publicly either for fear of raising suspicion.

On April 27 the government published a note on the front page of *Granma* clarifying exactly who was leaving in the boatlift as a way of justifying why they had become targets of the people's ire: "We call social misfits all those who travel to the United States in the boatlift. Social misfits are . . . people who have much in common with those who were at the embassy and others who missed their chance but have since solicited passport and exit papers. Traveling also are relatives of Cuban residents in the United States who are not necessarily lumpen. But, in general, they are people who lack a national identity and love of their country. People who long for the Yankee 'paradise' and who are full of false illusions about that unjust and selfish society that Martí once called a monster. Therefore, *Granma* will continue referring to all of them as social misfits."

So this is who I have become, I thought, an alienated member of the lumpenproletariat who has no feelings for her country. But the guilt was fleeting. I was old enough to understand how my government worked, and I saw the editorial for what it was: an attempt to inflame the sentiments of hatred that many felt, or thought they should feel, against those who were leaving.

It did not help the ugly mood of the country that on May 1 over a million people celebrated May Day by listening to Castro speak for an hour and a half. It was the biggest mass rally in Cuban history, the paper reported the next day. National Poet Nicolás Guillén read two of his poems, while Colombian writer Gabriel García Márquez sent a message of solidarity, attacking the United States for its provocations against Cuba. But the coup de grâce was delivered by Castro himself when he acknowledged that in the last few days a battle of the masses, unprecedented in the history of the revolution, had been fought in the streets of Havana. The enemy, Castro said, had to be shown that he couldn't play around with the revolution and that a people couldn't be threatened or offended with immunity. "Camarioca was nothing compared to Mariel," he said in his trademark hoarse voice, rising above the cheers of the always exultant crowd as his feet. "We really have an open road. Now let us see how they can close it."

His words were repeatedly met with chants of "Good riddance to the scum!," one of the many slogans hurled in the acts of repudiation, and "Fidel, for sure, hit the Yankees hard!," an old slogan that was resuscitated every time the masses were called upon for a display of patriotism. After the rally the intensity of the acts of repudiation increased, and it became impossible to walk on the streets of Havana without bearing witness to the misery of some poor person running from an angry mob.

On May 2 the street violence reached the offices of the U.S. Interests Section, provoking an international scandal and briefly shifting Washington's intermittent attention from the world at large to Havana. That morning about 800 impatient former political prisoners had gathered in front of the building, clamoring to know when they would be able to travel to the United States. American officials came to the door of the building and advised them to go home to wait for notification. Just as the crowd had begun to disperse, two buses screeched to a halt in front of the Interests Section, and dozens of men in civilian clothes poured out, armed with baseball bats, chains, and machetes. The armed mob and the former prisoners engaged in a furious battle, which the unarmed ex-prisoners, among them women and children, were sure to lose.

The marines who guarded the Interests Section had no choice but to admit the hundreds of people seeking shelter from the attacks, pressing their bodies against the shattered glass front door of the building. In less than ten minutes, about 450 bloodied former prisoners and their families filled the hallway and waiting room while a frustrated mob continued to mill outside, still itching to fight. In an editorial the next day, the government portrayed the attack as a provocation of the United States.

That same day, a victim of an act of repudiation, attempting to flee his tormentors, rammed his car into a crowd, killing a sixty-seven-year-old woman, who, like the soldier killed at the Peruvian embassy on April 1, became an instant martyr of the revolution.

For the next two weeks, as we waited for our turn to leave Cuba, I read the newspaper every day in disbelief, searching in vain for the country and the people I used to know. Where was our collective decency, our sense of right and wrong, our much-touted solidarity? The only place where I felt comfortable anymore was at home, sitting around the dinner table once my father had finished his shift and arrived home safely one more time. The world outside seemed foreign, dangerous, and unpredictable.

We tried to stick to some sort of normality, but there was no escaping the fact that we, too, had changed. My father, who had been so sure of my willingness to leave the country with the rest of the family, began to doubt me. He didn't say it, but I could tell he was worried every time he changed the subject when someone told us stories about teenagers who at the last minute had refused to accompany their parents and had been "rescued" by the government as revolutionary heroes. One evening, trying to disconnect from the events of the last few days, I went to the movies with two friends to see a French-Italian film that had just been released. I was in the theater lobby when, out of the corner of my eye, I noticed my father hiding behind one of the thick columns outside the theater. I pretended not to see him as I walked home with one of my friends but I could sense him following us all the way, hiding behind porticoes and bushes. Perhaps he was concerned for my well-being and thought he could protect me from an act of repudiation. But the possibility that the wave of mistrust that was sweeping the country had seeped into our family kept me awake that night.

BY THE FIFTH DAY of waiting, we were beginning to think that we were never going to leave, because we had received no word from Mariel or from Miami. My father was tense; my mother was sad. Both were worried about my uncle but didn't dare speak about it. Every morning my father skimmed the paper for news from Mariel. In the evenings he listened to the Voice of America to get weather updates.

One day thunderstorms unleashed winds of fifteen to twenty knots with gusts up to fifty miles an hour and six-to-twelve-foot-high waves, a frightful image that I couldn't shake. On April 29, the U.S. Coast Guard found two bodies in a capsized vessel—the first fatalities of the boatlift. Cuban officials had ignored requests by the coast guard to advise them of the approximate number of people who left every day and what boats they were on. Moreover, according to the news reports, every time a coast guard vessel approached Cuba's waters—

twelve miles offshore—to assist a boat, the Cuban government accused the
United States of territorial violation. My father hoped that somewhere in the
ocean, battling waves and the pressures from both the Cuban and the U.S. governments, his brother was still sailing toward us.

MY MOTHER AND MY AUNT continued to empty our house of anything and
everything my aunt could use or sell. Because we feared that the neighbors might
conclude we were leaving if they saw my aunt carrying large bags, we developed a
way to deceive them with the help of a friend, whose roof was level with our patio. He was an old orchestra conductor who quietly opposed the regime and was
generally left alone in deference to his status as a respected musician. He lived
with his middle-aged son in a house stuffed with mementos of his career. They
allowed my aunt to go up to their roof several evenings, and there, in the darkness
of the night, she would carefully balance herself over the low wall and reach for
the jam-packed bags my mother delivered. Then they would whisper good-bye
until the next night. Or until they saw each other again. There was no way of
knowing when the police would come for us.

When the police did come, forty-five minutes before noon on May 7, we were
unprepared. My father wasn't home to savor the moment he had long dreamed
about. My mother told the police that her husband had just left for work and
that she couldn't go anywhere without him and her younger daughter, my eleven-
year-old sister, who was in school. If she hurried, she told the officers, she could
probably still find her husband at the bus stop. One of the men offered to take
her in the police car. He said it would be faster, adding that the family had to
gather and be ready to leave in ten minutes, which wasn't that difficult since we
didn't have to pack; we had been told we could take only one small overnight bag.

One of the officers, burly and unshaven, wearing a dirty white T-shirt, stayed
behind, poking his nose into every drawer, cabinet, and shelf in the apartment.
He explained that he needed to do an inventory of the house. I left him in the
kitchen and went to the bathroom to change, while our neighbor stood by the
door, supervising the scene and making a mental note of the things she wanted to
keep for herself.

As I gathered what I wanted to take with me—a small calendar with a picture of Varadero Beach that had been a gift from a professor I had a crush on, a chocolate-colored lipstick, and two pens that my uncle had brought me the year before—I overheard a conversation between the officer and our neighbor.

Why don't you call the other neighbors and arrange something for these people? he asked her.

He was talking about a show of repudiation, the same kind of violent attack my parents had been avoiding for days. I recoiled when I heard the officer's words and hid behind the bedroom door, wondering what I would do if our neighbors turned against us. I was alone, trapped in the apartment. I began to search my mind for a way out, weighing whether or not I would have the courage to jump to a nearby roof from our patio. But I needn't have worried. Our neighbor, who held the rank of lieutenant and was married to an army colonel, looked the officer up and down and told him, Nobody touches this family. I've seen these kids grow up. After identifying herself by her rank, she ordered him to stand on a chair and get our pictures from the wall. I want to keep them, she said. Later, when the officer wasn't looking, she took the small, portable Soviet radio my parents had given me for my fifteenth birthday and hid it under her housecoat.

Just then my mother returned to the house alone. She had found my father at the bus stop, but he'd gone with the officer to fetch my sister from school. My mother's fast and nervous pace had attracted the attention of some neighbors, who had followed her home. Soon our small apartment was bursting with friends and neighbors who'd come to say good-bye. To the officer's astonishment, there were more tears of sadness than of anger. No one scolded us. All wished us well.

My father came back with my sister as the officer was wrapping up the inventory, which meant that everything we had owned was now the property of the government. He told us he had discovered that we had plenty of food stored. Meat packed in the freezer. Beans stacked in boxes on the kitchen floor. Garlic, watermelon, and papaya on the patio. That's a lot of food, he said. What else have you got hidden?

It was a moment of terror. Nobody else seemed to have anything, so what the officer was really asking was, How did you get what you have at a time when nobody else does? My mother pretended she was too busy to hear the question; my father couldn't think of anything to say except the truth. We have relatives in the country and they send us a portion of their harvest every year, he said. The officer let the moment pass, perhaps because our neighbor, the lieutenant, was still there, alert and watching.

We went back to packing. My sister wanted to take an old baby blanket, but my mother told her to save the space for more practical items, like an extra set of clothes in case we got wet on the way to Key West. My mother took a small image of Our Lady of Charity, who she was sure would protect us at sea, and, in a bow to nostalgia, a jeweled pin in the shape of a perfume bottle that my father had bought her during their honeymoon.

I finished quickly and stood on the balcony alone, saying good-bye to my house, my block, my friends, the view. I could see Dulce, the old lady in the corner house, hushing her dogs; Natalia, from across the street, sweeping her wraparound terrace while stealing glances at the commotion in our apartment. Two men I'd seen all my life but whose names I'd never learned were talking under a streetlamp. People were lining up at the bodega. Children in uniform were walking to school for the afternoon shift. A boy darted in front of a car, chasing a baseball.

And then suddenly my mother called me from the door. It was time to go.

Nobody took the keys.

Some of our neighbors accompanied us downstairs and, as we walked to the unmarked police car, parted ways as if we were leaving a wedding reception, not our home, our country. We all sat in the back, my sister on my mother's legs.

Write soon! our neighbors yelled.

Don't forget us!

We smiled back through tears. The driver pressed the gas pedal, and the car lurched forward, dispersing the crowd reaching out to us through the open windows. As the car rounded the corner toward the main thoroughfare, I felt an intense pain deep in my chest. I tried to concentrate on what was happening, but there was no coherence in my thoughts, only bits and pieces of long-ago events and snapshots of what I'd just left behind: The untouched lunch on the table. My schoolbooks on the top shelf in the bedroom. My dolls carefully arranged on top of the dresser. My underwear neatly folded in the second drawer from the top. My parents' seventy-two-piece set of rainbow-colored wedding china inside a cabinet. Pictures on the wall, dirty clothes in the hamper, dry linen hanging on the patio.

I realized I had left *The Catcher in the Rye* on a table next to my bed, where I had placed it to make sure I wouldn't forget to take it with me. I told my parents that I wanted the car to turn around to get the book. They wouldn't hear of it. Too risky. Too dangerous. There was no time to go back.

ABOUT TWENTY MINUTES LATER, we arrived at a recreational club called Abreu Fontán. Before the revolution it had been a playground for the rich; since the revolution it had belonged to the workers—and it showed. Pre-1959 it must have been a grand building, with its tiled floors, high ceilings, and carved stucco columns framing perfect views of the ocean. When we arrived there, it was in disarray: peeling paint, broken windows, and untended gardens.

Thousands of people sat on the grass or the wet sand, waiting, but for what, we did not know. Where was our boat? Where was my uncle? We joined the crowds near the water, under the shade of a sea grape tree. Uncomfortable and with no information, we were beginning to feel like refugees. It was clear that at that moment we had nothing and no one in the world except each other and the hope that my uncle was still at the harbor and that we would be allowed to join him.

At dusk the government started selling food, but there wasn't enough to go around; we managed to get only yogurt. We took a walk near the water. Sometime during the evening, a disembodied and amplified voice began calling names thorough loudspeakers. Ours were eventually called, and that's how we learned that the boat that awaited us was called the *Valley Chief*. From then on, *Valley Chief* was our new identity. No one from the government called us by name anymore. Could *Valley Chief* line up here? the uniformed officers would order when they wanted us to move. Where is *Valley Chief*? they would ask when they needed to find us.

There were eighteen people in our group, among them a family of four, a man who said he didn't remember the face of the brother who'd come for him, an old woman and her son, and a couple with a baby. At first we were wary of each other. After years of denying our political leanings and deepest desires, no one in the group was eager to share intimate thoughts. But by nightfall we had become a community, looking out for each other and making sure no one strayed too far. My family got particularly close to a couple who had two children. The father, fat and jolly, was a bus driver, the mother a homemaker. The children, a girl and a boy, played with my sister.

As the day began to slip away, I suddenly had the urge to call my friends. I wanted someone besides my family to register the fact that I was really and truly leaving Cuba. I searched in vain for a telephone inside the building. None had a dial tone. Then it occurred to me to go outside and find a pay phone. Somehow I convinced my mother that I would be forever miserable if I did not make those calls, and, amazingly, she agreed but said she would go with me. Without a pass or a passport, and still somewhat innocent of the wave of cruelty enveloping the country, we simply walked out of the club in search of a phone, leaving my father and sister behind but making sure the guard at the door saw our faces so that he would let us back in.

The street was clogged with demonstrators shouting revolutionary slogans. Halfway down the block, someone yelled, There are two of them! Let's get them! My mother and I ran back as fast as we could, dozens of people at our heels screaming insults. One grabbed my hair, but I pulled free and ran faster. I jumped over a cement barrier and, without even pausing to check with the guard, pushed open a side door to the building and ran in. My mother followed, and as we caught our breath slowly, leaning against a wall, she decided not to tell my father. We were safe after all, but I'd learned a lesson: I had become the enemy.

When it became obvious that we would spend our first night away from home on the floor, my mother and sister found a thin mattress and went to sleep. My father and I sat on plastic beach chairs in front of them. All night the names of vessels were called over the loudspeakers—a sign, we thought, that the boat was ready and the group needed to assemble fast. One by one, those who had responded to the call were interviewed by half a dozen uniformed and plainclothes officers at four long, school-cafeteria-style tables. If everything was in order, they boarded a bus and were promptly taken away. Since there were no boats near us, we assumed they were shuttled to the port. Nobody took the time to explain the process or how long it would take, and we didn't dare to ask.

My father and I did not speak much that night. I regretted not having a book; I needed distance from the misery that surrounded us.

I saw a chemistry professor from Santiago de Cuba begging an officer to let him join his wife and children, who were already in the bus. His wife's name had been called, while his, inexplicably, had been omitted. When the officer refused to let him go, his wife said she wanted to stay with him. The officer said no to that, too. She must go. He had to stay. And so he did, falling to his knees and weeping, begging for mercy on the floor, his tear-drenched face inches from the officer's boots.

There was also an old woman, sobbing inconsolably because her only son couldn't leave with her. Her sister had claimed them both, but because his name had been misspelled in some document, he was not allowed to go. Without her son, she wanted to stay. But her son pushed her back, into the arms of the officer who took her away as she kicked and screamed. The son turned around and quickly ran toward the gate, covering his ears from his mother's screams.

Dawn found us asleep in our chairs. At about 8:00 A.M., our boat was called. *Valley Chief, Valley Chief,* come to the main office, a voice blared from the speaker until all of us had gathered near the door. We sat together in front of two officers who asked our names and looked at our identity cards. Satisfied that our pictures matched our faces, he then asked why we wanted to leave. My father said what he'd said when asked before: We want to be reunited with our relatives in the United States. The man asked if we knew who had come to pick us up, and we said we did. Then he waved us off and called the next person in line.

Shortly after, we were seated in a bus with no windows—intentionally removed to expose us to the fury of the protesters outside. As we left Fontán, we crouched down in our seats, uncertain of what to expect. Those who did not were pelted with tomatoes and eggs thrown by the mob. Some people cried, while others cursed under their breath. An old lady prayed. The former bus driver, who had become our friend, was hit by a rotten egg on the back of his neck.

Our next destination was El Mosquito, a barren, dusty military base on the coast, perhaps named after the large pests that made swimming there unbearable. El Mosquito, some twenty-four miles from Havana, was a secluded holding station to the port of Mariel. We formed a long line in the midst of a woodsy, rocky area, where there was no relief from the relentless sun. We had no idea what we were waiting for. But because Cubans were trained to wait in line everywhere, often without knowledge of what awaited on the other end, we obeyed.

For lunch, soldiers distributed brown boxes with small rations of white rice and canned Spam. I entertained myself by trying to listen to the conversation in English between a woman with white plastic elephants hanging from her necklace and a fat man who said he was an English teacher. I couldn't understand a word. She told me she needed the practice; it had been years since she'd spoken English with anyone. At one point a young man who was standing in line a few paces ahead of us had an argument with a guard. Several guards grabbed him and said he needed "a little pill." His mother screamed, Don't take my son! but they took him anyway. We never saw him again.

I wondered what could have triggered such a response from the guards. Was it something the young man was carrying? Did we have anything on us that could harm our chance of leaving? Could we, too, be beaten at the whim of an officer? My parents did not say a word. We knew that our best bet was to say nothing, ask nothing, and move through the line to complete the process as smoothly as possible.

Sometime in the afternoon, our turn finally came, and we were asked to walk into a small building with a green roof. We were interviewed individually. An officer asked my name and what I was carrying. I showed him the lipstick, the almanac, and the two pens. He took the pens, put them in his pocket, and sent me to a booth with a flimsy beige curtain. There, a uniformed woman asked me to lift up my blouse, unhook my bra, and take off my pants and underwear. My face was hot from embarrassment and humiliation. The woman must have realized that I was hiding nothing from her but my nakedness and asked me to stop before I lowered my panties.

Unknown to us, my sister had hidden a plastic bag in her underwear. It contained a picture of our grandfather and a letter that our downstairs neighbor had sent her from the Soviet Union, where he'd gone for military training three years before. The officer who searched my sister read the letter carefully and handed it back to her without a word. My father was asked to turn in the last of his possessions, two hundred pesos, enough for a modest family vacation in Cuba, and all our identification papers. He protested mildly but was told that where he was going he would not need Cuban pesos.

We came out of the house through a back door and stepped into what looked like a tropical concentration camp. There's no going back now—we've left it all behind, my father said, surveying the scene in front of us. A pretty stretch of beach bordered it to the north; dense foliage hugged the camp from the south. Dozens of olive green tents dotted a dusty area, the size of two football fields, surrounded by barbed wire and protected by barking dogs. Men in fatigues patrolled the perimeter, holding rifles with bayonets over their shoulders. We were taken to one of the tents, filled with two rows of military-style bunk beds, and told to wait.

The word was that this was the last stop before Mariel, but there was no way of knowing how long the wait would be. We met people who'd been waiting for ten days. We couldn't fathom spending a day there, let alone a week. We had no towels, no sheets, no clean underwear. We hadn't taken a shower or brushed our teeth since we left our house the day before. We hadn't slept on a bed or taken off our shoes or had a minute alone. We also hadn't gone to the bathroom.

Someone pointed to a cluster of tents in the distance and said those were the showers and toilets for women. We marched in but were quickly rebuffed by the unbearable stench. Mounds of excrement lined the halls. Flies swarmed. My mother felt ill. We decided instead to take a bath in the ocean. Salt water, we thought, would be better than no water at all. But an officer told us that swimming was not allowed. We went back to the tent.

The camp was divided into three sections. One large area was reserved for people like us who'd been claimed by relatives from Miami. Another, without tents or cots, was for those who'd been in the Peruvian embassy. Yet another section, closer to the water and guarded by attack dogs, was reserved for people who'd walked into police stations across the country, declared themselves scum, and asked for a permit to leave. Anybody who described himself as, say, a homosexual artist or an unemployed dissident, even if he showed no proof, was allowed to go if the government considered the person dispensable. Doctors were held back. So were others who owed their careers to the so-called generosity of the revolution and were forced to stay until they paid back their schooling with years of labor.

Dusk was fast approaching. We'd been told that the loudspeakers would continue blaring during the night. If you missed the moment they called out your name, we were told, you had to wait for space on another boat. Nobody knew when the names would be called. Therefore, staying alert to hear the call of our boat was crucial.

We assembled around one bunk bed and decided to break the night into seven shifts, one hour each. One person from each family would stay awake to listen for the name of our boat, we agreed. My mother took the early shift. The breeze from the ocean cooled the tent, the loudspeakers droned on, and spotlights canvassed the entire camp. I don't think anybody in our group slept that night.

At about ten the next morning, we heard the call through the loudspeakers: *Valley Chief, Valley Chief, Valley Chief.* We rushed to an area where again we were ordered to form a line and board a bus. Once full, the bus refused to move. We had to disembark and push it forward, with the driver at the wheel, until the engine rumbled back to life. Two and a half miles later, we arrived at Mariel.

FROM THE BUS we could see the masts of the vessels. There were recreational yachts, shrimp boats, and even small speedboats whose owners must have raced down just to see what was going on. Good Samaritans were throwing apples and little shiny bags from boat to boat. I'd never seen apples before, but somehow I knew what they were. What was in the bags, I had no idea.

There was an atmosphere of energy and optimism around the boats: people coming and going, men in uniforms carrying bottles of water, foreign reporters interviewing refugees and exiles. A reporter boarded our bus and interviewed the fat English teacher and two children. We remained on the bus for such a long time that even the driver grew antsy. When he left to see what was holding us up, the former bus driver in our group went to the wheel and drove forward a bit, enough for us to see the *Valley Chief* a few feet away, bobbing in the water. The boat seemed old but sturdy, probably a fishing boat of some kind, not very big but, I hoped, big enough to accommodate all of us. From my window I caught a glimpse of my uncle, tanned and dirty and bearded. He was wearing jeans and a white T-shirt that contrasted sharply with his sunburned skin. Smiling, he waved at us.

Following the orders of the officers, my uncle waited for us on deck and didn't approach the bus. After a few minutes, we were allowed to disembark barely steps away from the boat. I got to my uncle first and hugged him long and hard. My father and mother reached over me and held on to his neck. My sister stayed somewhat behind, not sure of what to do until my uncle pulled her close. We remained in a tight embrace for a long time.

Then we scrambled into the boat, all talking at once in a vain attempt to calm our nerves by telling each other the stories of the last two weeks. We'd been afraid, we told my uncle. But why? he asked. You should have known I wasn't going to leave without you.

HE TOLD US about the sixteen days he'd spent waiting for us at Mariel, worried that we wouldn't be brought to him. The nights were the worst, he said. He couldn't stand the total darkness or the uncertainty of what the morning would bring. Unlike other people, who had accepted the Cuban government's offer to stay in a hotel, my uncle hadn't dared to leave the boat. He feared that immigration officers would come back when he wasn't there and that he would miss the chance to add our names to the growing list of claimed relatives. There were so many boats already at Mariel when he arrived that it had taken the authorities fourteen days to get to our names on the list, and then two more days to call the *Valley Chief* to the dock to pick up its passengers. As we listened to his story, he offered us soft drinks, ham, cheese, and bread, which he had purchased from a government-run supply boat, but we couldn't eat a thing.

Sometime in the afternoon, a bus parked in front of the *Valley Chief* and about 200 men, pale and disoriented, began to board our boat. My uncle explained that the captain had been ordered to take people from the Peruvian embassy. But the men from the bus didn't look as if they'd come from the embassy. Some were shoeless; others wore orange uniforms that retained the creases of clothes that had been folded for too long; most had their heads shaved. A few were crying, and many of them were smoking. After they were all on board, it became impossible to walk around. One of the men asked my father if he had a nail clipper. No, my father said, why? Because I want to slice my veins open, the man said, a vacant look in his eye and a toothless smile on his thick lips. The air was sticky, the heat was unbearable, and we all reeked of sweat and rancid food. It was becoming hard to breathe.

My uncle moved us to the wheelhouse and then went outside to assess the situation. The *Valley Chief*'s blue flotation line was already underwater, my uncle said when he returned, but there was nothing we could do. Either we took those people, whoever they were, to the United States, or no one left Mariel. My uncle and the other men from Miami pooled their last dollars and ordered food for everyone, including the unexpected passengers. The new arrivals were hungry, they'd told everyone aboard. The food arrived, and they quickly gobbled it: greenish scrambled eggs and white rice. My mother forbade us to eat, entertaining us instead with a guessing game. I spy with my little eye, she would say. But there wasn't much variety in the game: blue was always the water or the sky, green the uniforms of the soldiers, and red the triangle of the Cuban flags that fluttered atop the main building on the docks.

In the evening, when we thought we would soon leave to head toward Key West, a storm began to approach from the north. Dark clouds covered the harbor, and the air smelled of rain. It didn't rain, but the atmosphere remained charged and threatening all night. We found some thin cots on deck and huddled together on the floor. It was impossible to sleep, as people were trampling over each other to go to the bathroom or get some air. No one dared to step onto the pier, so we spent the night the same way we'd endured the day: shoulder to shoulder with the kinds of people we'd tried to avoid all our lives.

The following day, when we were given the order to leave in midafternoon, the

Valley Chief, creaking under the extraordinary weight of so many of us, refused to move. The captain said that the motor was damaged and we were not going anywhere unless someone returned to Miami in another boat and brought him the replacement part he needed. A mechanic from another boat offered to fix it for two thousand dollars. No one had that kind of money anymore. Before mass despair set in, my uncle, the only one in the group who spoke English, announced he would look for help. My father wanted to go with him, but my uncle insisted that he should go alone.

I saw him step onto the docks and followed him with my eyes until he was nothing but a speck of white in a sea of moving bodies.

NINE

Captain Mike Howell:
Sailing Mañana

Mike Howell, aboard the *Mañana* in 1980.

S EE THAT BOAT over there? said the man whom everyone on the docks called "Major Rafael," pointing to a sixty-foot wooden shrimp boat that looked like an enormous centipede: a bulging middle with hundreds of legs and arms sticking out.

Mike Howell strained to read the name on the stern: *Valley Chief*.

Yes, what about it? he asked, turning his gaze back to the uniformed man before him.

It's broken down, the major said.

So? Mike replied, thinking that it was a good thing the boat had malfunctioned. The flotation line was way below the water level. If it left Cuba like that, it surely would sink in the Florida Straits.

We'd like for you to tow it to Key West.

Tow it to Key West! Mike yelled, and immediately regretted it. This is Cuba, remember, he told himself, trying to stay calm. All you want is to get out of here. Pronto. What's that going to do for me? Mike asked in a softer tone.

I have your list. I promise to send your people out in the next few days if you take this boat off my hands, Major Rafael said.

Just then Mike noticed a tall, tired-looking man with a mustache, standing behind the officer. The man took a step forward and in heavily accented English addressed Mike directly.

My family is in that boat, he said, introducing himself as Oswaldo Ojito. I've been here for seventeen days, and I want to take them home with me. Now that we've finally received the order to leave, the boat broke down. Can you please help us?

This was not how Mike's unlikely 750-mile journey from New Orleans to Cuba was supposed to end, but it was clear that, for reasons he couldn't begin to discern, the people he'd come for were not going to be released to him anytime soon.

Like the Cubans who eyed him with hope from the decks of the *Valley Chief*, Mike, too, itched to leave. But unlike them, who had waited for two decades to shake Fidel from their lives, Mike had very little patience. Six days in Cuba, and the storied pleasure island of his parents' generation no longer appealed to him. After a series of unproductive and tense dealings with men in uniforms, Mike had begun to feel claustrophobic.

With or without the refugees, he was leaving Cuba today.

MIKE HOWELL had always felt he lived in a hurry, as if someone had pushed the fast-forward button of his life story and walked away, leaving him to the mercy of the rushed, blurred images.

He was born Michael Foley in Atlanta, Georgia, in 1947, but before Mike was two, his father had left home. Sometime around Mike's third birthday, his mother, Jean, married James Howell, an abusive alcoholic but wealthy man who owned thirty-six first-run theaters on the eastern seaboard. The family moved to New Orleans and bought a five-bedroom house with a pool in Lake Vista, a neighborhood where a boy could spend hours riding his bicycle along curving cul-de-sacs that fanned out into the shape of giant flower petals. The Howells went on to have five more children, and Mike was given his stepfather's surname.

When he was eight years old, Mike made an adult decision: He resolved to become a practicing Catholic, the religion of his birth father. Mike saw his new faith as a way to reclaim a part of who he used to be, the son of another man. Church was important to him also because, for a few hours a week, it took him away from his chaotic family.

In a home burdened by the antics of a drunken, violent stepfather, Mike had no escape, no shelter but the church and the life of his imagination. He became an altar boy, memorized the Latin mass, and began to seek refuge in books about solitary young men who confronted adversity and triumphed. He read all the books of Jules Verne and memorized lines from *Kon-Tiki*, the real-life tale of a man who'd sailed across the Pacific Ocean on a raft.

When he was ten, the family spent a summer in a vacation home they owned near Daytona Beach, in Florida. The last tenants of the house had left behind their books. On the bottom shelf, in a pile of old magazines and newspapers, Mike found an album of pictures of World War II. He was fascinated by the machinery of war and the glory attained by surviving against the odds. Some nights, after the grown-ups had gone to bed, he would sneak into the library and study the pictures by the light of the moon streaming through the windows.

On his twelfth birthday, his stepfather gave him a twelve-foot rowboat with an outboard motor. Mike was thrilled with the boat. He would steer it out to Lake Pontchartrain and spend hours alone in the water. That was the only act of kindness Mike remembers from his stepfather.

The senior Howell had his own ideas about male bonding. When he wanted to make peace with Mike, a square-shouldered teenager with thick arms and a Greek profile, his stepfather would rouse him from his deep sleep at two in the morning and challenge him to fight. Mike would do it, in part because he wanted to hurt the man he'd been instructed to call his father, but also because multiple beatings through the years had convinced him that there was no sense in opposing the will of an adult who reeked of alcohol. It was easier to oblige.

Mike attended Catholic schools until the end of high school. He dreamed of playing football and was good at it, but when the time came for college, he deferred a Louisiana State University football scholarship to join the army in October 1964, a more definitive form of escape than the church had been. He was seventeen. To pass the physical exam, he lied to recruiters about his chronic asthma attacks. When he turned eighteen, he volunteered for Vietnam.

Private Michael S. Howell arrived in Vietnam in December 1965, at a time when Americans were just beginning to comprehend that the war would be a long and costly one. Earlier estimates predicted that only 300,000 American troops would be needed to win the war, but those numbers ballooned to as high as 750,000. Mike had no sense of what Americans were doing in the region and didn't particularly care about the Vietnamese. He thought he was going to war to defend the United States, to somehow protect his country's way of life, and also to act out his childhood fantasies: He would finally wear a uniform, engage in combat, and, he was sure, earn the medals that would help him restore a little of the dignity his stepfather had robbed him of during his childhood.

Because he admired pilots almost as much as he revered sailors, Mike asked to be assigned to the 334th Armed Helicopter Company, which had served in Vietnam continuously since July 1962. Mike's main job was to fly at night in a three-helicopter unit called the Fire Fly Team. He was often the man in the middle helicopter, the one hovering at about five hundred feet aboveground, illuminating the targets for the soldiers in the other helicopters. Often he would be the man behind the machine gun, aiming .50-caliber bullets, at a speed of 550 rounds a minute, toward the Vietcong below. Some days he would go on one or two missions, some days five. He would do the same thing for eight days straight, then rest for two.

On April 13, 1967, when he had flown more than four hundred missions and won an assortment of medals, Mike's luck ran out. That day he had volunteered to train a new crew. Searching for a target, the armed helicopter team flew into Cambodia, a place where the war had not yet officially encroached. But the enemy, Mike and the others knew, was down there, within their reach. Why limit a war to the constrictions of parallels and latitudes?

Below them a great mass of equipment and men was moving about, readying antiaircraft guns and mounted artillery. Thinking that the troops were too well armed to be Vietcong, Mike, who was operating as a door gunner that day, reasoned they must be U.S.-supported Cambodians. But as the helicopters got closer, within shooting range of the men, Mike realized they had discovered North Vietnamese troops, more highly trained and better equipped than the peasants with rifles that he was used to facing from his perch behind the machine gun.

The pilot ordered the copilot to call for air support, but the copilot, young and inexperienced, radioed in the real coordinates, which guaranteed they would get no help because American helicopters weren't supposed to have flown into Cambodian airspace. Mike's team decided to fire their rockets anyway, to force the enemy to take cover. The Vietnamese fired back. Mike saw a puff of hot air and then heard a big explosion. It was about two o'clock in the afternoon, but he was drowning in darkness. His left arm was shattered, a bullet had pierced his left leg, and shrapnel had hit several other parts of his body. Mike was bleeding to death.

He held his arm and leaned back, keeping his eyes open. His crew chief, though wounded himself, pressed his hand against Mike's gushing arm wound during the fifteen-minute flight back to the closest base. In the cockpit the gauge for the engine exhaust gas was in the red, and the helicopter's right side had been blown away. The pilot came over the intercom and, voice crackling with fear and emotion, yelled, Mike, we're gonna get you back! and Mike believed him.

The helicopter hovered aboveground on the triborder area of Vietnam near an aid station where the soldiers knew that blood was stacked in refrigerated bags. Medics loaded Mike onto a stretcher and had started to run with him when the violent wind from the rotor blades startled them. They dropped the stretcher and Mike on the dirt, facedown. Still alert, Mike thought, Damn, I got dirty. And then he stopped breathing.

Quickly, the soldiers put him back on the stretcher and ran toward the medical unit. They got Mike on a stainless-steel table and stripped him of his uniform. The sudden coldness of the metal restarted his heart with a jolt. He realized he was alive because he felt broken and incomplete. As a Catholic, he was certain that there was no imperfection in death. Had he been dead, he wouldn't be hurting so much. He was aware of where he was and what was going on in the room, because he could still hear and see peripherally but he could neither move nor talk. He began to panic when he heard a male voice give up on him. Don't waste the blood on him! the man ordered. Mike's mind was screaming, Yes, please, waste the blood, waste the blood, please! but he had no way to convey his fears or his will. Then Mike heard the voice of a woman, a doctor or a nurse, yelling to the others, Bullshit! Cut him down! I'll take his legs. You do his arms.

When veins collapse, as Mike's had, doctors are trained to cut into ankles and arms searching for usable veins into which they can directly pump whole units of blood. When he felt the incisions, the warm rush of blood, and the soothing voice of the woman, Mike knew he would live, and he began to relax. He felt as if a dark veil had gently descended over his face.

The army sent Mike's mother a telegram telling her that her son was gravely wounded and expected to die. Contrary to this dire prediction, Mike survived, but his arm stubbornly refused to heal. Ten days after he'd been shot down, he was transferred to a hospital in Saigon, where doctors amputated his left arm. He was nineteen years old, and his first thought after waking up from the operation was that he would never again be able to hug a woman.

No longer useful for combat, in pain, disillusioned and traumatized by the ordeal of war, Mike was sent home. In his luggage he carried two Purple Hearts.

Before his arm had properly healed, and sometimes still in excruciating pain, he started to attend classes at Louisiana State University. What was left of his arm, a scarred chunk of meat at his elbow, was still shedding flakes of skin and pieces of bone. For a while he thought he would be a doctor. Like many other veterans he felt an urge to heal mankind, but having to take trigonometry classes soon dissuaded him of that dream. He enjoyed school, though, and found a particularly sweet irony in the fact that, because he was a severely wounded veteran, the government not only paid for his education but also provided a monthly stipend for his expenses through a vocational-rehabilitation program.

It was a conflicted time for a Vietnam veteran to be in college. The very same day that Mike was shot, April 13, 1967, the Beatles finished recording *Sgt. Pepper's Lonely Hearts Club Band*, the album that ushered in the so-called Summer of Love, unleashing the hippie culture onto the Western world. Mike, too, got caught up in the spirit of the times, but he kept a low profile. There was an increasing backlash against the war everywhere in the country, but especially on college campuses. Veterans like Mike were called baby killers and thought to be psychotic. They were routinely confronted at demonstrations and attacked in student newspapers. Mike never talked about his experience in Vietnam, but everyone knew he was a veteran; his wounds were in plain sight. He let his hair grow long, smoked marijuana, and, in endless conversations with his peers, tried to understand their antiwar sentiments. Though he never joined an anti-Vietnam protest, in time he, too, came to believe that the war was wrong.

He married the first girl he dated, and they had a daughter, but, in a repeat of his own early childhood, he divorced his wife before his daughter reached the age of two. Mike quit school six credits short of graduation and tried to figure out what to do next. A regular job was out of the question. He could never sit in an office all day or even work for someone else. No patience. Instead of searching for an office job, buying a house, and spending his life longing for the excitement he thought only the sea could deliver, Mike decided to bring together work, home, and passion: He would buy a boat to live on and become a sea captain.

To find his boat, he first bought a camper and, together with a new girlfriend and another couple, traveled throughout the United States for two years, stopping at every marina from the Florida Keys to Nova Scotia. He returned to Louisiana empty-handed in 1973. Shortly thereafter, less than two miles from his house, he found a fifty-five-foot motor yacht, roomy and sturdy but dilapidated. The U.S. government had built the *Mañana* in 1946 to put it to work in the conservation of wildlife and fisheries. A man named John Santos had bought it from the government, and he in turn had donated it to a group that taught boating to teenagers. When Mike found it, it was a rusted shell of its former self, rotting away in the waters of Lake Pontchartrain. But Mike thought the *Mañana* had potential. He used up all his savings, $1,200, to buy it.

It didn't occur to Mike that boating might be a difficult job for a man with only one arm. Ever since Vietnam he'd worn a rubber prosthesis that helped to keep him balanced and, from a distance, gave him an almost normal appearance. An exact copy of his right arm, the prosthesis even had freckles and small bulges where the veins of his formerly muscled arm would have been. The arm allowed him to hold a rope when he was throwing a line to and from the *Mañana*, but he couldn't grasp anything with the fingers. In his dreams he always had two arms. Awake, he felt the sensation of his lost limb. He did not think of himself as handicapped.

After seven years of exhausting work refurbishing the thirty-four-year-old *Mañana*, Mike thought she was ready to sail, and he ordered his new business cards. MAÑANA CHARTERS, the cards read in big, bold, black letters. And, underneath: CAPT. MIKE HOWELL. No more drifting and traveling for Mike. At thirty-two, he felt it was time to settle down to a business he enjoyed, ferrying passengers along Lake Pontchartrain, towing boats in trouble, and rescuing people at sea, if needed.

* * *

ON APRIL 26, 1980, as Mike worked on the *Mañana*, berthed at the docks of the New Orleans Municipal Yacht Harbor, a man and two women approached him.

We understand that your boat is for hire, the man said in a thick Spanish accent that Mike couldn't quite pinpoint to any country he was familiar with. He concentrated on the man's appearance: tall, white but tanned, standing erect, almost proud, his eyes fixed on Mike's face.

That depends, Mike said carefully, trying to keep the excitement out of his voice. These could be his first clients.

The man said he'd been sent by Luis Gómez, a former city fiscal officer and a well-known figure among Latinos in New Orleans, someone Mike had known for at least two years. Mike was paying close attention now, and he urged the man to continue.

He said his name was Rogelio Ventura, a Cuban, just like the friends who accompanied him. Without pausing, Ventura asked Mike to take them to Cuba to bring back relatives they'd not seen in at least a decade, relatives they desperately wanted to rescue from communism. He said they had about $3,000 with them and were prepared to pay more. The offer was tempting. After years of dedicating almost his entire veteran's pension, $1,300 a month, to the *Mañana*, Mike could certainly use the money. He owed about $160,000, money he'd borrowed from the bank to refurbish the *Mañana*. Still, Mike was cautious. He'd never ventured outside the territorial waters of the United States, and his boat lacked a crucial piece of deep-sea navigation equipment, which cost about two thousand dollars. Also, he had no idea what to expect in Cuba, a country whose history he was only vaguely familiar with.

The more he listened, though, the more going to Cuba seemed like a manageable—even desirable—good deed. Cuba wasn't too far; he could picture it in his head: the largest island in the Caribbean, shaped like an alligator at rest, warm weather, great beaches, ample harbors, a mariner's dream. The Gulf wasn't very dangerous, he thought. Saving people was part of the *Mañana*'s mission, and

Mike relished the idea of playing savior. The man and the women in front of him seemed determined to go. Mike took a look around the harbor and realized that of all the boats there, his was the largest and the best equipped for such a long journey. If he didn't take them, who would?

Ever since Vietnam he'd felt he was living on borrowed time, or lagniappe, originally a French word that means "something extra," like the extra doughnut bakers used to throw into the bag for customers who bought a dozen. Perhaps the time had come to put the lagniappe he'd been blessed with to good use.

Fine, he told them, but I won't charge you for it. I don't deal in human beings. Go back to your church or your community, get a list ready, and I'll take you to Cuba for the cost of expenses.

Rogelio Ventura, a forty-five-year-old carpenter who had left Cuba only ten years earlier, was astonished by Mike's generosity. With tears in his eyes, Ventura thanked him and promised to come back with others who would accompany them on the trip.

As soon as the trio left, Mike picked up off the floor his yet-to-be-read copy of the daily *Times-Picayune*. An AP story on page four told him part of what he needed to know: "The makeshift flotilla of small boats ferrying refugees from Cuba to the United States faced stormy weather Friday, but refugees from the communist country continued to stream across the Florida Straits," the lead story said. He read on: "State Department spokesman Thomas Reston said that as of Friday morning 16 boats had been served with notices of fines for defying the administration's call for a halt to the boatlift."

Mike didn't understand what he was reading. He'd been so busy tinkering with the *Mañana* that he hadn't paid attention to the world around him for a few days. Searching for more information, he rummaged through the pile of unread papers from the past week. On page one of the April 24 edition, he found another wire story from Miami: BOATS IGNORE BAN, SET SAIL FOR CUBA, the bold headline announced across the page.

As he read the story's first paragraph, he began to understand the intensity of his recent visitors' feelings. "Scores of boats—from tiny pleasure craft to big charter fishing boats rented for briefcases full of cash—set out for Cuba Wednesday in defiance of a State Department command to halt the sealift of refugees from the Peruvian embassy in Havana."

He realized that the commitment he'd just made to the Cubans was in fact a dangerous and apparently illegal act. As a veteran he couldn't see himself violating the law even if it entailed rescuing people from communism. While there was still time to change his mind, Mike decided to call his local senator and the White House to ask for guidance. An assistant to the senator gave him his blessing. At the White House, Mike told the operator who answered about the strange request he'd just received. The operator transferred him to a junior staff member.

I have only one question, Mike asked the young man after mentioning he was a Vietnam veteran. If I do what these people want, will I get in trouble?

No, was the succinct reply. Mike forgot to ask the man for his name or rank.

Still unsure, Mike called Joe Julavits, a local newspaper reporter he knew from the yacht club. Julavits, who wrote a regular boating column, didn't try to discourage him. What's more, he asked Mike to let him follow his story if he decided to go.

After all the calls, Mike wondered how much legal risk there could really be in bringing people from Cuba, an enemy country. In times of crisis, he knew, governments are prone to make threatening public statements that are ultimately meaningless and impossible to carry out. The boatlift, he concluded, could be one of those.

Mike's conclusion wasn't far from the truth.

Though by then both the State Department and the Immigration and Naturalization Service had issued repeated warnings against bringing refugees from Cuba illegally, few captains had paid any attention. These statements, delivered to the public without much fanfare by low-level administration officials, didn't seem to carry the full weight of the U.S. government. In addition, they contradicted each other. The State Department's warning carried the threat of prison, as well as a two-thousand-dollar fine and forfeiture of the vessel. The Immigration and Naturalization Service's announcement warned that it would fine boat captains a thousand dollars per passenger and seize the boat until the fine was paid. The administration had not yet spoken with one voice, cohesively and forcibly, against the boatlift.

THE WEEK THAT BEGAN on April 21, the day the first two boats of the flotilla—*Dos Hermanos* and *Blanche III*—returned from Cuba loaded with refugees, was the busiest and most stressful week of the Carter administration. It started off on an ominous note when, on Monday, Secretary of State Cyrus Vance told the president privately that he would resign, citing his disagreement with the administration's decision to rescue the American hostages in Iran after the failure of secret negotiations with the Iranian government.

Daily routine meetings between President Carter and his top advisers that week included briefings on the Iran hostage crisis, the rising price of oil, the Soviet occupation of Afghanistan, the Vietnamese moving toward Cambodia, the hundreds of thousands of Indochinese pouring into refugee camps in Southeast Asia, the crumbling of the Camp David Accords as the Israelis continued to establish new settlements in the Arab territories, and the deteriorating economy in an election year—inflation had reached 17 percent the previous month, and there was no hope for a balanced budget despite deep cutbacks in federal social programs.

On Thursday, April 24, when there were already more than three hundred boats in the Mariel harbor, the United States launched a disastrous mission to rescue the hostages in Iran, which resulted in the death of eight American soldiers and failed to bring the hostages home. With the world and the White House in such a convulsed state, no administration official had a clear idea of what was happening in Miami or Key West, much less in Mariel, a harbor that few if any of the president's top advisers had ever heard of.

It wasn't until April 26, the Saturday when Mike was approached by the Cubans, that the first high-level Mariel meeting was held in the White House. Vice President Walter Mondale chaired the meeting in the Theodore Roosevelt Room, a large office adjacent to the Oval Office that was nicknamed the "Fish Room," because President Roosevelt used to keep a fish tank there. Present were the chief of coast guard operations; the attorney general; the secretary of state; the secretary of health, education and welfare; the deputy secretary of defense; a deputy CIA director; and other top people in the administration, including Stuart Eizenstat, President Carter's chief domestic policy adviser and executive director of the White House domestic policy staff.

Everyone in the room seemed to be taken aback by the boatlift. For a long time, the signs of an impending crisis with Cuba had been clear, but everyone in the Carter administration had seemingly ignored them. There was one exception: Wayne Smith, the chief of the U.S. Interests Section in Havana, had alerted his government on repeated occasions, but to no avail. In February he'd sent his bosses at the State Department a cable titled "Cuban Intention to Reopen Camarioca," calculating that the mere mention of the word "Camarioca" would at least pique the curiosity of his superiors, who might remember the boatlift unleashed by Castro during the Johnson presidency. The cable sat untouched in a junior officer's in-box at the Department of State's Bureau of Legal Affairs. But even if the cable had moved through the channels as expeditiously as it should have, few people in the Carter White House would have understood the significance of Camarioca. Difficult to pronounce and impossible to spell for the majority of President Carter's advisers, the name had not become a code word for uncontrollable immigration.

During the rambling meeting about Mariel on April 26, Smith's warnings were not even discussed. It was too late for introspection by then. The session, which lasted several hours, had been hastily called to discuss options to stem the flow. One of the options was to persuade the Cuban-American community, which administration officials knew to be generally law-abiding, to stop chartering boats to Cuba; the other was to determine what if any legal routes the government could pursue to stop the boatlift.

Though the two alternatives were explored, many of those in the meeting knew instantly that there was very little they could do. It wasn't illegal for American vessels to leave the country. It was only illegal for them to return loaded with unscreened, unapproved refugees. But what to do with a boatful of refugees? They certainly could not be returned to Cuba, a communist country. Also, to force them back into Cuban waters would constitute an act of war against an enemy nation. The government could deny the refugees entry, but where would they go? In dangerously overcrowded, precarious old boats, to force them to remain at sea would have been tantamount to a death sentence. There was no immigration agreement that allowed a safe return to Cuba, say, by plane. And even if there were, once the Cubans had stepped on U.S. soil they had the right to stay and apply for residence, courtesy of a 1966 law granting Cubans that privilege. The Justice Department would be inundated with legal challenges opposing the deportation of people who, since the advent of communism on the island, had been received in the United States with open arms. More important, to turn them away would be contrary to the rhetoric and the image of the United States as a safe harbor for refugees fleeing repressive pro-Soviet regimes at the height of the Cold War.

Coast guard officials in Key West quickly established that the only way to stop the boatlift would be to use force, and they told White House officials just that. No one in an administration guided by human-rights principles was prepared to allow for such a thing. There was another motivation for not resorting to violence: In an election year, no one wanted to further alienate the Cuban-American community, an important voting bloc in South Florida. Thus, while Washington maintained that anyone piloting boats to Cuba would be detained and fined, in reality there was no way to safely and legally stop the boatlift. The meeting ended inconclusively.

When the first week of the boatlift came to a close, over 6,000 Cubans had arrived in Key West, more than double the number of people who arrived in the twenty-four days of the entire Camarioca boatlift of 1965.

In a public statement on April 27, Vice President Mondale called for the "orderly, safe, and humane evacuation of refugees" and asked the Cuban-American community to "respect the law and to avoid these dangerous and illegal boat passages." At the same time, the president ordered the navy and the coast guard to render all possible assistance to those at sea.

Both floundering and mutually contradictory attempts at setting policy left the shores of the United States wide open to Cuban refugees. And it left Mike Howell with no compelling legal or ethical reason to refuse the Cubans help. The *Mañana* would sail on.

MORE THAN 35,000 CUBAN exiles lived in New Orleans in 1980. Its relative proximity to Florida and access to the Gulf of Mexico made New Orleans a focal point during the boatlift. A local religious leader, the Reverend Leo Frade, who was in charge of Hispanic ministries at Grace Episcopal Church in New Orleans, was trying to raise $170,000 to secure a three-hundred-passenger ship to ferry Cubans from the island to their relatives in Louisiana. Just as their compatriots were doing in Florida, Cubans in the entire state of Louisiana began to mobilize to find jobs for the expected new arrivals.

The enthusiasm was contagious. Mike attacked his project with a military zeal, organizing the crew, studying maps, devising a route, checking and testing equipment. When Ventura returned accompanied by three friends on April 29, Mike was ready. He had hired two young helpers named David and Damien, and, with the Cubans' money, he had purchased the navigation equipment he needed to get oriented in the open seas. The Cubans had also bought seventy-eight life jackets, at six dollars each, and stocked the boat with more than five hundred dollars' worth of food.

On Wednesday, April 30, the *Mañana* left Lake Pontchartrain at 1:00 A.M. Mike had picked a good day. That same morning, just as he steered the *Mañana* along the coast of Louisiana toward Florida, the Pentagon announced that Cuban refugees would be picked up from the Florida Straits only when necessary to save lives and that no refugees would be returned to Cuba.

The *Mañana* ran into trouble as soon as it left home, doing justice to a bumper sticker Mike kept prominently displayed in the cabin: ANYBODY WHO OWNS A BOAT DESERVES IT. Outside Gulfport, Mississippi, the *Mañana* developed an oil leak. Then, near Pensacola, Mike discovered a fuel leak. After both leaks were fixed, one of the two generators began to malfunction, which wreaked havoc with the navigational equipment. Finally hurricane-force winds of fifty miles per hour and ten-foot waves forced the *Mañana* to wait out the storm in Pensacola, a time Mike used to replace the failed generator and to buy twenty-five gallons of additional fuel. About 130 miles out in the Gulf, past Panama City, Mike got a call from Julavits, the reporter who was chronicling the *Mañana*'s journey for New

Orleans's afternoon daily, the *States-Item*. "Nothing can stop us now," he told Jula-vits, brimming with his usual optimism. "We are on our way to Cuba."

It took the *Mañana* three days to navigate the 600 miles from New Orleans to Key West, where Mike and his crew rested for two nights and restocked the boat. On Sunday, May 4, a fine, sunny day with winds that reached up to eighteen miles per hour, the *Mañana* departed for Mariel.

The lead editorial of the *New York Times* that morning called on President Carter to "take the refugees, and stop being so grudging about it."

The *Mañana* dropped anchor at Mariel that evening, just hours after it had left Key West. Mike could see he was surrounded by hundreds of boats, close to two thousand, bobbing in the darkness. Some of the boats were so small and ill equipped that he wondered how they'd been able to make it to Cuba and how they would make it back, loaded with their human cargo.

THAT NIGHT AND for several nights after, the crew of the *Mañana* was kept awake by the powerful searchlights that scanned the harbor. In the morning, Mike was told the lights were searching for defectors. Cuban officials worried that some of the army men patrolling the harbor would swim out to one of the boats. A soldier had tried it the week before, but he'd been caught by his peers and viciously beaten.

Mike wondered how such a beautiful place could breed so much violence and misery. Mariel was a gorgeous harbor, about two miles long. The landlocked, in-dustrial harbor became known to the United States in 1962 when Soviet ships used it to unload the missiles that brought the world to the brink of nuclear war during the Cuban Missile Crisis. Now the port was home to a cement factory that spewed uninterrupted columns of white and gray smoke, the only obstruc-tion to the harbor's natural beauty. Overlooking the harbor, the old Cuban Naval Academy sat on a hill like a fairy-tale white castle.

Where the *Mañana* was anchored, about a mile and a half from the docks, there were no channels of official information. Someone from another boat told Mike they needed to turn in their list of wanted relatives at the Tritón, a hotel twenty-nine miles away, where the immigration service had established an office.

Mike and Ventura took the twelve-foot fiberglass dinghy to the docks and, after paying twenty dollars each, boarded a bus to the hotel. On the bus they were given a few pointers about civility in Cuba, including a request to dispose of chewing gum in garbage cans, not on the floors of the shiny new buses that the government had put at their disposal.

At the hotel, a modern white building twenty-three stories high in an exclusive beachfront section of Havana, they encountered a different world. Bands played Cuban *guarachas* while pretty waitresses sold cold beer for a dollar; a big meal cost six dollars, but an eight-minute call to Miami could cost more than sixty dollars. Since American dollars had not circulated in Cuba for two decades, the Cuban government arbitrarily determined, in the first days of the boatlift, an exchange rate of seventy Cuban cents per each U.S. dollar. About a thousand of those who had come by boat slept in the hotel's modest rooms; others went there every day to make calls, take showers, and return refreshed to spend the nights on their boats. A chain-link fence surrounded the building to prevent hotel guests from mingling with the regular Cuban population.

Mike took a quick look at the scene, concentrating on the teary-eyed Cubans who seemed to occupy every corner of the lobby. Several—women, mostly— were openly crying. After days at Mariel, they had just heard that their relatives would not be able to leave with them after all, either because the government did not approve their exit permits or because some families, afraid to be separated, had opted to stay put unless the entire family could leave, a nearly impossible feat given the stinginess of Cuban immigration officials and the size of what most Cubans considered family: not only parents and their kids but grandmothers and sometimes even aunts and uncles. Every captain Mike met at the hotel complained that only a fraction of those on their lists had been granted permits to leave. Then why are the boats leaving so full? Mike wondered. Who *are* those people, if they're not the ones on anybody's lists?

Immigration officials spent about an hour going over Mike's list of twenty-five names. When they finished, they told him to return to his boat and wait.

Life on the boat at Mariel soon became a tiresome routine. For entertainment the crew and the Cubans swam in the harbor, though the *Mañana* was equipped with a shower and carried 750 gallons of water. They cooked and ate and drank.

For variety in their diet, and to conserve what they'd brought from Key West, they bought supplies from two blue-topped government boats that cruised the harbor. Ham sandwiches cost a dollar at first, but then, when demand increased, the price was raised to three dollars and eventually to five. Bottles of Havana Club rum were priced at eighty-five dollars each, and water was three dollars a gallon, sometimes five.

Tourism had not yet developed in Cuba, but Mariel provided the first indication that the industry could be profitable. Boat owners were fined steeply if they threw garbage overboard; a wooden Cuban boat would make the rounds every morning picking up bags of garbage and selling bags of ice. The price fluctuated according to demand. Some of the men whiled away the night hours at the *Capitán Pinares*, a huge party vessel, courtesy of the Cuban government, where bands played until dawn.

THE DAY AFTER the *Mañana* arrived in Mariel, President Carter appeared to endorse the boatlift during a stop at the League of Women Voters convention in Washington on May 5. After his prepared remarks, the president opened the floor for questions. A convention participant, Marion Shapiro of Hays, Kansas, asked him what he intended to do "about enforcing current immigration laws."

"Ours is a country of refugees," the president began. "Those of us who have been here for a generation, or six or eight generations, ought to have just as open a heart to receive the new refugees as our ancestors were received [with] in the past." He went on to a lengthy explanation, which reporters later characterized as "brimming with compassion." The president concluded with an unexpected promise: "We'll continue to provide an open heart and open arms to refugees seeking freedom from communist domination and from economic deprivation, brought about primarily by Fidel Castro and his government." The audience responded with warm and extended applause.

If, up till then, stopping the boatlift had proved impossible, now that the president appeared to have asked the country to welcome the new refugees, the flotilla gained new momentum. His statement, much to the dismay of others in his administration who were pressing for a coherent and enforceable policy regarding the flotilla, made headlines in both Miami and Havana.

About 14,000 Cubans had arrived in Key West in the two weeks before the president gave what soon came to be known as his "open arms" speech. In the two weeks that followed it, 43,782 more arrived, and there were no indications that Castro was ready to stop his island from hemorrhaging people or that Cuban exiles had tired of following his game. On May 6 the president grabbed headlines again by declaring a state of emergency in South Florida and authorizing the release of $10 million to provide aid to the refugees. Later that day an exasperated State Department spokesman, Hodding Carter III, admitted to the press that the government had no policy toward Mariel.

"Hodding," a reporter asked during a State Department briefing, "are you saying the government hasn't had its act together?"

"I am saying, in the face of an extraordinary explosion of people seeking freedom, the answer is, yes, that is right," Hodding Carter replied.

"But you know what? It is not possible to get the act together," he went on, almost as if speaking to himself. "We did not envision that the man who held the keys to the jail in Cuba was going to let the people come out."

At a White House meeting with members of the Florida congressional delegation on May 7, President Carter was defensive about his utterance at the League of Women Voters. He assured everyone that he'd been misinterpreted. Reporters had overemphasized the "open arms" element of the quote and neglected the historical context in which he'd said it. What he'd meant to say was that the United States had a history of compassionate immigration policy and that compassion should also be extended to those who had already arrived. He did not mean to encourage the disorderly arrival of thousands of people. But that distinction, even the president himself knew, was far too nuanced for a press corps hungry for a decisive statement from the White House regarding Mariel. Now that he'd said it, he couldn't go back on his word. "I'm not going to sink any boats with people in them," the president said coldly before concluding the one-hour meeting.

Later that day, top administration officials, including National Security Adviser Zbigniew Brzezinski and the president's chief domestic-policy adviser, Stuart Eizenstat, held a meeting to assess the impact of the president's "open arms" comment. Everyone agreed that, in the absence of a coherent policy, the president's words had become the government's de facto policy regarding Mariel.

Brzezinski, a Polish immigrant who tended to view the world through the prism of the Cold War, thought, like Jimmy Carter, that the United States should be generous and accept the Cubans, but in an orderly way. Eizenstat, who had been a junior aide in the Johnson White House during the time of the Camarioca flotilla, argued that the administration was too focused on the foreign-policy ramifications of the boatlift. What was needed, he said, was what he termed "an acceptable policy," a safe, legal way to stem the flow of people he knew Castro had no incentive to curtail. Assistant Secretary of State Warren Christopher explained that whatever decision they ultimately came up with probably would not include any cooperation from the Cuban government. "Castro won't participate in talks," he said.

The next day President Carter telephoned Eizenstat and asked him to collaborate with Brzezinski in formulating an enforceable policy to stop the boatlift. It was time Washington sent a unified, clear message to both Miami and Cuba.

The following morning, May 9, everyone in the administration woke up to read a scathing *New York Times* editorial mocking President Carter: "At last, the President has pledged that the United States will provide 'an open heart and open arms' to the refugees pouring out of Cuba. Excellent, but does one open arm know what the other is doing?"

THAT SAME DAY Mike decided to go back to the Hotel Tritón to check on his list. After three days and three nights in Cuba, he was eager to go home and tired of being told he must wait. He didn't see what good he could do waiting around all day under a punishing sun until some bureaucrat or, worse, a man with a gun made a decision about when and if he could return to the States and even about whom he could take with him.

He asked David, one of his crew members, to accompany him. He didn't want to be alone with the Cubans in charge. Something about their starched uniforms and half-crooked smiles—as if they were privy to a joke he was too dumb or too gringo to get—made him uncomfortable, and he didn't trust himself to keep his cool in their presence.

At the hotel a Cuban soldier noticed the rigging knife David carried in his belt and took it from him before the two Americans could meet with immigration officials. A trio was playing a Cuban bolero when Mike walked into the office.

Okay, he said. We're ready to go. Where are my people?

Here's your list, a uniformed man with a gun told him.

Mike looked it over. That wasn't his list. His people were on it, but there were three hundred other names he'd never heard of before.

No, I'm not taking three hundred people in my boat, he said flatly. We are only going to take the people on my list. With that he threw the list on the table and turned around to leave.

You are going to have to do it! the man yelled after him, and then threatened to arrest him if he didn't. Mike rotated on his heels and looked straight at the officer. His open, dimpled face, framed by unruly hair that brushed against his eyes, made Mike look younger than he was and belied the anger that was always boiling just below the surface, hidden behind his smile. When angry, he stood erect, stretching his barrel-like torso so that he became taller, the fist of his overly strong right arm opening and closing quickly as if grasping for a weapon that, fortunately on that day, he didn't have.

If you're going to arrest me, you better get more people, Mike said, eyeing the expanding group of soldiers who'd come to the officer's aid. Then he stormed off, followed by David. Nobody moved.

MIKE COULD BARELY sleep that night. He feared that his mission had failed. Either he followed the orders of the Cuban government or he would have to leave without his people. The Cubans played hardball, he realized. They had their guns and their laws on their side, as well as the manpower to carry their threats out. Intimidation had worked for a few minutes that afternoon, but Mike doubted it would work again.

The following morning, May 10, just as he was mulling over what to do, a boat full of soldiers approached the *Mañana*. Mike froze, his mind reeling with possible scenarios. Though he had returned from Vietnam thirteen years before, Cuba had started to seem to him like a war stage. Underneath the bow, hidden in a compartment above the extra beds, Mike kept a small cache of weapons: a pistol, two shotguns, some rifles. He thought briefly about asking David to bring them up. He had no intention of getting arrested in Cuba. Then, just as it had appeared, silently and suddenly, the Cuban boat veered to the left and disappeared. Mike was convinced, more than ever, that it was time to leave Cuba. Now.

He pulled up the anchor and tried to approach the docks with the *Mañana* to inform the authorities that he was leaving. But a voice amplified by a bullhorn ordered him to stay put. The crew threw the anchor back into the water while Mike and Ventura got into the dinghy to find Major Rafael, the man who Mike suspected was in charge of the harbor operation. Mike simply wanted to let the major know that he was leaving. Without Rafael's approval nobody could leave the harbor.

The ships' docks were ten or twelve feet high and difficult to climb for a man with only one arm. Rounded timbers formed a sort of rustic ladder against the cement wall of the docks, which Mike climbed steadily but slowly, followed by Ventura. He concentrated on lifting a foot, grabbing the next timber with his one good arm, then lifting the other foot and again his good arm. If he faltered, he would fall into the water.

When he reached the top, he was sweating and panting, on his hands and knees, crouching on the hot cement. He looked up to see the barrel of an AK-47 rifle pointed right at his forehead. Mike wasn't afraid, but he was surprised. He hadn't had a gun pointed at him since Vietnam. He quickly jumped to his full height, and, as he did, he waved his hand to move the gun away from his face. But the movement carried such force that the barrel of the gun hit the young soldier on the forehead, splitting his head open. The man fell down, bleeding. Mike caught the rifle before it touched the ground. For the second time in less than twenty-four hours, a group of soldiers encircled Mike. Among them was Major Rafael, the man he'd come to see.

Mike dropped the rifle on the fallen soldier and walked over to the cluster of officers.

Major Rafael, nos vamos en cuatro horas, he said in Spanish to make sure his message was understood. *Punto.* We're leaving in four hours, and that's final.

Ventura stepped in and spoke in rapid Spanish to the major, but Mike couldn't make out the words.

He's crazy, Ventura was saying nervously, trying to gain some time. He's a Vietnam veteran. He's traumatized.

The major remained calm. He ordered the soldiers to take care of the bleeding man on the ground. Mike kept talking, gesticulating with his hand, while his rubber arm moved up and down stiffly, guided only by the force of his shaking, angry body.

And if you're going to shoot me, you better shoot me now, 'cause I'm leaving, he said, this time in English; he was too flustered to think of the words in Spanish.

Translate that! he barked at Ventura.

But Ventura, a family man who understood the nature of the regime, opted not to translate. He was afraid the Cubans just might shoot them both.

Mike then turned to the major again. *Un momento, por favor*, he said before running off and returning with another translator, the American-born son of Peruvian parents, whom he'd met at the harbor. The young man, a medical student, was there as a member of the crew of another boat. He translated for Mike, who wanted to make sure the Cuban officers understood that not even guns would thwart his resolve to leave.

No one is going to shoot anybody, Major Rafael said once he understood Mike's threats.

By then the soldier Mike had knocked down had awakened and someone had bandaged his head. He slipped the sling of the rifle over his shoulder and joined the group. Mike turned to him and apologized. *Perdóneme, por favor*, he said, hoping that with his words and conciliatory gestures everyone would understand that he hadn't meant to hurt the soldier. He'd simply acted out of reflex.

With the tension somewhat deflected, the major offered Mike a deal that, he said, would please everyone. Take the *Valley Chief* people and go home.

FOLLOWING THE MIAMI CUBAN, Oswaldo, Mike took a few steps toward the *Valley Chief* and scrutinized some of the faces of the men on board. Though there were women and children, the majority were men. He didn't trust most of the faces he saw. Like other captains in the harbor, he'd heard that the Cuban government was mixing convicted criminals in with regular people in the boatlift.

Mike hated the idea of filling his cherished *Mañana* with people he didn't know. But he also didn't want to return to the United States empty-handed. As an ex-soldier, Mike understood the depths of despair. A useless vessel in enemy territory can certainly drive a man to beg. In Oswaldo's voice he had sensed despair.

BEFORE MIKE and the others began to debate the fate of the shrimp boat, a *New York Times* reporter had noticed it, too. His name was Edward Schumacher, and after being at the harbor for about ten days, he was eager to go home. When he went looking for a boat that would take him back, the *Valley Chief* had caught his eye, at first because it was overloaded. Moored near it there was another vessel, double the size of the *Valley Chief* and grossly overloaded as well. It was called the *America*. Hundreds of men with glazed eyes, shaved heads, and what appeared to be prison or hospital garb were hanging on to any part of the boats that could keep them from falling into the water.

Schumacher smelled a story. Just a week earlier, the *Washington Post* had published a short article citing FBI officials' concern because "a small number of Cuban intelligence agents, criminals and prostitutes [had] been discovered among the flood of Cuban refugees entering Key West." But the piece relied on information that the FBI's director, William H. Webster, had shared with a group of *Washington Post* editors and reporters during a private lunch. The *New York Times* had not been invited—certainly not Schumacher, who was hundreds of miles away prowling the docks of Mariel.

Until Schumacher stumbled upon the *Valley Chief* and the *America*, no reporter from a major U.S. newspaper had actually been able to witness how the Cuban government was mixing "undesirables" with the regular boatlift crowd. For one thing, it was nearly impossible to assess whom it was that the Cuban government was granting exit permits to. There was clearly a group of people authorized to leave who had relatives waiting for them at the harbor. Then there were the thousands of refugees from the Peruvian embassy. But there was a third category as well: Thousands of Cubans were lining up in front of specially set-up immigration offices to petition for visas on the grounds that they were what the government called *escoria:* homosexuals, prostitutes, drug users, and enemies of the revolution. Whether or not those seeking exit permits were truly "undesirables" was unknown. A man could easily pretend to be gay; his wife, on another day, could pretend to be a lesbian. If both were believed, they could leave through Mariel and meet up again in Florida, and no one would know what they'd had to say to escape their country.

Schumacher had heard that the Cuban government had been using a formula in which only about 30 percent of the 30,000 refugees who'd already arrived in Key West—about 9,000—had relatives in the United States.

What Schumacher didn't know was that Castro himself manipulated the formula every day, balancing both Washington's tolerance and Miami's innocence against his own needs to cleanse the country of "scum." He had created seven categories encompassing every possible type of person he wanted to get rid of— from *gusanos* to child molesters. If Cubans in Miami monitoring the new arrivals noticed that too many criminals were arriving in the boatlift and protested too loud, Castro would adjust his numbers, increasing the percentage of relatives and lowering the percentage of criminals for a few days. If no one protested, he would reverse the numbers.

The *Valley Chief* provided Schumacher with the perfect anecdote for the story he'd been writing in his head for days. He got closer to the boat and began interviewing the men in Spanish.

By the time Mike approached Pier 3 to examine the *Valley Chief*, Schumacher had already sent the story to his editors at the *Times*.

YES, I'LL TAKE THEM, Mike said to Oswaldo. But because he was wary of the men staring at him from the boat, Mike said he would take the women, the children, and the elderly aboard the *Mañana* and tow the *Valley Chief* with the men on it to international waters, where the U.S. Coast Guard would help them. Oswaldo, eager for any offer that would take him far from Cuban shores, accepted.

Mike went back to the *Mañana* and announced his decision to the New Orleans Cubans. They, too, believed Major Rafael's promise and quickly warmed up to the idea that if they couldn't take their own relatives with them, at least they'd be helping other Cubans in need. The crew lifted the anchor and came bow-in alongside the *Valley Chief.*

Before the *Mañana* left, a Cuban soldier handed Mike an official departure authorization. Signed by an officer at the Ministry of the Interior, the form listed routine information about the boat's size and capacity and where it was headed. In the space reserved for a description of what kind of shipment the boat was taking from Cuba, the officer had typed the word *lastre.* Ballast.

The next morning Schumacher's story ran above the fold, in the center of the front page of the *New York Times*: RETARDED PEOPLE AND CRIMINALS ARE INCLUDED IN CUBAN EXODUS, the headline announced. The top of the story provided the first tangible and independently witnessed proof of Castro's macabre plan.

The young man's rib cage protruded from his chest and only a few teeth remained in his mouth. His speech was limited, apparently from mental retardation. His glazed eyes bulged with fear.

He was on his way to live in the United States.

The young man and a handful of people of similar appearance were among almost 200 Cuban refugees crowded aboard the Valley Chief, a 70-foot fishing boat that is scheduled to arrive tomorrow at Key West, Fla.

About 200 common criminals, Cubans here said, were to arrive at about the same time among 420 refugees aboard another vessel, a 120-foot red, white and blue catamaran called the America.

The two vessels, moored near each other this morning at a pier where Cuban soldiers have been loading refugees, are being used in a major effort, discussed openly by Cuban officials, to rid the country of criminals, mentally retarded people, delinquents and others the Government calls "scum" by sending them to the United States.

TEN

Tempest-Tost

Cuban refugees braving the waters of the Gulf on their way
to Key West at the height of the boatlift.

I HAD REMAINED in the same position—straining my eyes to follow my uncle in the distance—for too long. My neck hurt, and I no longer believed I could will his prompt return just by keeping my eyes fixed on his white T-shirt. I rubbed the back of my neck in an automatic gesture. Wispy clouds moved swiftly in the otherwise clear sky, and a slight breeze offered a break from the midafternoon heat. I squinted in the light.

The thought of losing my uncle frightened me. He was the only link we had to the rest of our lives. If he disappeared, we would be forced to stay in Cuba. And legally we were no longer in Cuba. We couldn't just pick up our lives where we had left off. They would never take my sister and me back in school. My father would not have a job, and no one would ask my mother to make dresses anymore. People would be afraid to be seen with a family that had tried, but failed, to escape.

My uncle's deep voice yanked me out of the darkness of my thoughts.

He was speaking to a tanned and muscular sailor, standing next to him. They were surrounded by armed Cuban soldiers. The sailor spoke English with an accent I had never heard in any of the black-and-white MGM films broadcast on Cuban television every Saturday after midnight. Although I had taken English lessons in school since the eighth grade, I didn't understand a word he was saying. He spoke as if the syllables had melted in his mouth. His eyes twinkled in the light, and he smiled when he looked at us. The man had sailed his yacht, *Mañana*, to the port of Mariel in a humanitarian mission, my uncle explained, and now he had come to our rescue. Everyone in the boat moved closer to him. Here was an *americano* we could trust.

The man began to give orders to the younger men who accompanied him. I sat on the hard cement surface of the docks. From below I noticed something peculiar about the man's left arm. It barely moved while he talked and gesticulated with his right arm. My eyes followed the muscles of his forearm. Somewhere above the elbow there was a bulge, a somewhat clunky connection to his shoulder. The arm was fake, I realized, but so similar to his other arm that it was almost impossible to tell them apart. The nails were perfectly shaped, veins formed an expanding web underneath the rubbery "skin" of his hand, and the coloring of the rubber precisely mirrored his skin tone.

The crowd dispersed to give the sailors room to maneuver. When the one-armed man threw a thick rope from the docks to keep the *Valley Chief* from drifting, his prosthetic arm got tangled and fell into the water. Everybody gasped. My mother fainted, her body hitting the cement with a thud.

A young man, a member of the American's crew, dove into the murky waters of the port and after a few seconds came out triumphantly holding the arm over his head, like a soldier in a war movie trying to keep his rifle dry. The American simply grabbed it, shook the water from it, and put it on. My mother came to. An explosion of applause followed.

It was a sign, I thought, of good things to come.

BEFORE MARIEL, I had never traveled anywhere outside the country or even very far inside Cuba. My longest, most exciting journeys had always been bus trips to my parents' small-town birthplaces in Las Villas. We would always arrive in Rancho Veloz, our first destination, around midnight. My grandfather Juan would be sitting in his wheelchair, waiting for us, wearing pajamas, his face fresh and smooth from a recent shave and his thinning hair carefully combed around his shiny bald spot. His gnarled hands would hold me by the shoulders away from his body, away from the hug I was aching to give him, and he would always say the same thing: My, my, how you've grown! You are a little woman already!

Folds of skin hung from his once-powerful arms, and his legs, no longer responsive, were nothing but bones covered by skin, purple and glistening from years of circulation ailments that had finally caught up with him. But his hands were still strong, his deformed fingers leaving red marks on my arms, as he finally relented and let me crush my face against his concave chest.

Abuelo, Abuelo, Abuelo! Grandfather! I would babble, not quite sure of what else to say. We would then sit and talk about life in Havana. My grandfather, who had lived with us for months at a time before his still-undiagnosed disease had confined him to a wheelchair for the past two years, would ask about old friends, about his barber, about the condition of certain gardens in the neighborhood from which we'd often stolen white roses, my dead grandmother's favorite flower.

When I was a small child, he had been my most tolerant and faithful playmate. He allowed me to stick him with my mother's sewing needles when I thought I wanted to be a doctor. He taught me to play checkers and performed magic tricks for my friends and me, insisting that his knowledge and strength derived from an invisible entity he called Caballo Blanco, White Horse, whose power only he could summon by clicking the fingers of his right hand.

During our yearly vacations in the country, I sat at the table well past bedtime, listening to my grandfather spin his tales as he sucked on his pipe. I hated leaving him at the end of the summer. I would wave to him from the windows of the train as it chugged along past his house, until I had run all the way to the last car and there were no more windows to wave from, always fearful that he wouldn't make it until my next visit.

And now I was certain I would never see him again. Tears ran down my face for the first time since I'd left my home, as I followed my mother to the *americano*'s boat.

I JUMPED OVER the railing and stood on the bow of the *Mañana*. The name was fitting, I thought. Without looking back to the *Valley Chief*, where my father had stayed with my uncle, I made my way belowdecks, where a woman named Blanca was asking for volunteers to help her make sandwiches. I wanted to keep busy, but my hands were shaking. First the mustard, Blanca gently guided me, then the ham and the cheese. I followed her orders automatically, not daring to imagine what was going on up above, where I knew the captain would soon begin steering us out of the harbor.

It was hot in this improvised kitchen. Beads of sweat ran from Blanca's face to her neck, collecting in a giant expanding stain on her pink cotton blouse. I heard the captain begin shouting orders, and felt the boat separating from the *Valley Chief* with a thud. Blanca handed me two more pieces of white bread, perfectly sliced as if no human hands had ever touched it. I thought of the fifteen-cent bread I stood in line for every other day: hard and coarse, uneven, clearly the work of a man and an oven, a communion of experience and fire.

I heard the sounds of the harbor: the Cuban officers barking orders through bullhorns, the thick lines of the sailboats—*ting-ling, ting-ling*—as they hit the masts, the waves lapping up against the sides of the *Mañana* with a deafening *whoosh, whoosh*. The sounds seemed distant now. We were pulling away.

A tear fell on my hands, and Blanca urged me to go up and give a good, last look to my land. You'll regret it later if you don't, she said sternly. I dropped the bread and the mustard, the ham and the cheese, and raced up the wooden stairs toward the bow of the ship, where I could see that the sun had begun to touch the waters of the harbor.

My heart was pushing against my throat as if it wanted to stay behind. I swallowed hard. I had always thought that I would leave Cuba during the day, when I could see my island in all its splendor just as I'd seen it on maps countless times: flat and green, with shimmering rivers crisscrossing its underbelly, bookended by mountain ranges, tall and regal like sentinels in the Caribbean that protected it from hurricanes and invaders and other perils of geography and history. Instead I concentrated on the contours of the land before darkness engulfed my scant view of the shores: patches of green, a flag flapping in the wind, a building on top of a hill.

Concentrate, I ordered my brain, urging it to record every small detail of my island. This is the last time I'll see Cuba. Take it in. Take it all in. I was momentarily distracted by the call of a bird before it dove into the water for its dinner, a silverfish, its scales sparkling with the last rays of the dying sun. I looked back to the land, but it had become more yellow than brown, the water more blue than green. I should have brought a rock with me, a little water, a handful of dirt, I thought, and stared hard at the horizon until my eyeballs began to hurt and the tenuous line of the shore melted into the horizon. Nothing but water now. I leaned over the bow and began to throw up.

NONE OF MY FRIENDS knew that I was leaving Cuba at this moment. I thought about Frank, still in Angola but due to come back any day now. I had not been able to tell him that I wouldn't be there when he returned. In fact, very few people beyond our immediate neighbors even knew that we weren't home anymore.

My friend Kathy surely was the first person outside my block to learn that I had left Cuba. For years I had picked her up every day at twelve-thirty so we could walk to school together. If I was late, which was often, she would walk the two blocks from her house to mine and call my name from the street, knowing that her voice would carry through the always open terrace door. I bet she had done the same on Wednesday. I bet she looked up, saw the bare terrace, the closed door, and she knew. I bet she saw my neighbors' faces and they saw hers, and I bet no one dared say a word.

Perhaps not even the government knew that I was in this specific boat. I felt free for the first time in my life, and the feeling was unsettling. There was no longer any need to hide my family's desire to leave Cuba, since everyone who surrounded me was, quite literally, in the same boat. Yet I felt very alone, disconnected, as if someone had cut the umbilical cord that had kept me attached to my sense of self and place for sixteen years. I was no longer the top student vying for a spot in journalism school. Nor was I the daughter of disaffected *gusanos*. I was nobody's friend or girlfriend. I was simply one more human being in a bobbing yacht heading north.

I had entered the world of exile, a zone where one must always walk alone, at one's own pace, and only after burying a part of one's soul.

I AWOKE WITH a violent stomach spasm, as if I were going to throw up, but my stomach was empty. I was totally disoriented. I didn't know where my head

was or in what direction my feet were pointing. I wondered if someone had
moved my bed. Then I realized I was not in my bed at all. I was on the cold, wet
metal floor of the *Mañana*. I tried to stretch my arms and uncurl my legs, but I
hit something soft. A person, perhaps? My sister was next to me, sleeping,
though I saw that she, too, had been throwing up. Her long hair was matted with
dried food. Someone was holding my ankle tightly. I sat up straight. A wave of
dizziness overcame me, and I fell back, my head hitting the floor hard. My
mother let go of my ankle and took my hands, caressing them. I could tell she was
scared.

She was forty years old and alone with her daughters for the first time in her
life. She didn't know how to swim, she'd never been in a boat, and she'd rarely ever
been away from my father. What's wrong? my mother asked. I thought for a
minute what to say. I was cold and hungry. I had an intense pain in my bladder
because I hadn't gone to the bathroom for hours, perhaps a day—I'd forgotten. I
couldn't feel my legs. My head hurt, as did my throat and stomach, from retching
up bile. My clothes were dirty. My hair was matted. I hadn't changed or washed
in almost five days. I felt like crying, but I was so dizzy that I couldn't even cry.
And of course there was the pain of all pains: I had left Cuba.

Nothing, I told her, and closed my eyes again.

I HAD NEVER BEEN seriously ill in my life, not so that I was practically im-
mobilized, as I felt now. In fact, except for occasional nosebleeds, I hadn't even
been to a hospital. The last time my nose had hemorrhaged, just a few weeks earlier, I'd sat in the waiting area of the emergency room in the country's top children's hospital for six hours. To avoid the spectacle of my gushing nose, I had
begun swallowing my blood. Finally, when I couldn't stand it anymore, I
opened the door of the nurse's station and demanded to see a doctor. A nurse
gave me some tissue to clean myself and gently told me that all the doctors were
in a meeting of the Communist Party and that there was no one to see me until
the next shift.

She led me to a bed and gave me a clean towel. There is nothing more I can
do, *cariño*, she said, in the endearing way Cubans talk when they empathize but

can't help you. Three hours later I was finally admitted. By then I had to be given shots to coagulate the blood and have the veins of my nose cauterized with electricity, which sent small, painful electrical shocks down my spine. I went home and seethed all weekend, convinced that even medicine had been contaminated by the politics that eventually choked everyone and everything around me.

MY MOTHER KNEW I was awake, though my eyes were closed. We've let go of the boat, she said, and I knew she meant that the *Mañana* had towed the *Valley Chief* to international waters, as arranged, and then let it go. I wondered where my father and my uncle were.

When? I asked.

Two hours ago, I think, she whispered.

Did you see them? Could you talk to them?

No, my mother said. I saw the lights in the distance.

What time is it?

She didn't know. I sat up with great difficulty and looked at her eyes, dark but dry. In the rush to leave Cuba, I hadn't even said good-bye to my father before we left the *Valley Chief*. I heard my uncle yelling after me to call his wife when we got to Key West, but I hadn't looked back. Darkness framed my mother's worried face and I felt the urge to touch her, to soothe her, but the effort of moving my head had been too much. I felt nauseated and lay back, trying to find a comfortable spot. A wave splashed us, and I tasted salt on my lips. It was Sunday, May 11, Mother's Day.

My mother was not going to get a card that day, I realized. I had mailed her one the day before we left our house. It was probably already under the door now.

Happy Mother's Day, I said just before the thick fog of seasickness enveloped me once more.

FOR AS LONG as I could remember, I had lived with the fear that this was the year in which I would lose my mother. Ever since I'd learned that my grandmother had died at the age of forty, the day after my mother had turned sixteen,

I'd dreaded that history would repeat itself, given the coincidence of our birth-days. My mother would be forty by the time I reached sixteen. She fueled my pessimistic rumblings by reminding me often that she was sure she would die young. One day, shortly before my sixteenth birthday, I'd awakened to the sound of her sobs. My mother, sitting next to my bed, was caressing my arms, my hands, my face. Frightened by the sight of her tears, I asked what was happening. Noth-ing, she said, but it will. And just like that, I began to live with the certainty that my mother wouldn't last me through the year.

She would be forty-one in October, and I was still sixteen. It was only May.

WHEN I WOKE UP AGAIN, the sun was hot on my sweaty skin, but I felt clammy and cold. People were rushing about, and I didn't know why. All my energy was concentrated on one immediate thought: I needed to get to a bathroom. My bladder was so full I couldn't move. I grabbed a roll of paper that my mother had given me earlier and carefully unzipped my pants. Under the navy blue blanket that covered me, I began to stuff the paper inside my underwear. I was sure I wasn't go-ing to be able to get to the bathroom in time. My mother saw my distress and called for help. Two young men, the sailors who had helped the captain earlier, grabbed my arms and carried me to the bathroom, my useless feet dangling behind me. The men stood at the door, turning their backs to us, while my mother held me so I wouldn't fall from the toilet onto the dirty floor. Where was my father now?

IN THE SUMMERS, when we traveled to Las Villas, my father made sure to be-friend the bus driver because he knew I would get sick on the trip and need fre-quent bathroom breaks. I often developed bouts of diarrhea or, worse, motion sickness while traveling. The buses lacked restrooms, so my father would search out the window for a bushy area, where even a large man like him could hide for a couple of minutes. Driver, can you stop for a moment? We have an emergency here, he would yell after taking a look at my pallid face. The driver would oblige.

For those inevitable moments, my mother carried a plastic bag full of colorful scraps of cloth, remnants of the dresses and pantsuits she sewed for her clients. Toilet paper was scarce. While I crouched on the fields, I focused on the intricate patterns of the scraps in the bag, trying to match each with the faces of my mother's clients. I knew that anything green and bold was usually Anita's, a young divorced woman who entertained my mother with stories of her torrid love affairs. Anything plaid or black and white belonged to the two fat sisters who always dusted their feet with talcum. Invariably, they left a chalky white trail on our floors whenever they came for a fitting. My mother would carefully pin the dress around their rolls of fat as I sat cross-legged on the bed and took notes of the alterations she needed to make.

I would walk back to the bus knowing that my father waited for me on the steps. He would tap my head softly as I, embarrassed but relieved, made my way to our seats, closed my eyes, and rested on his lap until the next needle-sharp ache pierced my stomach, bolting me awake.

I HEARD LOUD VOICES and running feet above deck as I left the tiny bathroom of the *Mañana*. We had arrived, it seemed. The sailors dragged me upstairs, where men dressed in military fatigues and carrying an olive green stretcher awaited. They fussed over me and, gesturing, indicated that I needed to be taken to a hospital. My mother refused, shaking her head forcefully, since she sensed that the men didn't understand Spanish.

Pull yourself together, she whispered in my ear. I can't let them separate us.

Slowly I got onto my feet, and as I did, I began to hear familiar loud cheers of *¡Viva Cuba libre!* Men and women stood behind a wire fence shouting "Long live Cuba!" until they were hoarse. Another group sang the Cuban national anthem in an endless loop. Yet others hurled slogans aimed at Fidel Castro: *¡Abajo Fidel!* Death to the tyrant! I wanted to cry. This is why I had left Cuba, I thought, so that I would never again have to hear another slogan, so that I would never have to hear another death wish against a political leader. I turned my face from the crowd and followed my mother, slowly, very slowly, to the end of a line that snaked around a two-story, sun-bleached white building. There was a mat on the floor in front of a door with a word printed on it in English: WELCOME. I studied each letter but couldn't come up with the meaning of the word.

The queasiness disappeared as I took my first steps in the United States, shuffling behind my mother and sister in the line. By the time we had reached the front, we were each holding a piece of paper bearing our name and the name of the boat that had brought us. Hold on to this. It's very important, a man in a crisp uniform said. I held mine in my closed fist as I prepared to board a bus.

Just then a kind woman approached the line and offered to make phone calls for anyone who needed to get in touch with relatives. In the day and night we'd spent on the *Valley Chief*, I had memorized my uncle's home phone number and address. I wrote it on a piece of paper she handed me and wrote my aunt's name on top, drawing a circle around it, to make it stand out amid the myriad other numbers the woman had already taken. The doors closed and the bus rumbled off, leaving the old wooden docks behind.

In a panic I realized that I'd just spent my first moments in the United States and yet I had no sense of where I'd been. I ran to the end of the bus and looked out but didn't see a name or a sign, only the bright green rear end of what looked like a small ice cream truck pushing through the crowd of Cubans at the fence. Two scraggly palm trees framed a squat building at the end of the docks. A woman frantically waved a small paper Cuban flag. This must be Key West, I thought, and went back to my seat.

WHENEVER WE TRAVELED from Havana to the country, to stave off boredom my father would tell me made-up stories of how the towns we were passing came to be named. Corralillo was named after a small corral where magical cows and sheep were kept, Sierra Morena after a beautiful dark-skinned woman whom every man desired but none could love. Rancho Veloz was so baptized because a lazy man had once had to build a shelter very quickly to protect his family against a furious storm. I would look out the windows of the bus as my father spinned his tales and see the children playing in the red dirt, the women cooling themselves with cardboard fans, and the men returning from the fields with their heads down and half-smoked cigars between their fingers. Some of them sometimes looked up and waved at the passing bus, knowing we were from Havana, a city they had probably never visited, but which I could tell they imagined as infinitely better than the plot of land they trudged on from dawn to dusk, every day except Sunday.

THE BLURRY IMAGES of Key West framed by the windows of the speeding bus confused me, and I wished that my father was there to explain it all to me. This couldn't possibly be the United States. Where were the tall, gleaming buildings? All I could see were old wooden houses, painted white or faded pastel colors, a thirsty dog sleeping in the shade of a screened porch, roosters crossing the streets as if this whole town were somebody's unkempt backyard. For a few minutes, the bus followed what looked like a toy train winding its way through short, narrow streets. When the little train turned and we passed it on the right, men and women with pink cheeks and white hats pointed their cameras at us. I suddenly became aware of what I must look like: My clothes reeked of vomit, my red-and-white checkered blouse had held up pretty well, but my red polyester pants were a shade darker than I remembered them. I would have given anything for a shower. I hadn't seen myself in a mirror for five days.

The bus stopped in front of a building that looked like a huge warehouse. Inside, the floor was lined with row after row of green army cots. Large windows, at least three stories high, let the light stream in like spotlights in a huge stadium. Crisscrossing iron beams formed random polygons in the high ceiling, and men in uniform—green, beige, white, navy blue—seemed to be everywhere. Long rectangular tables on two sides held sandwiches, soda, and gum.

I need to go to the bathroom, I said, and there was a metallic taste in my throat. My voice sounded hoarse, far away. It was the first time I had spoken to my mother and sister since our arrival.

On my way to one of the yellow portable toilets, someone called my name. I turned to see a blond woman with blue eyes and delicate features waving frantically at me, hoping to catch my attention. At first I thought she had confused me with someone else, and I smiled at her and raised my shoulders in a gesture of helplessness, but the woman insisted, and I began to walk toward her.

Halfway there, I realized who she was: one of my high-school literature professors, whom I'd known to be a die-hard revolutionary, the last person I ever imagined I would see in the United States. She had always been highly critical of people like my parents who did not support the regime. I turned and quickly walked away. The bathroom would have to wait. I could feel a blush spreading over my face and neck as I reached the cot where my family awaited. I was embarrassed that I had left Cuba and someone had caught me in the act. Never mind that she, too, had left. I felt like a traitor. Exactly whom I was betraying I didn't know. I covered my face so no one would notice I was burning with shame.

WE HUDDLED on one cot and waited for instructions and for a sign that my father and uncle were alive. At about 8:00 P.M., I heard my name called through a bullhorn. The name was somewhat distorted by the way the man pronounced it and by the echo of the bullhorn, but I was sure someone was calling me, and I ran toward the voice, my mother and sister following. Before we saw her, we could hear her voice: my uncle's wife, Tere. There they are! They are here! She was yelling to no one in particular. And then there we were, jumping with joy along with her and her children and hugging them in relief.

She urged us to leave with a brother-in-law who had driven her to Key West, while she stayed with Olimpia, one of the aunts who had visited us in Cuba the year before, and waited for her husband and my father. In the rush to leave, she kept our new documents, the flimsy pieces of paper with our names on them, which she said identified us as Mariel refugees. We were upset to leave without my father and uncle, but my aunt assured us there was nothing we could do. Go home and rest, she said as she gently guided us to a shiny moss green car right outside. The driver was Bartolo, the husband of my father's older sister and also my mother's second cousin, a man I'd never seen before. My mother sat in the front with him, while my sister and I stretched out in the back and immediately fell asleep, shivering from the extremely cold air-conditioning but too shy to ask Bartolo to turn it off.

I woke up startled by the beam of a flashlight on my face. A policeman at the car's window was talking to my mother's cousin in English. Without the identification papers we had left with Tere, we couldn't leave the Keys, he said. We got off the highway and pulled into the parking lot of a large roadside restaurant, which, my mother's cousin told us, purported to have "the world's best Key lime pie." I didn't know what a Key lime pie was and had to ask him to explain. Thinking of food—limes, pies, cream, cakes—I fell asleep, certain that in a few hours somebody would wake me up with the food that I had always dreamed would be plentiful in America: a warm ham-and-cheese sandwich, with the cheese melting and the borders of the ham curling up from the heat of the toaster, accompanied by a tall glass of orange juice. I couldn't remember the last time I'd had anything to eat.

Sometime later I heard the back door of the car open, and I felt a warmth enveloping my sister and me. A large, familiar hand caressed my face, and I opened my eyes to see my father hovering over me like a giant genie from a magic lamp. I leaped at his neck and remained there for a long time, hanging on to the anchor we'd all been missing for a day and a half.

For about six hours after the *Mañana* had left them behind, my father and the others on the *Valley Chief* had watched the boat slowly take in water. No one despaired, though, not even the disturbed men the government had packed in the boat. My father said he was worried about us, but not for his own safety. He was sure Americans would rescue them.

At around 7:00 A.M., two Coast Guard cutters approached the *Valley Chief*, squeezing it from each side with their pneumatic fenders. Pieces of old wood flew everywhere, and for a few minutes it seemed as if what was left of the boat would sink before everyone had been rescued. But the *Valley Chief* held on. The cutters took the men aboard a U.S. Navy amphibious-assault ship, the USS *Saipan*. The ship was so huge—almost a thousand feet long, my father calculated—that when he stood on deck the sea seemed a distant presence, hardly threatening. In its bowels the ship kept seventeen helicopters. Dozens of refugees from other rescue missions were already on board. All were checked by doctors and received a warm but spicy meal of rice and beans and meat. Sometime in the evening, my father, my uncle, and the others were placed on helicopters and flown to Key West, where they found my uncle's wife and drove off with her until they noticed our car parked in front of the restaurant that sold the world's best Key lime pie.

◆ ◆ ◆

WITH THE FIRST RAYS of the sun on May 12, we arrived at my uncle's house, in a city called Hialeah. Accustomed to seeing photographs of my relatives in New York, I found Hialeah a surprise and a disappointment, just as Key West had been. There were no tall buildings, no interesting architecture, no statues, bridges, or wide avenues, no sense of a city, really. And of course there was no snow. Outside the house, pretty with colorful gardens, it was unbearably hot. Inside, it was chilly, the hum of the air-conditioning following us from room to room as we examined our surroundings carefully, not daring to touch anything.

The ceiling sparkled, and the floors were slippery. Delicate porcelain figurines filled every table and shelf. Crystal lamps with tear-shaped pendants hovered over the living room, while thick, velvety drapes kept the sun out. The polished wooden table quickly filled with breakfast: ham-and-cheese sandwiches and orange juice poured out of a plastic jug, not squeezed from oranges. I drank three glasses and asked for more. My uncle happily obliged.

I took a long bath that left a ring of grime around the spotless white tub. A cousin I'd never met before came by and gave me her old, scratched sunglasses, but they fit perfectly, and I was glad. Another took me to a store, where she said we could look, but not buy. My uncle's wife bought me leather sandals, and someone else cut my hair. I pleaded for a copy of *The Catcher in the Rye*, and within hours I had one, except it was in English. It didn't matter, for I knew most of it by heart.

A picture of our family was taken in the yard, standing in front of flowering gardenias that, oddly, had no scent. I was assigned to my youngest cousin's bed, in a room decorated with sports memorabilia and lots of shiny golden trophies. That night, when I finally lay down to sleep on sheets printed with elongated orange balls and brown helmets, an irrational thought kept me awake: how to return to Cuba on the same boatlift that had just brought me to the United States.

A COUPLE OF DAYS LATER, we went to a makeshift immigration office near Hialeah to register our presence in the United States. A nurse drew our blood and took chest X-rays. As we waited for the results, we were called to a long table for an interview. A bald man with a military bearing but dressed as a civilian was in charge of my file. In flawless Spanish he asked my name. Before I could tell him, though, he said I could choose any name I wanted. It didn't have to be my real name.

You are in America now, he said. You can forget the past and begin anew.

I thought the man was joking, but his face remained serious, waiting for my response.

Thank you, I said, but I'll keep my name.

I didn't tell him that my name was all I had. My name and my memories.

ELEVEN

Teeming Shore

Rows of beds in a shelter for newly arrived Mariel refugees, 1980.

*O*N MOTHER'S DAY, Mercedes Alvarez woke up in the hospital, her arms wrapped around her baby's feverish body. Mercedes had known for days that her one-year-old son was sick. The boy was pallid and thin, and he had constant bouts of diarrhea. But for more than a month, ever since she'd walked onto the Peruvian embassy grounds with her husband and three small children, Mercedes had refused to return home, as both the Cuban and Peruvian governments had urged her to do. She had resisted her husband's pleas and her children's tears and even their illnesses.

The majority of the more than 10,000 people who had sought asylum at the Peruvian embassy in early April had heeded the government's advice and, trusting both Peru's and Cuba's promises, had returned to their homes with a pass until their permanent departure from Cuba could be arranged. Mercedes didn't know what had become of those people, but there were rumors that they'd been bullied and insulted and sometimes beaten by angry mobs waiting for them at home. She'd also heard that some families had been separated—the government allowing the mother to go with one of the children while keeping behind the father and the others.

And then there was the case that had kept her on edge, unable to fully rest at night. An eleven-year-old boy had gotten too close to the fence and, trusting a Cuban guard on the other side, had confided he missed his house, his friends, and his school. The guard quickly snatched the boy and took him away while his horrified parents yelled after him in vain. There were other rumors, but they were so good, so full of hope, that Mercedes simply could not believe them. She'd been told that many of the families who until recently had been at the embassy had left Cuba for the United States through a boatlift initiated by the Cuban government at the port of Mariel. She could not understand such generosity from her own government. Afraid, confused, and distrustful, Mercedes resolved to wait until the day the Peruvians took charge of her and her family and sent her to Lima, a city she couldn't locate on a map but that had become the repository of all her longings in the last five weeks.

In Lima, she visualized every day, she would take a bath, the longest bath of her life. She would finally brush her teeth and put on makeup and change her shoes and wear new clothes and have a healthy baby, the first of her children to be born in a land of freedom and, she imagined, abundance. The thought was so attractive to her that the buzzing stories about Mariel and Key West and Miami were nothing but unwelcome distractions in her daydreams, white noise for a crowded mind intent on following only its own compass.

Two days before Mother's Day, though, Mercedes's resolve collapsed. The doctors who oversaw the care of the more than 700 refugees still left in the embassy urged her to allow them to take her dehydrated baby to a hospital. They called an ambulance and told her the boy would die if he didn't get immediate help. Mercedes had no choice but to accompany her son, leaving her other two children in the embassy with their father.

When she woke up on Sunday May 11, Mercedes felt an intense heat in her heart that spread throughout her body: a desperate, physical need to see her mother. On Friday, when she arrived at the hospital, she had quickly given her mother's telephone number to a patient in the emergency room who had approached her, curious about all the security that surrounded her and her son. Call my mother and tell her where I am and that I need to see her, please, Mercedes pleaded with the woman. By now her mother should have received her message. In fact, she should have come yesterday, Mercedes thought, since today no visitors were allowed.

Careful not to wake her son, Mercedes unwrapped her arms from his lithe body and got up. Nearby she noticed two police officers guarding the access to her room. They, or a pair that looked just like them, had been there since she'd arrived at the hospital.

When the staff began their daily routines, Mercedes tried to busy herself with the care of her son, following the nurses' every movement and trying to concentrate on the doctor's words: diet . . . clean . . . wash his hands . . . home . . . home . . . you should go home. But all she could think about was the burning sensation that radiated from her pained heart. She is not going to come. She is not going to come, Mercedes kept repeating to herself to assuage her anxiety, to distract her brain from her real wish—that her mother might just get the message and show up at the hospital.

Sometime in the late afternoon, just when she had convinced herself that her mother was not coming, Mercedes looked up and saw her in the hallway, walking toward her, oblivious to the two police officers calling for her to stop. One called for backup. Her mother kept walking, a smile stretching her lips all the way to her ears, or so it seemed to Mercedes.

Mercedes started to get up from her chair. She felt trapped in a slow-motion movie scene, stretching the moment as if savoring the anticipated feel of her mother's chest crushed against her tear-soaked face. Instead she watched her mother being led away by a policewoman. Horrified, Mercedes saw that her mother, freeing herself from the policewoman's grip, turned around to blow her a kiss. Right then Mercedes began wailing. First softly, as if to herself, and then deeply and loudly, so that everyone in the hospital would learn, once and for all, that she had gone mad.

She finally got up from her chair, yelled her mother's last name—Navarro! Navarro!—just as she always did when addressing her on an important matter. Navarro! Navarro! she repeated, and ran to the door, but a police officer stopped her. No visitors today for embassy people, he said, and Mercedes felt the uncontrollable urge to spit on his face. But she didn't. She swallowed hard and did the only thing that could possibly give her more pain than not hugging her mother ever again: She ran to her son's bed, pulled all the needles from his arm, and lifted him up to her chest.

Get me an ambulance! she ordered to no one in particular. I'm taking him back to the embassy. There is nothing left for us to do here.

Alarmed, nurses and doctors rushed to the room and tried to reason with her.

Señora, the doctor said, calling her by the bourgeois title hardly anybody ever used anymore and that Mercedes realized she'd acquired by virtue of being a *gusana* in the embassy. She wailed even harder. *Señora*, the doctor tried again. If you take him from this room, he will surely die.

Mercedes's knees buckled, but she held on to her son even tighter.

One of the doctors rushed down the hall and returned to the room with Mercedes's mother in tow. Perhaps you can convince her, as a mother, he pleaded.

Navarro put her arms around her daughter.

You know what's best for him, she said, soothingly. And on she went, caressing her daughter's hair until Mercedes allowed the doctors to take her son from her and hook him up to the IV again. All Mercedes wanted to do was to hold her mother and never let go.

When Mercedes had calmed down, the doctors gave the guards a nod. Visiting time was over, the guards said softly. They had made an exception, they explained. Given the circumstances. But the mother had to go. Mercedes had to understand. Navarro glanced at the guards and doctors, asking for a little privacy for a proper good-bye. When mother and daughter were alone, Navarro pulled back her daughter's hair to whisper in her ear. Mercedes expected a loving farewell, perhaps a kiss. Instead, in a total reversal of what she'd just said publicly, Navarro spoke the only words her daughter was unprepared to hear: Listen carefully, my child. Do not leave the embassy. Do not leave. It's your only safe ticket out of this country. These monsters don't believe in women or children. Don't trust them. Take your son and go back.

Mercedes's face froze as she listened to her mother. She had the sense, even as it was happening, that her mother's advice would change the course of her life.

Without a word Mercedes watched her mother walk to the end of the hall, flanked by the two guards. Remember what I told you! her mother yelled before boarding an elevator. The next day Mercedes calmly told the doctors she needed an ambulance to take her son back to the embassy. This time the doctors complied. At the embassy everyone asked her what had happened. She didn't tell them, but Mercedes had begun to mourn her mother and her country. She was now certain that she would never again walk the streets of Havana.

* * *

TWO DAYS AFTER I'd settled in my uncle's house in Hialeah, President Jimmy Carter took the first firm steps to stem the flood of Cubans from Mariel. On May 14, all the television networks trained their cameras on the president as he outlined a five-point program aimed at regaining control of his country's southern shores.

The thrust of the plan, prepared by three of President Carter's closest advisers—Stuart Eizenstat, Zbigniew Brzezinski, and Jack Watson—was to force or embarrass Castro into stopping the boatlift while preserving the image of the United States as a nation that welcomed refugees, but on its own terms. The recommendations also attempted to extricate the president, ever so delicately, from the hole he'd dug for himself and his administration in his May 5 "open arms" speech.

The new policy stipulated that the United States would provide "safe and orderly passage" from Cuba to four categories of people: former political prisoners who'd been inside the U.S. Interests Section in Havana since May 2, when a club- and machete-wielding mob chased them down for wanting to leave Cuba; former political prisoners who'd been promised visas two years earlier and were still waiting to leave; people who'd sought asylum in the Peruvian embassy; and close family members of Cuban-Americans. But, the president warned, U.S. officials must screen all the refugees in Cuba before they set foot in Key West. The rules also threatened to impose stiff penalties, including prosecution and seizure of their boats, on those who continued to bring refugees illegally to the country, and left no doubt that Washington was aware of Castro's game: The president instructed the attorney general to begin exclusion proceedings against more than four hundred refugees believed to be hardened criminals.

With all other avenues exhausted and Castro showing no interest in negotiating an end to the mass exodus of people from his island, the administration had no other choice but to unilaterally halt the boatlift. Not that other options hadn't been contemplated and even, to some degree, attempted. The biggest effort so far had been geared toward two goals: internationalize the crisis by getting other countries involved and convince the Miami Cubans that sailing to the island to bring back refugees was not merely illegal but also dangerous.

Both efforts had failed. Only Great Britain and Costa Rica had sided with the United States in attempting to convince Castro to stop the boatlift, but Castro had so far refused to meet with anyone remotely close to the American government. And Miami Cubans, accustomed to playing by the rules of their adopted country, had not reacted well to the government's attempts to seek an orderly migration. The pull of family was too strong, while the repercussions for breaking the law were not serious enough. Nine vessels had been seized, but no fines had been collected. Top officials in Washington were convinced that the flotilla would continue as long as Castro wanted it to and as long as Cuban-Americans believed that it was their only chance to be reunited with their loved ones.

The impact of the May 14 announcement was not immediately felt, but at least now there was a stated policy to guide the many Americans dealing with the consequences of the boatlift, both immediate—such as overseeing the arrival and relocation of the refugees—and long-term—meeting their medical and educational needs and, more important, finding them jobs.

More than four hundred additional active-duty and reserve coast guard personnel from the eastern United States were called to the tip of South Florida to help enforce the new regulations. Six coast guard cutters, nine aircraft, six utility boats and fourteen boating-safety detachments were also sent in to reinforce coast guard and navy units. Customs agents immediately slapped seizure notices on more than seventy vessels, and the coast guard sent an urgent marine broadcast advising all boats to return to the United States empty and without delay, to comply with the president's new orders.

BY THE TIME the new policy was in place, most South Floridians were ready to accept it. More Cubans—86,488—arrived in May 1980 than in all of 1962, the year that up until then had seen the largest influx of Cuban refugees. More telling than the total numbers, however, was the composition of the boatlift. The majority were young, single men, many of whom admitted they had served jail time in Cuba, though their crimes ranged from attempting to leave the country illegally to having long hair or punching someone at a bar. In fact, the average Marielito, as Mariel refugees were contemptibly called, had no adult memory of pre-Castro Cuba and was unaware of the burdens and perils of freedom. After years of being told what to do by an ever-watchful state, Marielitos were eager to plunge into freedom, but many didn't know how.

Faced with the riddle of exile life in the United States, the daily struggle between wanting and fearing, between nostalgia and the wondrous possibilities of the American dream, some were unable to adapt. A few returned to Cuba or made the attempt while the boatlift was still going on by stealing boats or hijacking planes. Others turned to a life of crime, or chose death, as did Conrado Monés, a twenty-nine-year-old former biology teacher who climbed into a polar bear's cage at Central Park Zoo in New York City.

But the overwhelming majority of Mariel refugees were not so dramatic about their sorrow or so uncertain about their fate in their new country. They quietly slipped into the fabric of the city that had reluctantly welcomed them and went to work.

Still, there were inevitable clashes: between the Cubans who were already settled in Miami and the new arrivals; between African-Americans who saw their share of the pie get ever smaller with every refugee wave and the Marielitos who wanted more, better, and now; and between the old white Miamians, who were aghast that so many of their neighbors spoke a language other than English, and the fresh-off-the boat refugees who were too busy working to worry about their neighbors' fears.

A *Miami Herald* poll revealed that 68 percent of non-Hispanic whites and 57 percent of African-Americans in Dade County felt that Mariel refugees would have a largely negative impact in the area. Some people in Miami began sporting bumper stickers that read WILL THE LAST AMERICAN TO LEAVE MIAMI PLEASE TAKE THE FLAG? and newspaper stories with headlines such as DELUGE ADDS TO FEAR IN UNEASY MIAMI described a population torn between good intentions and self-protection. The influential *New York Times* columnist James Reston echoed the sentiments of many Americans when he wrote in a May 16 column that Castro was "exporting his failures." Castro's policy, he went on, "is to get rid of his unemployed opponents, even his criminals and mental cripples, and send them to the United States." An editorial in the same paper that day chastised Castro for dumping "criminals, even leprosy patients into the boats."

Rather than focusing on the unprecedented event of thousands of people taking to the sea to flee Castro's regime, the media repeated Castro's unfounded assertion that everyone who wanted to leave the island was scum. The unquestioned
acceptance of Castro's version of the boatlift demonstrated once again the hold he
still maintained over the imagination of Americans and, particularly, of Cubans
everywhere. In Miami, as well as on the island, they believed him.

SOUTH FLORIDIANS began to sour on the boatlift on May 11, the day I arrived in the *Mañana* just hours after the *America* had reached Key West at dawn.
The 120-foot catamaran carried on her three decks more than 700 refugees,
about half of them looking suspiciously unlike any other group of people who
had arrived before. The men on board, many wearing the same khaki clothes, did
not react as others had when reaching the land of freedom. They didn't cheer or
cry. They remained quiet, eyes fixed on the ground, as if still in chains. It was obvious to the authorities that many on the *America* had done time in jail.

The boat and its cargo made an immediate impression, in part because U.S.
reporters and authorities had been expecting it. The *New York Times* story that
Schumacher had dispatched from Mariel the day before had alerted the authorities to the particularities of the criminal population aboard two vessels, the
America and the *Valley Chief*. The men on board these two boats were said to have
committed crimes that ranged from theft and vagrancy to trying to leave the
country illegally, the article explained.

The *Valley Chief*, the boat that was supposed to bring my father and uncle to
Key West, didn't make it back. It probably sank after the USS *Saipan* rescued
them and the others. But the *America* arrived as expected. And when it did,
newspaper and television photographers focused their lenses on the faces of men
unaccustomed to having their pictures taken. Instead of mothers holding babies
and weathered old men kissing the ground upon disembarking—the images
weary Americans had grown accustomed to—people saw the faces of the boatlift
they would come to dread: thin men with sallow complexions, missing or rotten
teeth, averted eyes, shaved heads.

After an initial screening, U.S. officials did not detain any of the new arrivals as suspected dangerous criminals, demonstrating once again that the definition of crime, even delinquency, upheld by the Cuban government was not shared by U.S. authorities, who weren't in the habit of sending a man to jail for refusing to work, stealing a bicycle, or wanting to leave his country. The refugees from the *America* scattered, but the searing images of their despair, alienation, and displacement remained.

Eight weeks later Jim Hampton, the editor of the *Miami Herald*, published a column in which he pointed to May 11 as the day his support of the boatlift had begun to erode. As it happened, that was the day that broke all previous records for daily arrivals; 4,588 refugees aboard fifty-eight boats were processed between midnight Saturday, May 10, and 6:30 P.M. Sunday, May 11, among them my family and me. At the end of that day, the total number of refugees clocked in Key West had reached 37,000, or 10 percent of Miami's total population at the time.

RIGHT ABOUT THEN, Napoleón Vilaboa began to feel the heat. His telephone at home rang at all hours. You did this. You've turned Miami into an inferno. You will burn in hell! anonymous voices yelled into his ear. In the streets people openly called him a Castro agent, a worse insult in Miami than murderer. Vilaboa told his family not to answer the phone, and he began to look over his shoulder whenever he walked out of his house. His friend in Havana, René Rodríguez, advised him to leave town.

Of course, it didn't start out that way. At the beginning of the boatlift, Vilaboa had briefly been anointed a hero, the man of the hour, interviewed by reporters from radio, television, and newspapers. He became a fixture on the six o'clock news. He had urged Miami Cubans to follow him to Mariel, and he had delivered. Thousands of families were now reunited because of him. He'd been able to get his own twenty-two-year-old daughter out, the one he'd left behind as a toddler so many years earlier when he went to Mexico.

Eventually, though, the shine on Mariel wore off, and Vilaboa became the villain in the picture. Yet the more people tried to make him feel guilty, the more Vilaboa shied away from any responsibility for the boatlift. True, he had given the Cuban government the idea for the flotilla, or so he boasted. But he'd never intended it to become the repository of Castro's failures. He had wanted a repeat of Camarioca, a sort of orderly immigration to the United States that had brought families together and infused the Cuban community in Miami with energy and new blood. Instead Castro had twisted his idea in a macabre way. Vilaboa had become, he reluctantly admitted to himself, a victim of Castro's ploy.

On one of his trips to Cuba, Vilaboa asked Rodríguez why the government was sending over so many delinquents in the boatlift. Rodríguez told him that there was nothing the government could do, that those were the kinds of people who wanted to immigrate to the United States. Vilaboa knew that Rodríguez wasn't telling him the truth, but he never asked again.

DESPITE THE BACKLASH against the boatlift, or perhaps because of it, Castro remained undeterred and uncooperative. A *Granma* editorial on May 15 redefined the terms of the standoff: "Carter governs in Florida, but in Mariel, Cuba governs." CIA satellite pictures showed at least fifteen hundred boats waiting at Mariel harbor. Captains who returned to Key West with boats full of refugees they didn't know told coast guard officials that they'd been forced at gunpoint to take them. It was clear that President Carter had not managed to change Castro's edict that no boat shall depart Mariel empty. From then on, some top White House officials began to see the boatlift as an act of war.

"It's just as if he had planted a germ bomb in Miami," U.S. Coordinator for Refugee Affairs Victor H. Palmieri told other top members of the administration during a tense White House meeting at the height of the crisis.

Unlike other acts of war, though, this one had brought people, not bombs, to America's shores. And no one in Washington or in Key West was willing to respond with fire.

IN HIS HOSPITAL ROOM, Héctor Sanyustiz writhed in pain. The bullet that had ripped into his left leg during the embassy break-in had shattered muscle and bits of bone while drilling its way through his body; another bullet had pierced his right buttock. He'd been in the hospital for forty-five days, but he'd never been free of pain, and he'd rarely been alone.

Initially doctors told him they couldn't save his leg and would have to amputate it, but within hours that grim prognosis changed, and Sanyustiz kept his leg. The first night in the hospital, a woman captain from the Ministry of the Interior poured boiling wax on his right hand to test for gun-powder residue. She wanted to know if Sanyustiz had shot the weapon that killed the embassy guard. When Sanyustiz yelled out in pain, the woman yanked his arm and said, What are you complaining about if you had the balls to kill a guard? Sanyustiz stared at the wall and said nothing. He felt small, humiliated, and angry. From that day on, when doctors approached, he would shield his eyes because he couldn't take the hatred he read in their expressions.

Cuban officials who regularly visited him had told him that he should harbor no illusions: He was doomed to stay in Cuba forever. Sanyustiz believed his captors, but he no longer feared that prospect. What frightened him more than staying in Cuba was the certainty that he would be sent to prison or, worse, be executed by a firing squad, the regime's preferred method of disposing of its enemies. Every day mobs of people would congregate on the street in front of the hospital and demand that he and Radamés Gómez, his friend who had been wounded in the head and the back, be executed. ¡Paredón! ¡Paredón! ¡Paredón! To the wall! To the wall! To the wall! they shouted, and Sanyustiz felt like jumping out his third-floor window just so that he wouldn't have to hear their constant chanting.

Once, early in Sanyustiz's hospital stay, Foreign Minister Isidoro Malmierca came to visit and asked him just one question: Why? Sanyustiz told him the truth as he saw it—not the whole truth, but the part that he thought most palatable at the moment. He mumbled something about not being able to find a decent job. Malmiecea stared at him in disbelief and left without another word.

Sanyustiz was not alone in his hospital room. The minister of the interior in Peru had sent him a bodyguard, a young police officer deputized as a diplomat and placed in charge of Sanyustiz's and Radamés's safety. Sanyustiz and the man, named Federico Espinosa, had developed the sort of friendship forged when two people are alone in hostile surroundings. They shared code words and certain signals to deal with the unexpected. They agreed that if Federico ever tied a Peruvian flag to the bed, it would mean that the Cuban police were about to take Sanyustiz away.

That would be your end, Federico told him.

Federico kept a diary, in which he wrote down every drug Sanyustiz was administered and every procedure he was subjected to. He also wrote about every encounter Sanyustiz had with government officials. So the diary wouldn't be of use to the Cuban government, Federico wrote in hieroglyphics, which he'd learned in a history class at middle school in Lima. If Sanyustiz were ever in trouble, all he needed to do was bang on the wall, and Federico, who shuttled between Sanyustiz's and Radamés's adjacent rooms, would come to his rescue.

At 3:00 A.M. on April 19, the day of the scheduled demonstration in front of the embassy, Sanyustiz called upon Federico when he received an unexpected visitor. A tall man in full military regalia, who identified himself as a colonel of the Ministry of the Interior, had come to see him with an unusual proposition: Sign this document or we won't be able to vouch for your safety today, the man said menacingly.

The document stipulated that Sanyustiz should renounce the protection of the Peruvian government and put himself in the hands of the Cuban government. Sanyustiz didn't understand what the officer meant, but he was not about to trust an emissary of Castro. He turned his head to the wall and asked to be left alone.

Then anything can happen, the man said, getting his face close to Sanyustiz's. One million people, the people of Cuba, will march by your window today on their way to the embassy. They are angry at you, because you've caused all this trouble. If they decide to come to your room and drag you out, there is nothing anybody can do to protect you.

Sanyustiz didn't say anything. His wounded leg was in traction He could barely move because of all the needles poked into him and all the contraptions attached to his body. In despair, he began to bang on the wall. By the time Federico showed up two minutes later, the man had left and Sanyustiz was alone in the dark, trembling with anger and impotence.

When the march at last began, Sanyustiz was glad to be in the hospital and not in the embassy. On the street several floors below, a million people clamored for, among other things, his death. That night, and many others that followed, he was unable to sleep; he refused to take painkillers for fear of being poisoned. He was afraid of the Cuban officials who visited him constantly, and he couldn't stop worrying about his wife and four-year-old son, who were alone at home.

On the morning of May 16, Sanyustiz received another visit from a Cuban officer, a general in a starched olive green uniform with medals of valor pinned to his chest. Sanyustiz knew him well. The general had often brought him newspapers and cigarettes to keep him entertained. Besides Federico and one of the doctors, the general had been the only person to show kindness toward him during his hospital stay, which is why Sanyustiz was immediately interested in what the general had to say: Leave quietly through Mariel and all will be forgiven.

Though the general had made the same offer in the past, Sanyustiz was startled anew. It didn't make sense that the Cuban government would want to send him to the United States instead of punishing him. It was like offering a child dessert before dinner. Too good to be true.

The first time the general had made this offer, about one month into Sanyustiz's hospital stay, Radamés, much recovered from his wounds, had been brought to the room. The general had pressed them to take advantage of the revolution's generosity and leave the island in the boatlift. Sanyustiz had asked why the offer was made only to them and not to the other men and women who'd been on the bus with them. The general explained that the others were inside an embassy crowded with more than 10,000 people and protected by the Peruvian government; it was impossible for any Cuban official to reach them.

Sanyustiz suspected that the general was lying. In a speech shortly after the break-in, Castro had sworn that none of the embassy invaders, those who'd entered by force before he had ordered the withdrawal of the guards, would ever be allowed to leave Cuba. Sanyustiz himself had read the words in the newspaper; so had Radamés, who'd rejected the general's proposition right away. Sanyustiz, too, had dismissed it, but he was less sanguine about it because, despite himself, he liked the general and his gentle, almost European refinement.

Sanyustiz knew that by ramming the bus through the Peruvian embassy gate he'd managed to destabilize the country as had no other event in the last twenty-one years. Thousands of people had left the island, and hundreds of thousands more wanted to follow. Nobody seemed to have any time for work; all everyone talked about was who was leaving and who was staying. The economy, always in poor shape, was on a steep downturn. The world's top newspapers were saying that Cubans, unable to elect their leaders, had found a novel way to make their voices heard: They were voting with their feet.

In his lifetime, Sanyustiz calculated, there had been two decisive political events in Cuba: the revolution, fought and won by thousands of men and women intent on overthrowing the Batista regime, and the Peruvian embassy crisis that had led to the boatlift. Castro was the leader of the first event. And Sanyustiz, because he'd been behind the wheel of the bus, was the protagonist of the latter. He was convinced that the Cuban government would never forgive or forget his actions.

But the general wasn't ready to give up. For his visit on May 16, he had come prepared. He began to chat with Sanyustiz, telling him about his military training in Eastern Europe. You have a family, the general suddenly said. Would you like to see them? Later that same day, Sanyustiz's wife was brought to his room. They were promptly left alone.

Be careful, Sanyustiz's wife told him, confirming his worst fears. I think it's a trap. Don't sign it. Go back to the embassy.

Sanyustiz asked her if she had brought their son. She said he was downstairs, because children were not allowed on his floor. Before Sanyustiz could say anything or ask anyone to let him see his son, the boy was brought to his room by the solicitous general. Sanyustiz had not hugged his son in a month and a half, and when he held him, when he pressed him against his chest and kissed his ears and cheeks, Sanyustiz understood that the Cuban government had won. He would sign the papers. The thought of returning to the embassy without his family was unbearable. If the officer was telling the truth, he reasoned, his son would have a chance to grow up in the United States.

Give me my clothes, Sanyustiz said to his wife, who, following orders from the general, had brought a freshly pressed outfit for her husband. We are leaving today for the United States.

An immigration team was quickly brought to his bed, and in a matter of minutes Sanyustiz had a passport for the first time in his life. In a few hours more, accompanied by his family, he was walking the docks of Mariel with the general by his side. The general asked him to pick a boat, any boat. Sanyustiz, eager to leave, picked the one in front of him, a small pleasure craft. His wife, terrified of the water, saw a large vessel in the distance and pointed. That one, she said. That's the one, then, Sanyustiz repeated.

The general took them to the boat, the *Gulf Star*, which already had about 800 people on board. He shook Sanyustiz's hand and wished him good luck. Sanyustiz and his family sat on the bow of the boat for about six hours until the captain received the order to cast off. As if on cue, the skies opened, and it began to rain hard. Sanyustiz found a spot where he could stretch his legs without suffering too much pain. He didn't want to have to explain his wounds to anybody on the boat or even in the United States. The last words of the general were fresh in his mind: For your own good, don't tell anyone who you are, or you'll put yourself and your family at risk. Remember that.

IT WAS NOT DIFFICULT for Sanyustiz to remain anonymous once he arrived. America was otherwise preoccupied. On May 17, the day the *Gulf Star* reached Key West, an overloaded, thirty-five-foot pleasure craft, called *Olo Yumi*, sank in the Florida Straits with 52 people on board. Coast guard swimmers managed to rescue 38 people and recover 10 bodies. A fifteen-year-old girl lost her entire family, including both parents, her two sisters, and her grandmother.

The tragedy brought the total number of deaths during the boatlift to 24. Coast guard Rear Admiral Benedict L. Stabile sent a telex message to the Cuban border guard explaining the accident and blaming Cuban authorities for it: "This marine tragedy happened because too many persons were put on board the small boat," he wrote. There was no response, but Cuba continued overloading departing boats. Coast guard officials estimated that 90 percent of the vessels returning from Cuba were either overloaded or filled to their maximum capacity. The losses of life were mostly due to "Cuban policies or indifference," the officials concluded in a written report.

That same day in Havana, a huge demonstration was staged in front of the U.S. Interests Section, a near replica of the march in front of the Peruvian embassy in April. This time the marchers were protesting against the 400 Cubans who had sought refuge there to escape a furious government mob two weeks earlier. Close to a million people walked past the Interests Section that day. Though there was no violence, there was plenty of tension, since, per State Department orders, all nonessential personnel had left Havana a day earlier, and the building was manned by a skeleton staff.

Miami, too, was in turmoil on May 17. Violence broke out in Liberty City and other black neighborhoods after a jury acquitted four white Miami police officers accused of killing a black insurance agent. Police cars were burned and fires set at government buildings. Governor Bob Graham mobilized 1,100 National Guardsmen, 170 Florida Highway Patrol troopers, 75 state wildlife officers, and 50 Florida Marine Patrol officers to stop the looting and the riots. Schools were closed. When calm returned on May 21, the damage was assessed: Hundreds of business were burned, looted, or destroyed; 270 people were treated at area hospitals; and 14 had died. The Liberty City riots had cost the city $100 million.

By then Sanyustiz had quietly settled in a Miami Beach hotel, one more boat refugee beginning a life in the United States. Just as he had done in Cuba when he was trying to avoid the authorities, Sanyustiz managed to slip from the clutches of the FBI, the State Department, the CIA, and anyone else who might have had an interest in chatting with the short, unassuming man with the slight limp who had started it all.

ON THE AFTERNOON of June 1, Mercedes Alvarez and her family left the grounds of the Peruvian embassy after fifty-eight days. She was thinner, despite her bulging pregnant belly, and wore the same clothes she'd had on since April 5, the day she jumped over the fence: a tattered brown skirt and a dark brown blouse with a flowery print. Underneath, she wore her husband's briefs. Her own underwear had long ago succumbed to use and many soapless hand washes. Along with 730 others, who like her had refused to go home or leave through Mariel, Mercedes boarded a bus for the airport. Before the bus had left Fifth Avenue, Mercedes turned her head for a long, last look.

The once elegant Peruvian embassy stood abandoned and dilapidated, surrounded by muddy sludge, the remnants of what were once well-tended gardens.
The wire skeleton of a funeral wreath still hung from one of the gates, a memo-
rial to the soldier Pedro Ortiz Cabrera. Mercedes did not allow herself the time
to think about her life in the compound she was leaving behind. She just held her
baby tighter and closed her eyes. When she opened them again, the bus driver
was taking them through some of Miramar's prettiest streets. She tried to find
and store at least one beautiful image from every street she passed: a brilliant
swath of pink, a hummingbird perched on a branch, a yellow hibiscus in full
bloom. The last time, the last time, she kept repeating in her mind, since there
was no one to talk to. No one on the bus dared to speak, fearful of any misinter-
pretation by the armed men guarding them.

It wasn't until she was alone inside the airplane, tended to by solicitous flight
attendants who offered her food and drinks, that Mercedes relaxed enough to
hold her husband's hand. All around her she could hear the others shaking lose
their fears and beginning to talk. The main topic of conversation was, of course,
their fate. They were convinced that their stay in Peru—if indeed they were going to Peru, which Mercedes still doubted—would be brief, lasting only until
they could travel to the United States. That was what the group had understood
from their frequent talks with Peruvian officials.

When the morning light awoke her, the plane was hovering over Lima, but Mercedes, distrustful as usual, did not believe it. In her mind the plane had circled over
the island of Cuba and was landing in the easternmost province, where, she was
sure, they would be detained in a forced-labor camp. They were treated to a full military welcome. Hundreds of men in uniform, bearing long weapons, faced the airplane. No one smiled or cheered as the Cubans descended. Someone who seemed
to be in charge approached them and told them not to fear the display of force. It's
the customary welcoming for important visitors, he said. Not a threat at all.

The group walked into the airport terminal, and it was there that Mercedes
realized she was no longer in Cuba. Floating above a cafeteria, Mercedes saw the
distinctive red letters of a Coca-Cola sign, a sight she hadn't seen except in the
movies. Yes, she thought, this must be what capitalism looks like.

That same day the group was taken to what Mercedes and the others were told would be a temporary home: a park in the middle of Lima, outfitted with military-style tents and cots. The grass was as high as Mercedes's knees, and there was little privacy. She had traded the discomforts of the Peruvian embassy for the humiliation of life in a public park, only the thin material of an army tent protecting her from the sun and the rain and the curious stares of passersby. But Mercedes was thrilled. After the living hell she'd endured for so long, the sight of clean sheets and plentiful food under the stars of a friendly city was heaven. She was so grateful she cried. Paradise indeed.

ERNESTO PINTO, who had been assigned to a desk job in charge of economic development since his return from Cuba, knew about the arrival of the embassy refugees. The park where the Cubans were housed was about a half-hour's drive from his office, but he didn't feel the need to visit them. By profession and temperament, he was in the habit of compartmentalizing. Havana, Castro, and the Cubans were no longer his problem. He had been asked to stay in Lima after returning to his country to negotiate a high-level meeting between Cuba and Peru, and he was content with the way his government had handled the crisis. No one had died a violent death inside the embassy, the very thing he'd tried to avoid since the day of the break-in, and most had gotten out, one way or another.

However, a small detail kept nagging him. Better than anybody else in his government, he knew that the Cubans in the park did not want to be there. Their cherished destination, he knew, was the United States—more specifically, Miami—and he also knew that no one had promised them a visa to Miami. In Lima you will be free to go to the United States if you wish, he'd told the Cubans at the embassy, but he didn't tell them that no one in Peru held the keys to that golden door. Once in Peru, they had as much of a chance to travel to Miami as any other Peruvian of little or no means. In time, he hoped, they might even get used to Peru and stop wishing they were someplace else.

＊ ＊ ＊

THREE WEEKS AFTER President Carter had issued orders to stop the boatlift, the Panamanian freighter *Red Diamond* sailed from Mariel with 731 refugees on board, including 35 infants. The coast guard became aware of the *Red Diamond* on June 2, when the captain radioed for urgent medical assistance halfway across the straits. A three-day-old baby was severely dehydrated, and a woman was in labor. There were so many people on board that the officers who intercepted the boat asked their supervisors if such an overloaded boat ought to be sent back.

Admiral Joe Costello, the chief of coast guard operations in Washington, D.C., was one of the supervisors called. He in turn called the White House situation room and very quickly got top officials from the departments of State and Justice, as well as members of the cabinet, on the line. The choices were limited—shoot them or accept them—and we can't accept them, one official told Admiral Costello. "Are you telling me you want a coast guard officer to shoot an unarmed refugee to turn them around? If you're going to want that to be done, you're going to have to put it in writing, because that is an order I can't accept," the admiral replied. At that moment Jack Watson, the president's assistant for intergovernmental affairs, chimed in and stopped the conversation. "Let them in," he said. The refugees got in, but the captain of the *Red Diamond* was arrested.

The *Red Diamond* was the last big ship to come from Mariel. The following week only 1,684 refugees arrived, and the week after that, 564. By the middle of June, there were 113,969 Marielitos in Miami.

WITH MIAMI BURSTING with refugees, the authorities opened the Krome Avenue Detention Center at an abandoned missile site near the Everglades as a temporary processing station, primarily for 14,000 Haitians who had arrived in an earlier exodus that year. On July 25, a so-called Tent City was set up under the I-95 overpass near the Miami River to house 650 Cuban refugees who awaited resettlement and had lived since June on the grounds of the Orange Bowl stadium. More than 60,000 Cuban refugees who lacked sponsors had already been sent to military bases across the country, in Florida, Arkansas, Pennsylvania, and Wisconsin. In two days, 200 more had moved into Tent City. Quickly the collection of army tents under the rumbling expressway became a ghetto, a first for Miami's proud Cuban community.

Fourteen Miami city employees worked at the camp, where their main task was to keep hundreds of mostly single, unemployed men from fighting each other or rebelling against the policemen who watched over them. Two meals were served every day in the camp, but the refugees were responsible for everything else—from doing their laundry to keeping the newly poured asphalt clean and the trash neatly stashed away. People left daily for jobs that paid as little as a dollar an hour or for the homes of sponsors. Others—new arrivals or some who had been rejected by their sponsors—took their places.

As in all ghettos, life in Tent City became a revolving door of frustration, simmering desperation, and anger. An official inspection in August 1980 yielded sixteen violations of health and safety regulations, including dangerously exposed wires, broken plumbing, and plugged storm drains that created a lake in the camp when it rained. The men and women who lived there wanted jobs, homes, comfort, even just a little kindness. But a housing shortage, a deepening recession, widespread unemployment, and the dual influx of Cubans and Haitians had left South Florida all but depleted of resources, stamina, and goodwill. There was little comfort for anyone and at times an almost total absence of compassion. One young refugee in Tent City told reporters he had returned to live under the expressway because his sponsor, an uncle, had been repulsed by his homosexuality. Thirty-two requested to go back to Cuba, but there was no treaty that allowed for their repatriation.

There were glimpses of generosity in Tent City, though, and even the incipient sprouting of an entrepreneurial spirit. At least four coffee vendors roamed the camp offering tiny cups of Cuban coffee for twenty-five cents. One of them, a refugee named Nury Torralba, told a reporter he got paid for only one out every three or four cups he sold, but he couldn't turn anyone down for lack of money. If the refugees had imagined that the streets of America were paved with gold, in Tent City they learned that the gold was anywhere but in the steaming, dirty, often-flooded asphalt of their first home in Miami.

• • •

BERNARDO BENES, who had continued traveling to Cuba after the release of the prisoners, was moved by the plight of the refugees from the beginning. He could not fathom Castro's reason for sending over so many unwanted refugees in an election year, unless of course he was secretly rooting for Ronald Reagan to win the presidency. As a man attuned to the way U.S. politics worked, Benes understood that the boatlift would ultimately damage President's Carter reelection bid.

In one of his meetings with Castro during those days, Benes found an opportunity to make his point: Fidel, he said, I didn't know you had become a political sergeant for Reagan. Castro gave him a surprised look. Benes couldn't tell whether it was real or feigned. He could not conceive that Castro, a man who had survived and made a mockery of six American presidents, could be so ignorant of U.S. politics. Each Cuban you send through Mariel is one less vote for Jimmy Carter, Benes told him. Castro didn't respond. By then, though, Benes had lost some of his clout with the Cuban government, in part because he'd been unable to deliver a complacent White House. In June 1980, Benes sent a private memo to Castro inviting José Luis Padrón to his son's bar mitzvah. Castro never replied to the memo and Padrón missed the party.

Back in Miami there was little Benes could do to alleviate the refugees' situation. One day in May, he had an inspiration. He brought thirty-two handpicked new arrivals to the lobby of his bank in the heart of Cuban Miami's Calle Ocho. With the help of the bank's lawyer, Benes unfurled several maps of Dade County and dusted off some old books to teach the refugees what he thought they needed to know to understand their new home. Avenues run north to south, he told them, streets west to east. Flagler Street divides north from south. And on and on Benes and the lawyer went, talking nonstop for two hours—about how to get a driver's license, how the courts worked, how to enroll children in school, how to treat police, how to find a job. In the faces of his pupils, he saw that no one had taken the time to explain that in their new country rights entailed responsibilities.

At the time Benes had not yet realized that the wheels of Mariel had been set in motion three years earlier: the day he agreed to meet with the Cubans in

Panama. Mariel, he had concluded, was an aberration, a hiccup in the path of reconciliation that he'd envisioned for Cuba and the United States. When this blows over, if Carter manages to hold on to the White House, he thought, we'll go back to normal. What that would mean for Cubans on both sides of the Florida Straits, he didn't know, but Benes was confident that it would have to be better than what they now had.

FIVE MONTHS INTO the boatlift, in early September, the police updated crime statistics for Little Havana, where many of the new arrivals had settled: Robbery was up 775 percent, auto theft 284.2 percent, burglary 190.8 percent, assault 109.5 percent. LITTLE HAVANA STRUCK BY BOATLIFT CRIMINALS, announced the *Miami Herald* in a headline on September 18. Weary police officers in Miami Beach began writing the letter *R* on their report every time a suspect was described as a refugee, while the Beach's chief of police directly blamed Mariel arrivals for the wave of crime in his municipality. With little evidence as to who had committed a specific criminal act, police usually blamed Cuban refugees, because the victims invariably described their assailants as young men who spoke no English.

Very few voices rose to point out that crime—fueled by drugs and a sluggish economy—had been on the upswing since the year before the Cubans arrived, or that Mariel refugees were more often the victims than the perpetrators of violent crimes. For the first time in the history of Dade County, in 1980 the tally of Hispanic homicide victims surpassed that for black men. A *Herald* story detailing 53 murders in July—one of the most violent months of 1980, up till then the deadliest year in Dade County history—demonstrates the point. Out of the fifty-three persons slain that month, four were Mariel refugees. Among the killers, two were Mariel refugees, but one, a watchman, had acted in self-defense.

The first Mariel refugee to meet a violent death in Miami was Juan José Toledo, who was killed by a police officer. Police said that Toledo pulled a box cutter on an officer at a health clinic on May 17. The officer shot him twice. Witnesses claimed they saw no weapon on Toledo, only a cardboard sign that clinic workers had hung around his neck: I AM A PARANOID SCHIZOPHRENIC.

* * *

IN MID-SEPTEMBER, Peter Tarnoff, executive secretary of the Department of State, flew to Havana to meet with Castro to convince him to put a stop to Mariel.

The president's May 14 plan had succeeded up to a point. Few boats remained at Mariel; most returned empty. While during May and even early June, anywhere from 17,000 to 22,000 refugees had arrived per week, in August the number had dwindled to as low as 280 in the first week of the month. Clearly, Mariel was dead, and the Carter administration was eager to bury its unsightly corpse.

Accompanied by Wayne Smith, the top U.S. diplomat in Cuba, Tarnoff held two brief conversations with Castro, in which he brought up only the issues the U.S. government was willing to negotiate once the boatlift was halted, including a widening of relations, a relaxation of the embargo to exempt food and medicine, and the formulation of an orderly immigration program, as suggested by President Carter's new plan.

Castro didn't seem to need any convincing. He told Tarnoff and Smith he had already decided to stop Mariel and also end the crisis at the U.S. Interests Section, where at least 50 Cubans remained from the original group of 400 that had sought asylum there in May. Castro, however, did not want to give the impression that he was responding to any kind of pressure from Washington and thus refused to discuss any of the other points until after the U.S. presidential election.

Tarnoff assumed that Mariel had taken its toll on Castro. The state of anxiety and paralysis in which Mariel had immersed the country since April could not linger forever. Castro may also have been concerned by the backlash he was beginning to feel from the boatlift. The anger in the United States toward his rhetoric and behavior regarding Mariel was so widespread that he may have feared he'd finally managed to alienate even his staunchest supporters.

ON SEPTEMBER 23 the last of the Cubans in the U.S. Interests Section left the building safely, on their way to the United States. Three days later, on Thursday,

September 25, boat captains still at Mariel heard the Cuban bullhorns ordering them to shore. The crews of more than a hundred boats boarded dinghies, hopeful that the calls signaled that relatives awaited at the docks, ready to be picked up. Instead the captains were diverted to a warehouse for a meeting with a Cuban army colonel.

"Good morning," the colonel said, adding without preamble, "Mariel is closed. You all must go."

The colonel gave them thirty-four hours to leave Cuba. Some of the boats had been waiting at Mariel for more than a month. Everyone understood that there was no use arguing against rules set by the Cuban government. Fifty boats made it back to Florida on Friday, empty. A hundred more arrived on Saturday. The last boat to carry refugees from Mariel was a fifty-five-foot pleasure craft called the *Hedonist*. With 188 Cubans aboard, it had reached Key West the Thursday before the announcement, bringing the total number of Cuban arrivals in the flotilla to 125,266; about 600 who were left at the port when the boatlift was halted were flown to the United States two months later.

Just as it had started 159 days earlier, suddenly and unilaterally, Mariel shut down. No note appeared in *Granma*, which dedicated most of its pages to the adventures of the first Cuban astronaut in space aboard a Russian mission. A single sign was left behind in the streets of the town of Mariel. It read CLEAR THE COUNTRY OF BUMS!

TWO MONTHS LATER President Carter lost the election, receiving just 41 percent of the popular vote. Only six states—including Georgia, his home state, and the District of Columbia—supported his reelection. Floridians overwhelmingly rejected him, choosing instead Ronald Reagan, a conservative Republican with a strong anticommunist rhetoric, viewed as someone who could easily put Castro in his place and never allow another Mariel. Among other pressing tasks, Reagan was expected to right the wrongs of the boatlift.

Indeed, in December 1984, after months of secret negotiations, Washington and Havana signed an agreement to deport to the island 2,746 undesirables of Mariel. The announcement met virtually no resistance. Marielitos had yet to find their voices, while the Cubans who had come in earlier immigration waves were more concerned about what the boatlift had done to their pristine image as the country's most successful group of Hispanic émigrés than about the fate of 2,746 human beings whom nobody seemed to want anyway. Few in Miami or in Havana understood that the deportation of Mariel refugees was the first step in the gradual erosion of the white-glove treament Cuban immigrants had thus far received.

TWELVE

With Open Arms

Meeting Gustavo Pique, one of the Mariel detainees involved
in the takeover of the Atlanta Federal Penitentiary in 1987.

I WAS AT the movies with my cousins in the fall of 1980 the first time I understood a complete sentence in English: "It seems you are coming down with a cold," the main actor told his costar. The phrase is etched in my memory, because understanding it marked the moment I began to feel, not just intuit, the possibilities of life in the United States. It was as if I'd been handed a key, a how-to manual that would allow me to decode my new world. If I could understand, I would eventually speak. And if I managed to speak, I could learn to write. Writing was important because I never seriously considered a career other than journalism, and I was determined not to lose myself, even if I had lost my country.

At times, though, it was difficult to conceive of a future without Cuba. The island and my sixteen years there exerted a strong pull that on some days threatened to drown me. With my socialist-trained eye, I cast a quizzical look at everyone and everything around me. Invariably I came up mildly disappointed. Fashion seemed decadent, drugs epidemic, and freedom overrated.

During the months of Mariel, all I could dream about was returning to Cuba in the same boatlift that had brought me to the States, but I was too busy just trying to get by from day to day to actually carry out any plan, no matter how many times I rehearsed in my head my return to our Santos Suárez apartment, to my friends, even to my boyfriend, Frank, whom I knew had already returned from Angola. From 1980 to 1984, I remember little but my near-constant pining for Cuba and my relentless drive to learn English. I read only English-language books and magazines, sometimes one word at a time with the aid of a dictionary. Past tenses of irregular verbs confounded me; prepositions to this day baffle me. Still, I managed to graduate from college with honors in 1986, and the following year I landed a job at the *Miami Herald*.

Through journalism, I thought, I could achieve distance. Distance was vital, because seven years after Mariel I was still limping through life, maimed by my exile condition. I enjoyed the new freedoms but, paradoxically, missed the restrictions that I had rebelled against in Cuba. Overwhelmed, I stuck to routines, and sought the company of other Marielitos. My pain then was too raw and too precious to share, and to them I didn't have to explain how and why longing and repulsion shared the same chamber of my heart. Journalism was a way to delve into the sorrows of others, while leaving my own intact.

Three months into my budding career as a *Miami Herald* journalist, I took a better-paying, more exciting job at *El Nuevo Herald*, a Spanish-language newspaper launched on November 20, 1987, by Knight Ridder, the *Herald*'s parent company. That same day the U.S. government announced a resumption of the 1984 immigration agreement that Castro had suspended in May 1985, angry at the launching of Radio Martí, a U.S. station broadcasting into Cuba. After a two-year hiatus, the governments had gone back to the negotiating table to proceed with the deportation of jailed Mariel Cubans, proving once again that, for Washington and Havana, refugees were pawns in a never-ending game of Cold War politics neither was able to win or willing to concede.

In November 1987, there were roughly 7,600 Mariel Cubans imprisoned in the United States; about half had finished their sentences but were being held in indefinite detention, while the others were still serving time; 210 of the total number of Marielitos in jails, however, had been held continuously since 1980, either because they were mentally unstable or because the authorities suspected they had committed serious crimes in Cuba. Marielitos under the custody of the Justice Department became known as "lifers" or "excludables," which meant they could be held until either Cuba took them back or they died. Despite their dire situation, few of them wanted to return to Cuba, preferring prison in the United States to an uncertain life in their own country.

The day after the agreement became public, a group of Mariel detainees held at the Federal Detention Center, in Oakdale, Louisiana, took over the prison to protest their imminent deportation to Cuba. Two days later a news flash popped onto my editor's computer: "Atlanta is on fire!" Marielitos held in the Atlanta Penitentiary were also rebelling against deportations. My editor scanned the newsroom looking for a willing person to hop on a plane to Georgia, but she didn't have to look far; I was right behind her, peering at the screen over her shoulder.

WITHIN FIVE HOURS I was in Atlanta, standing in front of the penitentiary, shivering with cold in my Miami autumn outfit—a loose cotton skirt and open-toed royal blue sandals—and wondering how I was going to cover an event happening inside a burning building surrounded by men with guns from every law-enforcement branch of the federal government. I had two advantages: I spoke Spanish, and I understood the plight of the detainees and their families. For the next two weeks, I paced up and down the sidewalk in front of the penitentiary, searching for—and often finding—stories to tell.

One dreadfully cold night, I joined a group of reporters who were interviewing the very talkative wife of one of the detainees. She and her husband had a three-year-old child, she said. He was a good man, but he had a temper. She looked about thirty-five, most of her teeth were gone, and her lithe figure couldn't conceal the telltale signs of alcohol abuse: swollen face, slightly protruding belly, bulging red eyes. Because the ink of my pen had frozen, I put it inside the front of my jeans to warm it up and retreated from the group, trying to guess where she was from. I couldn't place her heavily accented English, but assumed she wasn't Cuban, mainly because I'd never met a Cuban who looked as ruined by life as she did.

When the other reporters left, I went back to the woman and tried to make conversation.

¡Qué frío! she said, bracing against the cold. And with that phrase and the way she hugged her body with her own arms I realized that the woman in front of me was Cuban, like me. Instinctively I took out my pen, by now warm and ready, and began taking notes.

When did you come from Cuba? I asked.

Por el Mariel, she said, as if I should have known. I kept writing, trying not to allow my face to reveal my surprise. Marielita, like me, I thought.

I didn't say or even think the word "Marielita" lightly. To me, it was a badge of honor, a recognition that I belonged to a group of people who had once left their country as ballast and had managed to stay afloat, and even attain a measure of success. But many other Mariel refugees shunned the term, even pretending they had come from Cuba in 1979, as relatives of former political prisoners. To them, having left Cuba in 1980 as opposed to, say, a year earlier, implied not an act of courage, as I viewed it, but a weakness of character: What was wrong with me, with my family, that the government had had to kick me out? People never actually asked me that question, but I could feel their brains churning out unspoken and impolite questions such as that one the moment I revealed that I was a Marielita. Castro had managed to dominate the narrative of Mariel from the beginning and, in the process, had stripped all of us of free will. We didn't leave our country, see, we were kicked out, tossed overboard like bags of ballast in a sinking ship, or so the story went.

And now here was this woman in front of me, someone I was both repelled by and drawn to. I desperately wanted to hug her, and tell her I, too, had come in the boatlift. I understood, I wanted to say, but I had been well trained. I kept my distance and went on with the interview.

And how old are you? I asked, dutifully running through my memorized list of required questions. What she did for a living was next. I never got to it.

Twenty-three, she said suddenly.

Twenty-three, like me. I put my pen down and looked her in the eye. What happened to you? I wanted to ask but didn't. Instead I scrutinized her face for signs that she was lying.

She said her life had changed when she arrived in Key West, alone and scared, following a boyfriend who left her after about a month in Miami. She had tried to return to her family in Cuba but had not been able to. Then she met the man who was just across the street from us, one of the leaders of the prison takeover, and here she was, standing on a cold Atlanta street, chasing her version of the American dream. All she wanted was for the government not to deport her husband so her child could grow up with a father. All I wanted, I realized as soon as she finished talking, was a chance to tell her story.

THE RIOTS ENDED when the Justice Department promised a review process that would eventually free many of the detainees. In Atlanta, I was one of only two reporters allowed to witness the signing of the agreement inside the federal penitentiary. My first-person account of the events of that night, December 4, ran on the front page of the *Miami Herald* with my picture. I was a Marielita, too, I wrote. For years afterward I became the recipient of hundreds of letters sent by Mariel detainees and their desperate relatives. As I write this, in January 2005, about 1,700 Marielitos have been returned to Cuba and close to 750 remain in detention, but they will soon be freed. The Supreme Court has ruled that the United States can't indefinitely detain Mariel Cubans as it had done for almost twenty-five years using the argument that they had never been officially admitted in the country; they had been granted only a humanitarian parole. In the eyes of the law, during all these years Marielitos remained where they were in the spring and summer of 1980: treading the murky waters of Mariel. With the court's decision, they have finally reached the shore.

Epilogue

ERNARDO BENES, the man who started it all by daring to negotiate with Castro, woke up on the morning of March 6, 1980, to read a *Miami Herald* story revealing how the FBI had uncovered a terrorists' plot to assassinate him. Three years later, in the late evening hours of May 27, a bomb exploded at the Continental National Bank, where he worked, causing extensive damage but no injuries. Though the attempts on his life rattled Benes and his family, they came as no surprise. Unable to shake the label of traitor since his role in negotiating the release of the political prisoners became public in 1978, Benes knew that he had become a pariah in the community. At restaurants in Miami's Little Havana, while he was out dining with his wife and friends, strangers often walked up to his table and yelled, Son of a bitch, you are a communist and a Castro agent! Men and women whom Benes had considered his friends stopped returning his calls and some even looked the other way when he stretched out his hand to greet them. For years, community newspapers ran vicious editorials against him, and more than once the FBI placed him under watch because a fresh threat against his life had been issued.

No one attacked Benes more than Jorge Luis Hernández, the news director of WQBA, once the highest-rated radio station in Dade County. From his perch behind that powerful microphone, he organized a boycott against Benes's bank and urged his faithful listeners to repudiate the man who had licked the tyrant's boots.

But Mariel was unkind to Hernández as well. His early support of the flotilla was so total and so reckless that when public opinion turned against the Marielitos, Hernández was caught off guard. The station's ratings slipped, and WQBA lost its number-one spot. Less than a year after Mariel, Hernández lost his job. Now working for Radio Martí, the same station that in 1985 provoked Castro's ire, Hernández is certain that exiles hold him directly responsible for the chaotic and unchecked arrival of thousands of refugees.

Benes, too, lost his job. In 1984 he left his post at the bank that had been the center of so much of his community and political activism. Since then he has been employed only sporadically. In the last twenty years, he's held paying jobs on and off for a total of ten years. Seeking assistance to find a steady job, he once turned to the publisher of the *Miami Herald*, David Lawrence Jr., a newcomer to Miami who couldn't understand why a person as connected as Benes would need his assistance, but pledged to help. "I do know a lot of people in this town," Lawrence wrote Benes, "but you've been here for so many years, many more than I. Your contacts will probably be better than mine." They weren't. Today Benes and his wife live off the dwindling savings he amassed early in his career.

LIKE HERNÁNDEZ AND BENES, Napoleón Vilaboa was punished for Mariel. In 1981, lured by business opportunities in Costa Rica and fearing for his life, he moved to San José. Penniless, Vilaboa returned to Miami in 1989 and for a while worked as a night watchman at a Miami Beach building. A *Miami Herald* reporter found him there. In her story she quoted a former agent of the Florida Department of Law Enforcement who claimed that Vilaboa was indeed a Castro agent, an accusation Vilaboa still vigorously denies.

His friend and conduit to Castro, René Rodríguez, was indicted in Miami in 1983 for conspiracy to transport drugs to the United States; seven years later, Rodríguez died suddenly in Cuba. Vilaboa says he hasn't been to Cuba since 1987. His old friend Jorge Luis Hernández has hired him to host a thirty-minute talk show on Radio Martí on Sunday evenings so that Cubans on the island can hear him pontificate about history and democracy. The only group he belongs to now, he says, is the church. Approaching seventy, he claims that his only business is to save his soul. Neither Vilaboa nor Benes harbors any regrets about the boatlift, except one: More people should have been allowed to come to the United States.

◆ ◆ ◆

AMONG THOSE THEY THINK deserve to be in Miami is Mercedes Alvarez. After living for almost four years in a Lima park with dozens of other embassy refugees, she moved to a small home provided by a Catholic charity, with help from the United Nations, in a dusty neighborhood named Pachacamac, where packs of flea-infested dogs roam freely amid the piles of trash accumulated on every corner. The house is, in fact, a series of cement-walled shacks connected by low doors covered by flimsy cloth curtains. Mercedes lives as a poor Peruvian and has not been able to hold a steady job since she left Cuba. She often lacks money to buy food for her family, which, in addition to two of the three children she brought from Cuba, includes three born in Peru and four grandchildren. A few years ago, her first-born son paid his way to travel to the United States illegally. Mercedes has not heard from him in a long time and is not even sure where he lives.

Cubans from Miami periodically visit and promise to help her and the other eighty-two Cubans who remain in Pachacamac. But so far, no one has offered her a visa to the United States. There is no legal reason for Americans to consider her a refugee. In theory she lives in the country that she chose when she sought asylum in the Peruvian embassy. She says she was told in Havana that she could travel to the United States from Peru. But no one that I've talked to in the Carter administration or the Peruvian government recalls making such a promise.

The last time I talked to Mercedes, she told me she no longer harbors any illusions of ever living in the United States.

ERNESTO PINTO, the Peruvian diplomat who for about three days took charge of the more than 10,000 Cubans who sought refuge in the embassy in 1980, remains unscathed by the events he helped unleash. After stints in Germany and China, he was sent to Switzerland in 1997 as consul general in Zurich, where he worked on returning to Peru some $90 million deposited there by former president Alberto Fujimori. In 2001 Pinto achieved the rank of ambassador. Back in Lima now, he is in charge of coordinating the work of European embassies for the Ministry of Foreign Relations, and he teaches law at the University of Lima. He has written two books on international law. His expertise: human rights.

In many ways the most tortured of all the Marielitos I know is Héctor Sanyustiz. Disabled after several heart ailments, he lives alone and nearly destitute in a small studio apartment in a remote neighborhood of Miami-Dade County.

Unable to comprehend why he was encouraged—and allowed—to leave Cuba only forty-five days after breaking into the embassy, he lives with the kind of angst that burdens survivors of catastrophic events. In every conversation we've had in the last six years, he's always asked the same questions: "Do you know why me and not the others? Why Fidel wanted me out of the way?"

None of the five people who rode in the bus with Sanyustiz left Cuba in 1980; two are still there.

His stepson, Arturo Quevedo Martínez, then seventeen, was caught trying to leave the Peruvian embassy, arrested, and sentenced to three years in prison. He eventually made his way to the United States as a political refugee. All the others—María Antonia Martínez and her son; Francisco Raúl Díaz Molina; and Radamés Gómez—were detained in Cuba for four years and seven months. Technically they lived in a house under the protection of the Peruvian embassy in Havana. In reality they were prisoners of the Cuban government, which forbade them to receive visitors or communicate with the outside world for so long that most Cubans, including those who came in the boatlift, forgot that they, together with Sanyustiz, were the ones who opened the gates of Mariel.

After his release, Díaz Molina was allowed to leave for Peru, where he still lives and works as a taxi driver. Radamés was caught trying to leave Cuba on a raft and was sent to prison for three years. On September 26, 1991, eleven years after Castro put an end to the boatlift, he arrived in Miami as a political refugee. His two sons were born here. María Antonia and her son are still in Cuba.

For years, the Peruvian embassy became a museum of the events that transpired there. It was called the Historic Museum of the March of the Combatant People. For ten dollars, visitors could watch a grainy video loop of Sanyustiz's bus crushing the embassy's gates, supposedly taken from a security camera. Later, when Cuba opened its doors to tourism in the early 1990s, the museum was razed and a hotel was built in its place.

I have not been able to find an answer to Sanyustiz's question. I don't know why he left when the others didn't, but I think Sanyustiz was allowed to leave because in the end he didn't matter. Why waste time and resources keeping a man in a country where he didn't want to stay? Or perhaps the reasons were more sinister than that. He was, after all, a man with the courage to sit at the wheel of a bus as it plowed through iron gates guarded by armed officers. In jail he could have become a liability; in the streets of Havana, a personality; dead, a martyr. In the United States, however, with its vast spaces and its self-absorbed culture, Sanyustiz would surely get lost, which is in fact what happened—until 1998, when a nephew called the *Miami Herald* to reveal his story.

In December 2001, Sanyustiz joined a procession in the streets of Hialeah honoring San Lázaro, fulfilling the promise he'd made in 1978 when he prayed to the saint to free him from jail. Despite his physical ailments—he still has no feeling in parts of his left leg, where the bullet ripped tissue and shattered bone—he helped to carry the large statue of San Lázaro, the pitiful likeness of a man supported by crutches and surrounded by dogs licking his wounds.

THE PEOPLE OF CUBA, too, were forever changed by the boatlift. Mariel demonstrated that Fidel Castro's carefully controlled utopia had deep fissures. For the Cuban government, it meant the end of a virtual monopoly on its people and their ideas. If a bus driver was able to poke a hole through the system, the end of Fidel Castro was not only desirable but also attainable. The perceived vulnerability of the system gave rise to a vocal human-rights movement that had been quietly working since the 1970s and, lately, has attracted the attention of former president Jimmy Carter. At Castro's invitation, President Carter went to Cuba in May 2002. He met with members of the outlawed opposition and, in a public speech, urged Castro to consider a petition—signed by more than 10,000 Cubans—for a referendum on changing the laws of the country. Castro applauded politely but ignored Carter's call for democracy.

The Cuban government is now known internationally not as a beacon of progressive thoughts and revolutionary ideals but as a repressive regime routinely abandoned by its brightest sons and daughters. Actors, musicians, and painters defect whenever they can. So do skilled surgeons, prominent writers, and even professors of Marxism. Many, as five ballet dancers did in the fall of 2003 in New York and Florida, simply hail a cab or walk away from the hotels where they are staying during their tours. Invariably, they describe a Cuba today not unlike the one Marielitos left behind almost a quarter of a century ago.

Economically, Cuba is worse off now than in 1979, despite the legalization of the dollar in 1993. Foreign investment and revenues from tourism are down; malnutrition, disease, and desperation are up. The dollar brought with it all the scourges of capitalism without the benefits of democracy and personal freedoms. Young people in Cuba cannot yet choose the careers they wish to pursue, but university students and even graduates roam the streets selling their bodies to tourists for a silk scarf or a meal. Cubans cannot read the books they want, but they can hawk their families' old leather-bound encyclopedias. Cubans can't stay in hotels reserved for foreigners, but they are still expected to go to the Revolutionary Square to listen to Fidel Castro speak for hours and then applaud, applaud, applaud.

In April 2003, in a show of force not seen on the island for decades, the Cuban government arrested, convicted, and sentenced to long jail terms seventy-five journalists, economists, librarians, doctors, and human-rights workers—all dissidents accused of writing for foreign publications, setting up independent libraries, or collecting signatures to petition for the referendum Carter had praised a year earlier. Around the same time, three young men were executed by a firing squad for attempting to leave the island in a stolen vessel. An aging Castro is still in charge of the government, the Communist Party, and the state. His brother Raúl controls the armed forces.

The boatlift is not taught in Cuban schools, nor is it ever discussed on television or in any other public forum, though in recent years Castro has been willing to discuss with his foes formerly taboo topics such as the 1962 Missile Crisis and the Bay of Pigs invasion. When a *Miami Herald* reporter visited the port of Mariel five years ago, few in the dusty town of 41,000 wanted to talk about the thousands of people who had left in the flotilla. "They might as well be ghosts," a man said.

* * *

TWENTY-FIVE YEARS AFTER the events that altered so many lives, Mariel lives on as a much-abused point of reference in political rhetoric on both sides of the Florida Straits. U.S. lawmakers talk about never allowing another Mariel— which has become a code phrase for uncontrollable immigration—while their Cuban counterparts play the Mariel card: the implied threat that Cuba has millions of people who are desperate to leave and a government ready to let them loose whenever it is politically convenient. In the summer of 1994, when thousands of people left the country in overcrowded boats or floating in the inner tubes of truck tires, and it seemed as if Castro was again preparing a mass exodus, President Bill Clinton, surely remembering the political lessons of Mariel, ordered that Cuban "rafters," as those refugees came to be known, be picked up at sea and sent to Guantánamo, a U.S. military base in Cuba's easternmost province. At one point, Guantánamo held more than 35,000 Cubans. With this one action, and with the support of the leadership of the Cuban-American community, Clinton managed to change the status of Cuban refugees from freedom seekers to immigrants. Though the Cubans in Guantánamo eventually were flown to Miami, the presidential order remained in place. Since then, Cubans who touch land are allowed to stay in the United States, while those who are stopped on the high seas are routinely returned to the island, even though to this day Cuba and the United States have no formal relations and no official embassies in each other's country.

In Miami, Mariel is barely ever mentioned. The stigma is gone. Nearly 97 percent of those who arrived in the boatlift, according to U.S. government estimates, are law-abiding men and women who work and pay taxes and can be found throughout the United States but especially in Miami-Dade County, where they have helped the vibrant and established Cuban community transform South Florida into the gateway to Latin America. Today, Marielitos own restaurants and nurseries. They work at Disney World and the National Broadcasting Company. They tend to customers in supermarkets and make house calls as plumbers. They teach at prestigious colleges, receive accolades in the art world, and work abroad as engineers for oil conglomerates. They are poets, journalists, factory workers, bakers, soldiers, and even army doctors. They have an aggregate annual income of $2.2 billion, an amount that exceeds the estimated total cost of the boatlift: $2 billion.

A poll conducted in 1990 revealed that Marielitos were virtually indistinguishable from earlier exiles, except in one regard: They are much less politically inclined, shunning political activism and allegiances to any particular group. Like other Cubans, though, the majority of Marielitos want to stay in the United States, even if the alternative were a democratic Cuba; they vote Republican but have sympathies for elements of the Democratic agenda; they support a woman's reproductive choice; they believe that the United States should institute a free national health-care plan. And, like other Floridians, they are ambivalent about immigration. To a pollster's question on whether or not the United States should allow another massive boatlift from Cuba, almost 50 percent said no.

My father fits squarely into that mold. An American citizen since 1994, he still works as a chauffeur, driving patients to medical appointments and physical therapy sessions. My mother, who worked in a factory earning the minimum wage for almost ten years, stays home in one of the suburbs that are stretching Miami-Dade to the edge of the Everglades. My sister, the mother of two boys, rarely talks about Cuba, though her sense of longing, I've discovered, remains intact. They, as do I, remain close to my Uncle Oswaldo, who is now an accountant at a state university in Miami. Neither he nor my parents or my sister have ever been back to Cuba.

I FOUND the *Mañana* at 12:31 P.M. on June 13, 2002, three years after I began searching for it. It was berthed at the end of a pier on New Orleans's Municipal Yacht Harbor, gently swaying in the waves. I walked toward it carefully, tentatively, afraid to get close and realize that a coast guard historian had punched in the wrong boat registration number and led me to a different *Mañana*—there are about ninety vessels in the United States with the same name. No one was on deck, but someone was taking a shower. I could see soapy water gushing out of the hull. I boarded and looked inside the closed cabin, cupping my hands around my face to avoid the glare of the noon sun. On top of a table strewn with papers and what appeared to be photographs, I saw a rubbery arm. That's it! I thought, and checked my watch, as I always do when I'm working to record the instant a story comes alive. Before I spotted the arm, there had been only the possibility of a story. Now I had no doubt that the man taking a shower belowdecks was the captain I'd been looking for.

The *Mañana* was less elegant than I remembered, less imposing, smaller even. In my memory, the yacht that brought me to the United States was large, white, and spotless, with graceful lines and polished wooden panels. Instead, I found an old towing boat, with peeling paint and rusty corners outside. Inside, it had the frayed and rumpled look of an aging bachelor's pad; dog hair covered the furniture and the floors. But it didn't matter. The *Mañana*, I thought, was perfect. For after all, I was lucky to have found her twice in one lifetime.

The captain of the *Mañana*, Mike Howell, turned out to be an uncomplicated man who crinkles his eyes when he smiles, and he smiles a great deal. He seems unburdened by life. He lives alone, with his dogs, in his boat, the only home he's ever bought for himself. Until I found him, twenty-two years after the boatlift, he had not known the fate of any of the people he brought from Cuba. The trip to Mariel had been intense, he said, and then he repeated that word for emphasis. The return was emotional. "We wept when we saw you all walk away," he told me.

He understood my need to reach out to him, because for years he has been searching for the woman—either a nurse or a doctor, he's not sure which—who saved his life in Vietnam, refusing to give up on him when the other medics had. When he finds that woman, all he wants to do, he says, is thank her, which is how I started the journey that led to these pages: by wanting to find the captain of the *Mañana* just so that I could thank him. Because in May of 1980, I didn't know the words to express thanks and because, even if I had, I wasn't sure if I felt grateful to have left Cuba.

CUBA IS NO LONGER an obsession in my life. Rather, it is the imprint of my life, a dull pain that throbs at the slightest provocation: a word I thought I'd forgotten; a hymn that only former Communist Pioneers, like me, can still sing; a black-and-white picture of my family circa 1970 that my mother keeps on her night table; and that chocolate-colored lipstick I brought with me and is now tucked inside my medicine cabinet, just as my parents always kept the nearly empty container of Vicks VapoRub in theirs.

Home, that elusive concept for refugees everywhere, continues to evade me, like a desert mirage that grows farther the closer I seem to get to it. When I returned to Cuba in 1998, I was at home walking the streets of my childhood, among the people I grew up with, but oddly out of place elsewhere. I felt incomplete, besieged by a familiar feeling of restlessness, of not really being anywhere at all. Exile, I learned then, is not a temporary condition that dissipates in the euphoria of the return. Exile, like longing, is a way of life, much like a chronic, but not terminal, disease with capricious symptoms: an avowed preference for a certain shade of blue—the color of my old house, I realized once I stood in front of it again—and a formerly inexplicable, almost childish delight at the way the light filters through the fiery blossoms of some South Florida poinciana trees—just as it does in the trees that still shade my old neighborhood, even if I'm no longer there to see them.

Acknowledgments

I HAVE LONG KNOWN that journalists are privileged with the task of writing the first draft of history, but as a journalist for almost two decades now, I had been too busy crafting that first draft o ever truly benefit from the work of others. That is, until I began researching this book. I'm indebted to the work of dozens of journalists who covered the boatlift, especially Jo Thomas, Joseph B. Treaster, and Edward Schumacher of the *New York Times*; Helga Silva, Guillermo Martínez, Dan Williams, and Guy Gugliotta, all former *Miami Herald* reporters; and a host of others from the *Washington Post* and *Newsweek*. Joe Julavits, then working for the now-defunct *New Orleans States-Item*, recorded Captain Mike Howell's Cuba adventure with the kind of attention to detail that researchers swoon for.

I'm also indebted to the work of librarians and researchers, such as Martin I. Elzy, former assistant director of the Jimmy Carter Library; Gay Nemeti at the *Miami Herald*; Linda Lake and Vincella Miller at the *New York Times*; Esperanza de Varona and her team at the Cuban Heritage Collection of the University of Miami, especially Zoe Blanco-Roca; Nancy Burris of the *Times-Picayune*; and Traci L. Hahn at the National Vessel Documentation Center, U.S. Coast Guard. In my search for Captain Mike Howell, I was helped by Mona Porter and Robert Sanchez of the State of Florida's Division of Motor Vehicles; they provided the original list of boats named *Mañana*. Chris Havern, a historian in the U.S. Coast Guard's office in Washington, D.C., whittled the list of fifty-five down to four by using a mariner's logic and a historian's hunch. Manolo Fallat, a fellow *Mañana* traveler blessed with a wonderful memory, picked Mike's name among the four I tossed at him close to midnight one day, twenty-three years after we had both disembarked the *Mañana* in Key West.

Few writers are as lucky as I am to have had an academic write a book on a similar subject. During the course of my research, I came across a jewel of a book, *Presidential Decision Making Adrift: The Carter Administration and the Mariel Boatlift*, written as a doctorate dissertation in 1992 by David W. Engstrom, now an associate professor in the School of Social Work at San Diego State University. Dr. Engstrom not only shared with me his insights but he also allowed me to use and keep for more than two years the precious files he had accumulated in six years of research. Two other books have helped immensely: the acutely observed and sharply written *The Closest of Enemies: A Personal and Diplomatic Account of U.S.-Cuban Relations Since 1957*, by Wayne S. Smith, and *Secret Missions to Cuba: Fidel Castro, Bernardo Benes, and Cuban Miami*, by Robert M. Levine, a University of Miami professor who passed away before I could thank him for writing Benes's story before I did. Through the years, Wayne Smith has always been gracious enough to grant me several interviews when he could have just as easily directed me to his thoroughly written book.

Many other people contributed to *Finding Mañana*, in ways large and small, from recommending a book to delivering a letter in Peru. I cannot mention them all, but here's an attempt: Eida de la Vega found Engstrom's book; Rogelio Ventura unearthed and mailed a crucial document; Teresa Mlawer made the initial contacts in Lima, Peru, through her friends Aida Marcuse and Martha Fernández, that led me to ambassadors Ernesto Pinto-Bazurco and Edgardo de Habich. My dear friend Jorge Koechlin happened to have the home phone number of the former president of Peru, General Francisco Morales Bermúdez. Salomón Haddad, one of the few Miami Cubans who have not forgotten the Mariel Cubans still in Peru, led me to Mercedes Alvarez, and Hugo Díaz Pizarro drove me to her home and everywhere else in Lima, no matter how far or how late or how many times.

In the United States, I'm grateful to all the former members of the Carter administration who searched their memories for details of the Mariel story: Stuart Eizenstat, who shared his handwritten notes with Dr. Engstrom, and, therefore, with me; Zbigniew Brzezinski, who had the patience for sitting through my still unfocused interview; Robert Pastor, who recognized that I was working on a book when I did not yet know it and answered all my questions with that instinct in mind; Peter Tarnoff, who quickly understood the essence of all my questions; Victor Palmieri, who allowed me to sift through his as yet unpublished manuscript; and President Jimmy Carter, who faxed a response to the only question I really wanted to ask him: Why did he urge Americans to receive us Cubans with open arms if he really didn't mean it? Though he responded that he never intended to welcome an illegal boatlift, his answer is still unclear. No matter. I'm grateful to him for having had the kindness to welcome us in 1980. He and his staff insist they had no choice. I think they underestimate their humanity.

Among Miami friends I have found a wealth of information and a willingness to help: Norberto Fuentes introduced me to two Cuban defectors who had answers to many of the questions I would have asked Cuban government officials if I had been granted the interviews I repeatedly requested. They'd like to remain unnamed. Another defector, Carlos Cajaraville, who has since died, steered me in the right direction at the beginning of my research in 1999. Guillermo Martínez trusted me with the manuscript of a book he cowrote with Victor Palmieri. Siro del Castillo granted me the first interview and shared documents and books. Guarioné Díaz, David Shahoulian, Antonio Jorge, María Cristina Herrera, and Teo Babún shared information, documents, and memories.

Lissette Elguezabal, C. M. Guerrero, and Héctor Gabino, of the *Miami Herald*, helped with pictures, as did Pam Prouty and Minla Shields of the *Atlanta Journal Constitution*. Bob Mack graciously allowed me to use pictures he took more than twenty-five years ago in Havana.

I'm also thankful to a woman I never met and whose name I never learned. Knowing that she was deathly ill, she called Rafael Peñalver, a well-known Miami lawyer who is also my friend, and offered him several boxes containing hundreds of clippings about the Mariel boatlift and its consequences. That woman's treasure unlocked for me many of the secrets of Mariel.

Fabiola Santiago shared my daily angst with writing. Ana María Rabel, a fellow Marielita, nourished my soul and body more than once, cooking dinner for my family when I couldn't. And Ingrid Fuentealba lovingly took care of my children while I worked. My parents and sister, Mabel Junco, were invaluable sources of information. My husband, Arturo Villar, read every word I wrote and read them again after the rewriting. He managed never to be bored and sacrificed much in the almost three years of work I invested in this book, including a move to Miami from his beloved Carnegie Hill neighborhood in New York. Our youngest children have never known me not writing this book. I hope they find in these pages worthy reasons for so many postponed evenings of play.

Andrés Reynaldo, one of the best writers I know and a Mariel refugee as well, and Marifeli Pérez-Stable, who possesses one of the clearest minds in the U.S. on Cuban issues, read versions of this book and saved me from embarrassment. Sam Freedman, my professor and colleague, believed I could write this book before I did and urged me to take his book-writing seminar at Columbia University in the spring of 2000, surely a life-altering event for me and all his other disciples.

I could not have asked for a better agent than Heather Schroder, who had the foresight to intuit a book in my endless ramblings during our nearly monthly breakfast meetings in New York. She led me to Ann Godoff, who had the grace of recognizing vestiges of her own life in my refugee story and who so deftly turned my manuscript into a book. Her assistants, Sophie Fels, first, and, later, Liza Darnton, have been lifelines in the darkness of the editing and design process. Maureen Sugden copyedited the manuscript with such precision and knowledge that I was certain she was an undercover Marielita. Heather's and Ann's trust in my work allowed me to summon the courage to leave my day-to-day job at the *New York Times*, where my bosses were supportive of the book from the beginning. Gerald Boyd, the paper's former managing editor, told me I was born to write this book. I hope he was right. Along with Howell Raines and Bill Schmidt, he paved the way for my eventual return to the newspaper. The paper's current executive editor, Bill Keller, has nudged me to finish the book gently enough so that I feel wanted but never pressured.

And finally, but only because my gratitude is so vast that I thought I would leave them for the end, I owe a huge debt to the men and women who people this book: Bernardo Benes, Héctor Sanyustiz, Radamés Gómez, Francisco Raúl Díaz Molina, Ernesto Pinto, Mercedes Alvarez, Napoleón Vilaboa, my Uncle Oswaldo Ojito, and Captain Mike Howell. They gave selflessly and often, answering every question, taking every phone call, sharing my obsessions for accuracy and details. I would not have been able to write this book without their trust and cooperation. Indeed, without them, there would have been no Mariel story to tell.

Notes

Prologue

4 Information on the number of Cubans who left in the Camarioca boatlift and in the Freedom Flights: David W. Engstrom, *Presidential Decision Making Adrift: The Carter Administration and the Mariel Boatlift* (Lanham, Md.: Rowman & Littlefield Publishers, Inc., 1997).

5 More than a hundred Cubans sheltered in Latin American embassies in Havana: Wayne S. Smith, *The Closest of Enemies: A Personal and Diplomatic Account of U.S.-Cuban Relations Since 1975* (New York: W. W. Norton & Co., 1987).

8 Description of a woman with a fake arm and perfectly shaped nails comes from Elsa Wash, "Strange Love," *New Yorker*, April 5, 1999.

One: Worms Like Us

30 Fidel's speech after the bombing of the Cuban airplane: Michael Taber, ed., *Fidel Castro Speeches* (New York: Pathfinder Press, 1981).

Two: Bernardo Benes

Unless otherwise specified, the information in this chapter comes from repeated interviews in Miami, Florida, with Bernardo Benes, from November 1999 to June 2004.

38 Bernardo Benes's conversation with Alberto Pons in Panama and their subsequent meetings were confirmed by Alberto Pons. Interviewed on October 7, 2002.

45 Details about Bernardo Benes's father as well as Bernardo Benes's childhood in Cuba were supported by Meg Laughlin, "Bernardo's List," *Tropic* magazine, *Miami Herald*, November 6, 1994.

41–44 Information about the political dynamics in pre-Castro Cuba: Hugh Thomas, *Cuba: The Pursuit of Freedom* (New York: Harper & Row, 1971).

45 Confirmation of how Benes shared information with the White House comes from a telephone interview with Peter Tarnoff, April 2004.

46 Details of the last few hours of American diplomats in Cuba in 1961: Smith, *Closest of Enemies*.

46   Information on President Carter's goals when he reached the White House comes from an interview on December 6, 1999, in Atlanta, with Robert Pastor, former director of Latin American and Caribbean Affairs for the National Security Council in the Carter administration.

46   Details about treaties signed by Cuba and the United States in the 1970s: Smith, *Closest of Enemies*, and Taber, *Fidel Castro Speeches*.

47   Interpretations of President Carter's intentions for getting close to Castro: Smith, *Closest of Enemies*, and interview with the author in Washington, D.C., November 22, 1999.

47   The cost of Cuba to the Soviet Union: Jimmy Carter, *Keeping Faith: Memoirs of a President* (Fayetteville: University of Arkansas Press, 1995).

47   Interpretation of Castro's intentions in getting close to Carter as well as details about the dialogue were culled from interviews with Cuba expert and dialogue participant Marifeli Pérez-Stable, in Miami, Florida, in June 2004.

50   The number of businesses owned by Cubans in Miami in 1978: Robert M. Levine, *Secret Missions to Cuba: Fidel Castro, Bernardo Benes and Cuban Miami* (New York: Palgrave, 2001).

51   Information about press conference on September 6, 1978: Taber, *Fidel Castro Speeches*.

52   Details about the secret meetings between the Cuban and U.S. governments in the late 1970s: Smith, *Closest of Enemies*.

52   Information about how the United States didn't negotiate the release of the prisoners and agreed only to work on the logistics of getting them out of Cuba was confirmed by Peter Tarnoff during a telephone interview in April 2004.

52   Details on the arrival of the just-released prisoners in Miami: William R. Long and Guillermo Martínez, "Long Wait Ends for Prisoners," *Miami Herald*, October 22, 1978.

54   Quotation from Bernardo Benes at the beginning of the dialogue and details of the meeting of the exiles with Castro, including Castro's "constructive and cordial" comment: Ward Sinclair, "Cuban Exiles Await Word on Release of Prisoners," *Washington Post*, November 22, 1978.

54   Number of former prisoners leaving Cuba per month and Castro's anger at the U.S. for delaying the ex-prisoners' visas: Smith, *Closest of Enemies*.

55   The September 12, 1979, memorandum Bernardo Benes sent to Phil Wise, as well as Wise's forwarding note to Bob Pastor and Pastor's handwritten reply, came from the Carter Library, Atlanta: "Confidential Memo from Dr. Bernardo Benes and Alfredo Durán to Phil Wise re: the issuance of parole status to 5,000 ex–political prisoners of Cuba."

Three: Butterflies

63   More than a hundred thousand Cuban-Americans traveled to the island, adding about $100 million to the government's coffers: Smith, *The Closest of Enemies*.

66   Bodies left behind in the Angolan War: author's interview with Juan F. Benemelis in Miami, June, 2004.

71   Abolition of religious holidays in Cuba in 1969: Thomas, *Cuba: The Pursuit of Freedom*.

Four: Héctor Sanyustiz

Unless otherwise specified, the information in this chapter comes from interviews with Héctor Sanyustiz, from 1999 to 2004, and Radamés Gómez, June 15, 2004, in Miami, Florida; as well as with Francisco Raúl Díaz Molina, in Lima, Peru, on April 5, 2002.

77 Reluctance of the U.S. government to prosecute hijackers and the number of Cubans seeking asylum in Latin American embassies in 1979: Smith, *Closest of Enemies.*

78 Information about Edgardo de Habich's actions comes from an interview with de Habich and with Peru's former president, General Francisco Morales Bermúdez, in Lima, Peru, in April 1, 2002.

85 A picture of Sanyustiz after the accident was published with the article "Los Accidentes de Tránsito Siempre Son Perjudiciales," *Juventud Rebelde,* April 12, 1980.

86 Information about the right to asylum comes from an interview with Arturo García-García, Peru's former foreign minister, in Lima, Peru, on April 5, 2002.

90 Raúl Díaz Molina's pulling out a gold medallion of Our Lady of Charity: Fabiola Santiago, "The Mariel Story That Hasn't Been Told," *Miami Herald,* September 6, 1998.

91 Portions of Raúl Díaz Molina's story was confirmed by an article written in Cuba by Jorge Luis Blanco, "Los Sucesos de la Embajada del Perú," *Verde Olivo,* April 13, 1980.

Five: Ernesto Pinto

Unless otherwise specified, the events in this chapter were described by Ernesto Pinto and Mercedes Alvarez during several interviews in Lima and New York and by telephone, from 2002 to 2004.

100, 107–109 Pinto's version of the shootout, as well as his encounters with Fidel Castro, were confirmed by his wife, Lily Barandiarán, in a telephone interview on May 12, 2004.

101 How the soldier was killed was explained by Carlos Cajaraville, former captain in the Cuban counterintelligence, during an interview in Miami, on October 21, 1999.

101 The death of the soldier was published in "Síntesis Biográfica del Soldado Pedro Ortiz Cabrera, Custodio de la Misión del Perú, Muerto el Primero de Abril," *Granma,* April 4, 1980.

103 Details of the priorities of Peru in 1980 come from an interview with General Francisco Morales Bermúdez in Lima, Peru, April 1, 2002.

104 Description of how Cuba removed the guards from the Peruvian embassy: Guy Gugliotta, "How a Trickle Became a Flood: Origins of the Freedom Flotilla," *Miami Herald,* May 5, 1980.

104 Explanation of why the Cuban government removed the guards from the Peruvian embassy: "Declaración del Gobierno Revolucionario de Cuba," *Granma,* April 4, 1980.

105 The role of the Special Troops in the embassy crisis was explained in a January 10, 2003, interview by a former member of that group who now lives in Miami and wishes to remain anonymous.

106 Details of the kinds of people in the embassy: Guillermo Martínez, "Thousands Jam Embassy in Attempt to Flee Cuba," *Miami Herald*, April 7, 1980.

109 Information about Peru's dire economic situation: Gugliotta, "How a Trickle."

114 Castro's December 27 speech was cited by Engstrom, *Presidential Decision Making Adrift.*

115 Composition of the committed formed by Cubans in the embassy: Gugliotta, "How a Trickle."

115 A detailed discussion of Castro's troubles in 1979 and 1980 is found in Smith, *Closest of Enemies.*

116–117 Descriptions of life in the embassy, including Castro's visit, can be found in Juan Casanova, "Diez Mil Buscaban Refugio y Hallaron el Infierno," *El Herald* (no date available) and Gugliotta, "How a Trickle."

116 Cuba's position regarding the embassy crisis can be found in "La Posición de Cuba," *Granma*, April 7, 1980.

117 How the distribution of food in the embassy was manipulated by the Cuban government comes from an interview with Carlos Cajaraville, former captain in the Cuban counterintelligence, in Miami, October 21, 1999.

117 A characterization of those who were leaving Cuba was published in "Noticias de Mariel," *Granma*, April 27, 1980.

117 Description of how those leaving the embassy were treated, as well as the list of countries that offered to take some of the refugees: Guillermo Martínez, "Flights Carry First 250 to Costa Rica," *Miami Herald*, April 17, 1980.

118 Explanation of García-García's plan comes from an interview with him in Lima, Peru, April 5, 2002.

118 The Cuban government's assertion that Key West was closer than Costa Rica was published in "Salieron del País 309 Elementos Antisociales, pero de Nuevo Se Enreda la Madeja," *Granma*, April 18, 1980.

118 President Carter's comment on April 9, 1980, was cited by Smith, *Closest of Enemies.*

118 Washington's offer to accept 3,500 Cubans from the embassy: Gugliotta, "How a Trickle."

118 Number of Cubans flown to Costa Rica: Engstrom, *Presidential Decision Making Adrift.*

119 Description of what the Cubans did upon arrival in Costa Rica: Martínez, "Flights Carry First 250."

119 How the government began to promote the April 19 march: "¡Todos Mañana a la Marcha del Pueblo Combatiente!" *Granma*, April 18, 1980.

Six: Unwanted

123 The exhortation to the March of the Combatant People ran in "¡Todos Mañana a la Marcha del Pueblo Combatiente!" *Granma*, April 18, 1980.

130 Sketches of Sanyustiz and Ortiz: "¡Todos los Demás que Se Vayan, pero Ellos, de Aquí No Salen!" *Juventud Rebelde*, April 12, 1980, and "Los Hechos," *Juventud Rebelde*, April 12, 1980, and "Síntesis Biográfica."

132 Description of the posters the marchers held: Jo Thomas, "Marchers Rally Around Cuba, Castro, Communism," *New York Times*, April 20, 1980.

Seven: Napoleón Vilaboa

Unless otherwise specified, the information in this chapter comes from several interviews with Napoleón Vilaboa, in Miami, from 2002 to 2004, and from two interviews with Jorge Luis Hernández in Miami, February 2003.

139 Sentiments of Cubans in Miami as well as Washington's initial response toward the "Havana 10,000": Gugliotta, "How a Trickle."

139 How the U.S. government missed the signals of Mariel: Staff Report, U.S. House of Representatives, Subcommittee on Oversight, Permanent Select Committee on Intelligence, "The Cuban Emigres: Was There a U.S. Intelligence Failure?" June 1980, Washington, D.C.

140, 146 Political atmosphere in pre-Castro Cuba, as well as details about the Bay of Pigs invasion: Thomas, *Cuba*.

148 Samples of Vilaboa's writings come from Napoleón Vilaboa, "La Política Doble de Washington Hacia Cuba," *Patria*, July 23, 1965, and Napoleón Vilaboa, "Panorama Desde Hialeah," *Debate*, April 27, 1977.

148 Information about de la Guardia brothers: Andrés Oppenheimer, *Castro's Final Hour: The Secret Story Behind the Coming Downfall of Communist Cuba* (New York: Simon & Schuster, 1992).

149 Tony de la Guardia brought rum to his FBI contact: Interview in Miami with Norberto Fuentes, author, and friend of de la Guardia brothers, February 26, 2003.

149 FBI's investigations of bombings in Miami: Felix Masud-Piloto, *From Welcomed Exiles to Illegal Immigrants: Cuban Migration to the U.S., 1959–1995* (Lanham, Md.: Rowman & Littlefield Publishers, Inc., 1996).

149 Description of Vilaboa's house in Miami: Dan Williams and Iván A. Castro, "Boatlift Leader Set for More:'150,000 Want to Come,'" *Miami Herald*, June 1980 (exact date not available).

150 Bernardo Benes's pitch to Vilaboa to participate in the 1978 dialogue was confirmed by Benes during the course of multiple interviews from 2002 to 2004.

152 President Carter's announcement that the United States was prepared to welcome up to 3,500 refugees: Gugliotta, "How a Trickle."

157 Information about the forty-one boats that followed the *Ochún's* lead and Napoleón Vilaboa's comments to a reporter before he left for Cuba: Augustín Alles, "El Segundo Camarioca," *Réplica* (no date available), and Gay M. Nemeti, "Chronicle of an Exodus," *Miami Herald*, April 18, 2000.

Eight: Leaving Cuba

Much of the information in this chapter comes from repeated interviews through the years with Oswaldo Ojito, my uncle, and my parents, Orestes and Mirta Ojito.

161 Cuban government note about Mariel: "Noticias del Mariel," *Granma*, April 22, 1980.

161 A description of the *Valley Chief* is available in that boat's certificate of registry, filed with the National Vessel Documentation Center, U.S. Coast Guard, Falling Waters, West Virginia.

164 How the *Valley Chief* had been used comes from a telephone interview with Charles Caraker, nephew of its deceased owner, July 2002.

165 Number of boats going south on April 23: Robert L. Scheina, "Coast Guard Operations During the Cuban exodus" (Washington, D.C.: The United States Coast Guard, 1980).

171 Portrait of those leaving the country, according to the Cuban government: "Noticias del Mariel," *Granma*, April 27, 1980.

171 Details of May 1, 1980, speech by Castro, as well as his quote about opening another Camarioca: "The Biggest Mass Rally in Cuban History" and "We Have Been Waging a Mass Battle Whose Scope and Depth Is Unique in the Annals of the Revolution," *Granma*, May 11, 1980, International Edition.

172 Attack on Cubans gathered outside the Interests Section: Smith, *Closest of Enemies*.

172 Cuba's version of events at the Interests Section: "Yankee Provocation at U.S. Interests Section," *Granma*, May 3, 1980, International Edition.

172 How a driver ran over a woman trying to escape a violent mob: "A Large Demonstration of Heartfelt Grief," *Granma*, May 11, 1980, International Edition.

173 Details of how the boatlift was developing—fatalities, Cuba's overcrowding boats, and messages sent by the coast guard: Scheina, "Coast Guard Operations."

Nine: Captain Mike Howell

Unless otherwise specified, the information in this chapter comes from repeated interviews with Michael S. Howell, from 2002 to 2004. Howell's description of events during his trip to Cuba was confirmed by one of his crew members, David Bolyard. Some of the details were also confirmed by two Cuban-Americans who accompanied him, Rogelio Ventura and Antonio Ramón Rodríguez, and by a series of articles written about the *Mañana*'s voyage to Cuba written by Joe Julavits and published in May 1980 in the *States-Item*, a now-defunct New Orleans newspaper.

191 How the strategy of the Vietnam War was changing when Mike went to Vietnam: David Halberstam, *The Best and the Brightest* (New York: Ballantine Books, 1993). Note: Though in 1965 the projection was that as many as 750,000 Americans could be sent to fight in Vietnam, in reality, as Mr. Halberstam points out in his book, no more than half a million Americans were involved in the war.

192 Portions of Mike Howell's Vietnam story were first written by Bill Grady, "Vietnam Vet Surmounts Cruel Twist," *New Orleans Times-Picayune*, April 18, 1999.

194 Summer of Love information: Jon Pareles, "At Age 20, Sgt. Pepper Marches On," *New York Times*, May 31, 1987.

197 What Mike Howell read before he left for Cuba: Steve Wilson (AP), "Refugees Still Pouring into U.S.," *New Orleans Times-Picayune*, April 26, 1980, and Mimi Whitefield (UPI), "Boats Ignore Ban, Set Sail for Cuba," *New Orleans Times-Picayune*, April 24, 1980.

198 The White House's initial confused response to the boatlift: Engstrom, *Presidential Decision Making Adrift*.

199 Details of Cyrus Vance's resignation: Carter, *Keeping Faith*.

199 The troubles of the Carter presidency in April 1980: Victor H. Palmieri and Guillermo Martínez "An Act of War: The Inside Story of the 1980 Mariel Boatlift" (unpublished manuscript).

200 Descriptions of April 26 meeting in the White House, as well as of the mind-set of members of the Carter administration, were culled from handwritten notes kept by Stuart E. Eizenstat, assistant to President Carter for domestic policy, and from an interview with him in Washington, D.C., September 9, 2002.

200 How Smith's warnings of Mariel were ignored: Smith, *Closest of Enemies*.

201 How President Carter's human-rights stance played a role in the boatlift: interview with Robert Pastor in Atlanta, December 6, 1999.

201 Number of refugees who had arrived after the first week of the boatlift: Juan M. Clark et al., "The 1980 Mariel Exodus: An Assessment and Prospect," (Washington, D.C.: Council for InterAmerican Security, 1981).

201 Number of refugees who arrived in the Camarioca boatlift: Engstrom, *Presidential Decision Making*.

201 Vice President Walter Mondale's message to Cuban-Americans: Alex Larzelere, *The 1980 Cuban Boatlift* (Washington, D.C.: National Defense University Press, 1988).

202 Enthusiasm in New Orleans toward the boatlift: Joan Treadway, "Louisianans Charter Ship for Refugees," *New Orleans Times-Picayune*, May 3, 1980.

202 The Pentagon's announcement that no Cubans would be returned to Cuba: compiled from press dispatches, "U.S. Sending Ships to Assist Cubans," *New Orleans Times-Picayune*, May 1, 1980.

203 Challenge to Carter to take the refugees: "Castro's Black Eye, and Ours," *New York Times*, May 4, 1980, lead editorial.

203–205 Details about life in Mariel Harbor: Edward Schumacher, "Misery and Merriment Are Filling Nights in Havana for the U.S. Kin," *New York Times*, May 9, 1980, and Alex Larzelere, *1980 Cuban Boatlift*.

205 President Carter's May 5 "open arms" statement: Tom Fiedler and Carl Hiaasen, "Dilemma of Cuban Exodus: Does U.S. Try to Halt Boatlift and Risk Unrest as a Result?" *Miami Herald*, June 15, 1980.

206 Number of refugees who arrived after the president's "open arms" speech: Clark et al., "The 1980 Mariel Exodus."

206 President's decision to declare a state of emergency in South Florida: Fiedler and Hiaasen, "Dilemma of Cuban Exodus."

206 Hodding Carter comments: Graham Hovey, "President Declares Florida Emergency," *New York Times*, May 7, 1980, and Tom Fiedler and Guy Gugliotta, "SNAFU: How Refugee Resettlement Became a Mess," *Miami Herald*, June 1, 1980.

206 President Carter's own interpretation of his "open arms" speech comes from an e-mail exchange with author on February 24, 2000.

207 President Carter's comment on May 7 about not wanting to sink boats full of people: Fiedler and Hiaasen, "Dilemma of Cuban Exodus."

207 Details of the May 7 meeting among top administration officials come from the author's interview with Stuart Eizenstat in Washington, D.C., September 9, 2002, and from Mr. Eizenstat's own handwritten notes of his White House meetings.

207 Information about President Carter's order to formulate an enforceable policy to stop the boatlift comes from Stuart Eizenstat's own handwritten notes of his dealings with the president in 1980.

207 Brzezinski's position regarding the boatlift: author's interview with Mr. Brzezinski in Washington, D.C., September 9, 2002.

207 The *New York Times'* call to the administration to get the boatlift under control: "One Open Arm, and the Other," *New York Times*, May 9, 1980.

211 How Edward Schumacher found the *Valley Chief*: interview with Mr. Schumacher in February 2003.

211 The *Washington Post's* story about undesirables in the boatlift: Charles R. Babcock, "FBI Discovering Some 'Undesirables' Among Flood of Refugees from Cuba," *Washington Post*, April 29, 1980.

212 Description of how Castro manipulated the number and kinds of people who left through Mariel: interview in Miami with a former member of Cuba's Ministry of the Interior who wishes to remain anonymous, November 2002.

213 Story about the retarded people aboard the *Valley Chief*: Edward Schumacher, "Retarded People and Criminals Are Included in Cuban Exodus," *New York Times*, May 11, 1980.

Ten: Tempest-Tost

227 Descriptions of Key West in May 1980: Sara Rimer, "Key West: Life Goes On," *Miami Herald*, May 12, 1980.

229 Deployment of the USS *Saipan*: Alex Larzelere, *1980 Cuban Boatlift*.

Eleven: Teeming Shore

235 Information about Mercedes Alvarez's leaving Cuba and her life in Lima, Peru, comes from multiple interviews with her from 2002 to 2004.

239 Purpose of the May 14 recommendations: interview with Stuart Eizenstat in Washington, D.C., September 9, 2002.

239 Points of the May 14 announcement as well as an explanation of the failed options contemplated by the administration to stop the boatlift and the number of vessels seized but not fined: presidential statement, Cuba/Refugees 5/14/80, and Memorandum for the President from S. Eizenstat, Jack Watson and Zbig Brzezinski. Subject: Cuban Boat People. May 13, 1980. Carter Library, Atlanta.

240 Steps taken by the Coast Guard, the navy, and customs after the May 14 announcement: *Coast Guard News*, May 15, 1980, release no. 69-80, by Miami's Public Affairs Office; and Scheina, "Coast Guard Operations."

240 More Cubans arrived in May 1980 than in all of 1962: Clark et al., "The 1980 Mariel Exodus."

240 Composition of the boatlift: Guillermo Martínez, "Crush of Refugees Has Built a Whole City Within a City," *Miami Herald*, Special Reprint, 1980.

241 Story of Conrado Monés: Samuel G. Freedman, "The New New Yorkers," *New York Times*, November 3, 1985; and Sydney H. Schanberg, "Death of a Biology Teacher," *New York Times*, October 5, 1982.

241 *Miami Herald* poll: Richard Morin, "Deluge Adds to Fear in Uneasy Miami," *Miami Herald*, May 11, 1980.

241 James Reston's column: James Reston, "The Carter Cuban Policy," *New York Times*, May 16, 1980.

241 *New York Times* editorial about Castro dumping criminals in the boatlift: "A Clear Policy for the Castro Tide," *New York Times*, May 16, 1980.

242 The *America*'s arrival in Key West: Joseph B. Treaster, "Tide of Refugees Swells as Vessel with 500 Docks, *New York Times*, May 12, 1980; and Janet Fix and Anders Gyllenhaal, "Boats Bring 4,500 More to Key West," *Miami Herald*, May 12, 1980.

243 Jim Hampton's change of heart: Jim Hampton, "Una Segunda Mirada al Puente Marítimo," *El Herald* (no date available).

243 May 11 broke all records of daily arrivals: Fix and Gyllenhaal, "Boats Bring 4,500 More to Key West."

243 Vilaboa's experiences during the boatlift: author's multiple in-person and telephone interviews with Napoleón Vilaboa in Miami, Florida, from 2002 to 2004.

244 *Granma* editorial asserting Cuba's governance over Mariel as well as the charges that the Cuban government was preventing boats from returning to Florida empty: Margot Hornblower, "Cuba to Disregard U.S. Effort to Halt Refugee Boatlift," *Washington Post*, May 16, 1980; and Karen DeYoung, "Mariel to Remain Open for Exodus; Cuba Scorns Carter's Effort to Halt Refugee Boatlift," *Washington Post*, May 16, 1980.

244 Information about the CIA's satellite pictures: author's telephone interview with Victor Palmieri, June 2004.

244 Mariel as an act of war: Palmieri and Martínez, *An Act of War*.

244 Details about the hospital stay of Héctor Sanyustiz and Radamés Gómez come from interviews with Sanyustiz (from 1998 to 2004) and Gómez (June 15, 2004) as well as with Federico Espinosa (June 16, 2004).

249 *Olo Yumi* tragedy: Janet Fix and Fitz McAden, "Sea Takes 14 Refugees' Lives When Boat Capsizes in Straits; Survival Brutal for 38 More," *Miami Herald*, May 19, 1980.

249 Coast Guard's message to Cuba about the *Olo Yumi* and overcrowded boats: Schema, "Coast Guard Operations."

249 Demonstration in front of the U.S. Interests Section in Havana: Smith, *The Closest of Enemies*.

250 Description of the 1980 race riots: Nemeti, "Chronicle of an Exodus."

250 How Sanyustiz avoided detection: interviews with Sanyustiz, from 1998 to 2004.

252 Update of Ernesto Pinto in Peru: author's multiple interviews with Mr. Pinto, from 2002 to 2004.

253 *Red Diamond* story: interview of Admiral John Costello conducted by Stuart Eizenstat, no date available. A transcription of the taped interview was provided by Eizenstat.

253 Number of Cuban refugees who had arrived by the middle of June: Clark et al., "The 1980 Mariel Exodus."

253 Opening of Krome Avenue Detention Center and Tent City and military bases where Cuban refugees were sent to: Nemeti, "Chronicle of an Exodus."

254 Description of Tent City: Guillermo Martínez, "Life Is Tense in Miami's Tent City," *Miami Herald*, August 24, 1980, and Mike Clary, "Bajo las Carpas, Pueblo en Transición," *El Herald*, July 28, 1980.

255 Update on Bernardo Benes's activities during the boatlift: Author's multiple interviews with Mr. Benes, from 1999 to 2004.

255 How Benes had lost his clout with Castro: Levine, *Secret Missions to Cuba*.

256 September crime statistics: Nemeti, "Chronicle of an Exodus," and George Stein and Guillermo Martínez, "Little Havana Struck by Boatlift Criminals," *Miami Herald*, September 18, 1980.

256 Police officers in Miami Beach writing the letter *R* in their reports and the chief of police blaming newly arrived Cubans for the rising wave of crime in Miami Beach: Dan Williams and Joan Fleischman, "Beach Sees Crime Rise Since Refugee Influx," *Miami Herald*, July 25, 1980.

256 Crime was in the upswing since the year before the Cubans arrived: Peter Elkind, "Violent Crime Jumps Statewide," *Miami Herald*, August 16, 1979.

256 More Hispanic homicide victims in 1980 than black victims: Seymor Gelber, "A Little Perspective, Please, on Crime in Dade," *Miami Herald*, July 12, 1981.

256 Story about the city's deadliest month: Edna Buchanan, "July Became a Month for Murder in Miami," *Miami Herald*, September 8, 1980.

256 First Mariel refugee to die: Bob Murphy and Ana Veciana, "Cuban Finds Death at Journey's End," *Miami News*, June 12, 1980.

257 Peter Tarnoff's trip to Cuba to negotiate the end of the boatlift with Castro: Smith, *The Closest of Enemies*, and a telephone interview with Tarnoff, June 2004.

257 Arrival statistics for May, June, and August 1980: Clark et al., "The 1980 Mariel Exodus."

258 The Cubans leave the U.S. Interests Section: Smith, *The Closest of Enemies*.

258 How Mariel ends and last boats to arrive in Key West: Guillermo Martínez and Robert Rivas, "Mariel Is Closed; You All Must Go," *Miami Herald*, September 27, 1980.

258 *Granma*'s ignoring the end of the boatlift and its preoccupation with a Cuban astronaut: "Feliz Regreso de la 'Soyuz-38,'" *Granma*, September 27, 1980.

258 Sign left behind in the streets of Mariel: Guy Gugliotta, "Redúcese Masivo Éxodo a Discretas Salidas," *El Herald*, 1980 (no specific date available).

258 President Carter lost the election: *Congressional Quarterly's Guide to U.S. Elections*, Third Edition (Washington, D.C.: Congressional Quarterly Inc.: 1994).

Twelve: With Open Arms

264 Number of Mariel Cubans imprisoned in the U.S. in 1987: Mark S. Hamm, *The Abandoned Ones: The Imprisonment and Uprising of the Mariel Boat People* (Boston: Northeastern University Press, 1995).

267 Number of Mariel Cubans still in detention and deported as of June 2004: author's telephone interview with Holland & Knight lawyer and detainees' advocate, David Shahoulian, June 2004.

Epilogue

269 Update on Bernardo Benes: author's interviews and Levine, *Secret Missions to Cuba*.

269 Update on Jorge Luis Hernández: author's interviews, February 27, 2003.

270 Dave Lawrence's letter to Bernardo Benes: Copy of a *Miami Herald* stationery letter, dated February 2, 1996, was provided by Bernardo Benes.

270 Update on Napoleón Vilaboa: author's interviews and Liz Balmaseda, "Exile: I Was Mastermind of Mariel," *Miami Herald*, July 31, 1989.

270 Update on René Rodríguez: Pablo Alfonso, "Fallece en Cuba Presidente del ICAP," *El Nuevo Herald*, October 16, 1990.

271 Update on Mercedes Alvarez: author's interviews, 2002 to 2004.

271 Update on Ernesto Pinto: author's interviews, 2002 to 2004.

272 Update on Héctor Sanyustiz: author's interview, 1998 to 2004.

272 Update on what happened to the Peruvian embassy and to the five people who accompanied Héctor Sanyustiz in the bus: interviews with Raúl Díaz Molina (Peru, April 5, 2002) and Radamés Gómez (Miami, June 15, 2004), and Fabiola Santiago, "In Havana, a Nervous Encounter with History," *Miami Herald*, September 6, 1998.

273 Former president Carter's visit to Cuba in 2002: "Text of Jimmy Carter's Speech," The Associated Press, May 14, 2002; and John Rice, "Carter Wraps Up Landmark Cuba Trip," *Los Angeles Times*, May 17, 2002.

273 Cuba's situation today: Marifeli Pérez-Stable, "Politics, Economy Stuck in the Past," *Miami Herald*, February 19, 2004.

274 Cuba's show of force in 2003: "Mr. Castro's Prisoners," editorial, *New York Times*, March 26, 2004.

274 How the boatlift is ignored in Cuba: *Herald* Staff Report, "In Mariel, Massive Boatlift Struck from Official Memory; Embarrassing Exodus a Sad, Distant Taboo," *Miami Herald*, April 21, 2000.

275 Mariel Cubans are virtually indistinguishable from other Cuban exiles: Elinor Burkett and Liz Balmaseda, "Mariel Cubans Melt into S. Florida," *Miami Herald*, April 22, 1990.

Other Sources

The following books and newspaper stories informed the writing of this book, though they were not directly cited. Several of the sources of information I used were in Spanish, either because they were originally written in that language or because they were translated for publication. I have cited them in the language in which I read them. Some clippings, as noted, were incomplete or torn; therefore it was impossible to determine authorship and/or publishing date.

David M. Alpern, "Carter and the Cuban Influx," *Newsweek*, May 26, 1980.

Atlas de Cuba (La Habana: Instituto Cubano de Geodesía y Cartografía, 1978).

Teo Babún, "Port of Mariel," a report (undated and unpublished).

Liz Balmaseda "Precipitó Mariel la Fuga Anglo de Dade," *El Herald*, April 22, 1982.

Juan F. Benemelís, *Las Guerras Secretas de Fidel Castro* (Fundación Elena Mederos, 2002).

Shula Beyer, "Hialeah to Put More Cops on the Streets," *Miami Herald*, September 11, 1980.

Thomas D. Boswell et al., "A Bibliography for the Mariel-Cuban Diaspora" (Center for Latin American Studies, University of Florida, Gainesville, Florida, 1988).

Zbigniew Brzezinski, *Power and Principle: Memoirs of the National Security Adviser 1977–1981* (New York: Farrar, Straus and Giroux, 1985).

Siro del Castillo, "Cubans of 1980" (paper presented at the Office of Refugee Resettlement, ORR, Washington, D.C., February 16, 1983).

Alfonso Chardy, "Afecta el Puente Marítimo a Negocios Hispanos," *El Herald*, July 6, 1980.

Juan M. Clark, *Tercer Aniversario/Puente Mariel–Key West* (Miami: F.A.C.E., 1983).

"The Cuban Blockade Is Working—So Far," *Newsweek*, June 2, 1980.

John M. Goshko, "Cuba Offers to Free Political Prisoners," *Washington Post*, September 1, 1978.

Edgardo de Habich, *Traspiés en el Paraíso* (Lima, Peru: Triunfaremos, 1984), and *Embajador en Cuba* (Mexico: Premia, 1980).

"In Wake of an Exodus—the Mariel Mystery," *Miami Herald* (author and date not available).

Levi Marrero, *Geografía de Cuba* (New York: Minerva Books, Ltd., 1966).

Guillermo Martínez, "Dade Struggles to Cope with Refugee Influx," *Miami Herald*, June 2, 1980.

Guillermo Martínez and Dan Williams, "Nations Debate; Embassy Crowds Wait," *Miami Herald*, April 10, 1980.

"Mr. Castro's Prisoners," *New York Times* editorial, March 26, 2004.

Robert A. Pastor, *Exiting the Whirlpool: U.S. Foreign Policy Toward Latin America and the Caribbean* (Colorado: Westview Press, 2001).

Marifeli Pérez-Stable, "Politics, Economy Stuck in the Past," *Miami Herald*, February 19, 2004.

Federico Prieto Celi, *Regreso a la Democracia* (Lima: Realidades S.A., 1996).

Howell Raines, "Banker Is Proud of Role in Freeing Cubans," *New York Times*, December 27, 1978.

Steven Reddicliffe, "Exodo Cubano Influyó en Lucha de Radioemisoras por Audiencia," *El Herald* (no date available).

Derek Reveron, "Fears That Refugees Would Overburden Economy Fading," *Miami Herald*, April 22, 1990.

Fabiola Santiago, "In Havana, a Nervous Encounter with History," *Miami Herald*, September 6, 1998.

Ward Sinclair, "The Two Sides of a Negotiator for Castro's Prisoners," *Washington Post*, December 3, 1978.

Index

Italics denote illustrations.

FOR THE BEST IN PAPERBACKS, LOOK FOR THE

In every corner of the world, on every subject under the sun, Penguin represents quality and variety—the very best in publishing today.

For complete information about books available from Penguin—including Penguin Classics, Penguin Compass, and Puffins—and how to order them, write to us at the appropriate address below. Please note that for copyright reasons the selection of books varies from country to country.

In the United States: Please write to *Penguin Group (USA), P.O. Box 12289 Dept. B, Newark, New Jersey 07101-5289* or call 1-800-788-6262.

In the United Kingdom: Please write to *Dept. EP, Penguin Books Ltd, Bath Road, Harmondsworth, West Drayton, Middlesex UB7 0DA.*

In Canada: Please write to *Penguin Books Canada Ltd, 90 Eglinton Avenue East, Suite 700, Toronto, Ontario M4P 2Y3.*

In Australia: Please write to *Penguin Books Australia Ltd, P.O. Box 257, Ringwood, Victoria 3134.*

In New Zealand: Please write to *Penguin Books (NZ) Ltd, Private Bag 102902, North Shore Mail Centre, Auckland 10.*

In India: Please write to *Penguin Books India Pvt Ltd, 11 Panchsheel Shopping Centre, Panchsheel Park, New Delhi 110 017.*

In the Netherlands: Please write to *Penguin Books Netherlands bv, Postbus 3507, NL-1001 AH Amsterdam.*

In Germany: Please write to *Penguin Books Deutschland GmbH, Metzlerstrasse 26, 60594 Frankfurt am Main.*

In Spain: Please write to *Penguin Books S. A., Bravo Murillo 19, 1° B, 28015 Madrid.*

In Italy: Please write to *Penguin Italia s.r.l., Via Benedetto Croce 2, 20094 Corsico, Milano.*

In France: Please write to *Penguin France, Le Carré Wilson, 62 rue Benjamin Baillaud, 31500 Toulouse.*

In Japan: Please write to *Penguin Books Japan Ltd, Kaneko Building, 2-3-25 Koraku, Bunkyo-Ku, Tokyo 112.*

In South Africa: Please write to *Penguin Books South Africa (Pty) Ltd, Private Bag X14, Parkview, 2122 Johannesburg.*